RAG-OYLE TOWN FAMILY

Brian Hirst was born December 1st 1946, in Batley West Yorkshire, where he lived until 1965. He came in the middle of nine brothers, and he also had four sisters. He was the first in his family to undergo higher education. He took a teacher-training course at Bingley College during 1965–68, and then gained a Birmingham University B.Phil., and a University of East Anglia M.Phil., in English and Education. He taught secondary school English in Dunstable, Luton, Leytonstone, Iver and Denby, from 1968 to 1996. He began writing in 1999, when he moved from Derby to Scarborough. In August 2004, he was diagnosed with leukaemia. Since then, much of his time has been spent on hospital treatment and writing two memoirs, of which 'Rag-Oyle Town Family' is the first.

RAG-OYLE TOWN FAMILY

BRIAN HIRST

FOR MY FAMILY

Cover design by Clare Brayshaw

Front cover photograph – "Woodsomers" – Malcolm, David, Brian, John. Early 1950s.

Prepared and printed by:

York Publishing Services Ltd
64 Hallfield Road
Layerthorpe
York YO31 7ZQ
Tel: 01904 431213

Website: www.yps-publishing.co.uk

CONTENTS

BOB

Robert Hirst was known as Bob to his friends and family. He was born in October 1912 in Batley, a Yorkshire Pennine town, surrounded by the bigger towns of Dewsbury, Huddersfield, Wakefield, Bradford and Leeds. Batley in 1912 was full of heavy woollen and shoddy mills hugging the sides of the Bradford Road in a valley bottom, with terraced streets of sooty stone back-to-back mill-workers' houses running up the slopes of the valley. The town had several integral settlements and outlying villages and some of these areas were to play a large part in Bob's and his thirteen childrens' lives: places such as Batley Carr, Woodsome Estate, Purlwell, Staincliffe, Birstall and Healey.

Bob's Mam, Winnie Hirst (née Coleman), was born into a Batley-Irish-Catholic family around 1890. Like many northern industrial towns at that time, Batley had a sizeable Irish population consisting of people escaping poverty and famine in Ireland by finding work in the ever-expanding job markets of industrialised England. In 1912 Batley, the Irish community was already well established and had created its own little bit of Ireland in the small terraced streets leading off the main street of the town centre and in the Cross Bank area nearby. The sacred focus of life for "Batley-Irish fowk" was St. Mary's Roman Catholic Church at Cross Bank, where the priests were always Irish. The profane focus, tucked away in one of the little central Batley side streets near where Bob was born, was the National Irish Democratic League Club, more popularly known as the "Nash." At St. Mary's and at the Nash, the Batley-Irish developed and perpetuated their own culture and thereby maintained a measure of identity and dignity.

Not everyone found identity and dignity through living and worshipping within their own community. Some of the Irish incomers felt persecuted, belittled and ashamed, finding themselves in a minority, surrounded by an uncomprehending and suspicious majority indigenous population. Some turned to drink and other palliatives to escape a cruel world, and Winnie might well have been one of the drinkers in the Batley-Irish community. Bob's wife Mary certainly thought so:

"Shi wor a bad un. Nivver ad nowt good teh seh abaht nubdi. Yeh cud see er on a Fridi neet, slipping on teh Club wi a jug fer er beer, er else gin, spending er wages frum mill. Shi luvd er drink did that lady. Shi chased me an Bob all dahn roo-ed, yeh knaw, wen wi towd er wi wah gooin ter av teh get married."

And Bob, in one of his sanctimonious moods, sometimes agreed with Mary. Hunched up in his chair in the living room he would point at the ceiling and heaven beyond and blame Winnie for his own heavy drinking.

"It wah that lady. Er up yonder. *She* started me off ont ale, tha knaws."

Winnie's heavy drinking was shameful for Bob. He thought much of the blame for her boozing was due to her Irish blood; the Irish blood she passed down to him. Heavy drinking did feature in Winnie's life but her drinking habit must have been as much due to grief and desolation as it was to her Irish descent, after losing her husband in the First World War, when Bob was three and his younger brother James just a few months old.

Bob's father, also called Robert, came from a respectable non-Catholic working class Batley family. No one knows now how Robert and Winnie met or how they came to be married. But mixed marriages, usually through the force of strong mutual attraction and love, have always happened, even between people living in the most entrenched and divided communities. Robert's and Winnie's must have been one such marriage. There was probably strong disapproval in the Hirst family over Robert marrying an Irish Catholic girl. In pre-First World War Batley, rough Irish Catholics and respectable English Protestants were as segregated from, and alien to each other, as Republicans and Orangemen at the height of the troubles in Northern Ireland in the 1970s. Right up to the 1950s, when Bob's middle son Brian was at junior school, long after the waves of Irish immigration into the town ended, Catholic and Protestant kids used to taunt each other in the street, calling out "Catty Cats" or "Proddy Dogs;" the Cats being Batley Irish Catholic kids and the Dogs Batley English Protestants.

It must have taken strong will and deep love to make Robert and Winnie take the plunge into marriage, against the tide of disapproval from their respective families. But Robert's and Winnie's marriage did not last long. Robert was slaughtered on September 24th 1915 in France, the day before the Battle of Loos began, a battle in which 50,000 British and 25,000 Germans died. Throughout his life Bob found it difficult to talk about his fatherless childhood, except to Mary, especially when they were young and courting, or when he was drunk, later in his life. Mary said there was always tension between Winnie, and Robert's mother and sister, when Bob and James were growing up.

"Yeh see, Bob's Granma Est, an is Anty Mary, wah respectable fowk. Thi dint owd wi Winnie's drinkin, an way shi dragged them two bairns up. Ah dooern't knaw

3

what Bob an Jimmy'd've ended up like wi'aht Granma Est an Aunty Mary looking after em, while *she* wah boozin in pub."

Despite Granma Hirst's and Aunty Mary's efforts to save Bob and James from their mother's ways, they both became heavy drinkers when they grew up. James died in his early-sixties, quite probably largely from long-term alcohol abuse. Bob lived to eighty but illness, some of it related to heavy drinking, was a major problem in his life, from his fifties onward. Childhood was not entirely harsh and bleak for Bob and James. The two boys were fast and powerful swimmers and both were cup-winners in local school galas held at Batley Town Baths during their early teenage years in the mid-1920s. Bob also trained in boxing and fought in local competitions. Someone must have encouraged the boys to compete; someone must have planted the aspiration in them to become champions in sports. Perhaps it was Winnie who sowed that ambition in them, willing them to follow in the footsteps of her lost brave young husband. Or perhaps it was Granma Hirst and Aunty Mary who encouraged the boys to race and win: in memory of their Dad.

Mary once described Bob and James, as children, spending much of their time at Aunty Mary's and Granma Hirst's respectable houses in a respectable part of working class Batley, away from rough Winnie and her drunken goings-on. They spent hours gazing at the street outside from behind the net curtained window of Granma Hirst's and Auntie Mary's immaculate front parlours. Who knows what was in their young minds as they gazed? Were they thinking of returning to their Mam after the day spent with Granma and Auntie Mary, wondering if she would be angry, and drunk, when they returned home? Or perhaps they gazed into their hoped-for futures, seeing themselves as glorious heroic men like their father, spurred on to think like this by their adoring Auntie Mary and Granma Hirst.

The achievements of Bob and James did not end with the swimming trophies. Both brothers, in different ways, were successful young men. Before James became an inveterate drinker, he was a highly skilled master builder and that fact was often spoken of with great pride by Bob and Mary to their children.

"Yer Uncle Jimmy's a master builder, tha knaws. E's not just any owd brickie. Aye, lad. E's wekked all ovver, on sum gran big bildins. Yow name it, e's bin theer – Lundun, Leeds, Manchester, Liverpool. All bluddy ovver. An nor arf!"

Bob also was not without talents. There was a side to him, especially when he was young, which transcended the harsh and bleak in his life. He wrote beautiful copperplate handwriting and his grammar, spelling and punctuation were of a high standard. He was a soldier in the Second World War and sent wonderful, loving, pencil-written letters, in clear upper-case, to his son Barry and three daughters, Shirley, Margaret and Moira. He loved the poetry of Robert Burns and often recited it in later life at great length when he was drunk. It was after the war that he started drinking heavily and the habit continued well into his seventies. During those long years, he often returned home from the Nash after closing time, his breath reeking from the pints of Tetley's Mild he had consumed over the previous three hours, full of inchoate, rambling, slurred words; words which cut through the love book Mary was trying to read, curled up on the settee in the sitting room; words which ruined the TV programme his children were watching.

"Mary, lass. Mary, owd lass, grrr, er, gurr. Mek me a cupper tee, owd, owd, owd … lass."

Mary would throw him a withering furious look and then pretend to go back to reading her book, while Bob sank in his chair, clumsily undoing his tie and shoe laces. Apart from the noise of the telly, there was silence for a moment. And then:

"Brian, Brian? David? David, owd cock. Aster read Rabbie Burns ut yon school tha gus teh? Aster? Aster read Rabbie Burns?"

Brian and David studiously ignored him, pretending to concentrate on the television. They had neither heard of, nor cared about, Rabbie Burns. They just yearned for Bob to shut up or go to bed. The rambling, slurred monologue continued until everyone gave up and Mary and the children went to bed, leaving Bob alone in the living room, maundering on about Rabbie and disjointedly reciting a poem Burns wrote to his own Mary Lass.

Bob's life went awry for him in its later stages, at the end of the Second World War and after, when he could only express himself after drinking. But he was a happy and contented husband and father who enjoyed the adventure of going to war – at first. He was initially placed in the King's Own Yorkshire Light Infantry as a private, the same regiment and rank as his father when he joined the First War in 1914. Bob went to war with his lifelong mates, Tommy Tighe and Paddy Mac. Years after the war ended, some time in the early 1960s, Paddy and Tommy arrived at Mary's and Bob's house one day to collect Bob for an all-day drinking party, celebrating Paddy's birthday down at the Nash. Paddy was a squat, garrulous, barrel of a man with a beery red face, whereas Tommy was quiet and slim; dark, oily and weasel-like. When the two men arrived, Bob was still upstairs "preenin hissen," as Mary caustically put it, preparing to look his best for the birthday bash. Paddy started reminiscing while he was waiting for Bob, telling the middle Hirst boys – John, Malcolm, Brian and David – about those early days in the war.

"Oo aye, lads. We was all in bluddy Egypt. Me, yeh Dad, an Tommy-ay-tie-ay. All three on us. In desert. Wi Monty, an Rommel, an all them bluddy lot. By! It wor ot. Thas no idea wor ot is, until tha gus teh desert in Egypt. Wi wah Prince Farouk's body guards tha knaws. Aye. Bluddy

King en Egypt's lad. E wor a reight bugger, an nor arf, wah Farouk. Dusta remember, Tommy, that time in 'Xandria? Farouk tuk us teh ivvry bluddy bar i town. By ell, did we-er sup sum stuff between us that neet. Eh? Eh, Tommy, owd cock?"

There was an influential Uncle Bill in Bob's life, his father's brother, who was lucky enough to survive the First World War. Bill could never forget the slaughter of his brother, and the lessons war taught him about the rulers and ruled of this world. Uncle Bill was already working in the Yorkshire mines when Bob followed him there after he left school at the age of fourteen in 1926 – the year of the General Strike. Bill was active in the Strike and served a short prison sentence for taking part in it. He exerted a strong influence on young Bob politically, giving him a fire in his belly for right against wrong and for justice against injustice, especially when it came to the working man's eternal subjugation to his bosses.

So there was bleakness and harshness in Bob's life as a child and young man. There was alcohol, guilt and shame. But there was fun and comradeship with his mates. There was talent and natural ability, especially in sport. There was aspiration, political idealism, and a love of poetry and words.

Bob had been hewing in the mines for seven years by 1933, the year he met Mary Wolstenholme. He was twenty one and Mary was eighteen. Only months after they met, Bob and Mary married and less than nine months after their marriage they had their first child Barry, in May 1934. At the time of his marriage to Mary, Bob was a confirmed, devout Roman Catholic: his Mam Winnie made sure of that. Mary's parents, John and Elsie Wolstenholme, were not religious and nor was Mary. The bigoted elderly Irish Catholic priest at St. Mary's, Father Shine, refused to marry Bob and Mary unless Mary promised to devote herself to understanding Catholicism before she married. It was all mumbo-jumbo to Mary, this business of Catholicism, and so Bob, with great bitterness and sorrow, and against Winnie's wishes, renounced the Catholic Church (though never the faith) and was married in the Church of England instead. Bob and Mary had thirteen children, born over the first twenty-four years of their fifty-nine-year-long marriage, from Barry the oldest, to Shirley; Moira; Margaret; Robert; John; Malcolm; Brian; David; Richard; Stephen; Lynne and Michael, the youngest.

After he married, Bob continued working in the mines until 1939, when Britain declared war on Germany. By that time he had also joined the Territorial Army and when war broke out, he was already a physically fit Territorial soldier and the right age, and he was immediately recruited into full-time military service. He served with Paddy Mac and Tommy Tighe only for a short time in Egypt. When the army discovered he was a miner, Bob was moved to the Sappers and was posted to Gibraltar, then Malta. While serving in Malta, Bob received a letter telling him of Winnie's death, and not long after, he received even more terrible news: his fourth child Margaret had died of meningitis, aged four. Apart from the grief and pain that losing a child brings to any parent, Margaret's death, according to Mary, was to prove momentous for Bob, changing the whole course of his life and deeply affecting his personality; for the worse. In her nineties, Mary told Brian the story of what happened after Bob learned of "Ower Margaret's" death.

" E asked feh funeral leave, yeh knaw, luv. But army wouldn't gi it ter im. Thi towd im if ower Margaret'd still been alive, but seriously ill an dyin, then thi'd've gi-en im leave. But thi said what wah point er doin that, when she wor already dead? Well, yeh can guess wor appened then, can't yeh? He carried on, dint e? Said e *had* teh gu ter is own dowter's funeral Yeh know wor e wah like. E went mad. What do thi call it these days? E went ballistic. Shoutin an swearin. Smashin things up. Lashin aht at ivvribody."

Due to Bob's bad behaviour, the corporal stripes he had only recently been awarded were withdrawn and he was put in army prison for a spell, to calm him down. But he did not calm down. He ranted and raved until eventually he had a nervous breakdown and was invalided out of the army. Bob never fully recovered from his nervous breakdown. The war, and Winnie's and Margaret's deaths, scarred him deeply psychologically and on top of that he was scarred from being forced to leave the Catholic Church when he married Mary. He was incapable of speaking of these mental wounds for most of his life and they festered inside him always, only coming out in garbled words and actions when he was drunk.

Bob's quality of life began to decline after the war. One of his knees was damaged and he lost most of his sight in one eye, in accidents in the mines, which forced him above ground for good. He also caught what the army medics called sand fly fever (a form of malaria) during his time in Egypt and this, he claimed, gave him a poorly stomach for the rest of his life. Bob's occupation, written on Brian's birth certificate of December 1946, is "coal miner (hewer)," but he gave up hewing just a few years later and was employed in various unskilled jobs after leaving the pit. Sometimes he was a builder's labourer, sometimes a dustman.

Bob became ill with stomach ulcers around the age of fifty. Brian arrived home from school one day to be met on the door step by a desperate Mary, and the sound of Bob groaning in agony on his bed upstairs.

"Oo, thank God yer ere Brian. Yeh Dad's be-ern browt back frum wek errli. Ah dooern't knaw what's up wi im. Ark at im. E's been like that since e got back. Run dahn teh phone box, luv, an ger an amblance."

It was 1963 and neither the Hirsts nor any of their neighbours owned telephones. The nearest public telephone box was a good three-to-four minute fast run from where they lived. Brian made it to the phone box in three minutes and an ambulance soon arrived to take Bob to hospital. A stomach ulcer had perforated and the discharge was poisoning his stomach. Within hours of his admission to hospital he was given emergency surgery and part of his stomach was removed. He never worked again properly after that, living on sick pay and small army and mining disability pensions, doing only brief periods of unskilled work which gradually stopped altogether by the time he reached his late-fifties.

Bob went into terrible dark moods after drinking; moods which often lasted weeks. Brian's earliest memories of his father are all of a dark, distant, unloving man, except when he was drunk, when he would sometimes show affection for his children. He did not mistreat his post-war children in a physical way but he was distant and apparently indifferent to them. He did not seem to notice them and rarely spoke to them directly. He often treated Mary with a callous indifference, or a maudlin affection when it suited him, or when he was drunk, like the times he came back from the Nash, garbling on about Rabbie Burns and his Mary Lass.

During his childhood years in the 1950s and early-1960s, Brian's predominant memories of Bob are of a dark brooding man who maintained a big distance between himself and his bairns, in a household which was always full of children. Bob and Mary lived in four child-filled houses over the nearly-sixty years of their marriage, from 1934 to 1993:

1934 – 1947: Wainwrights Buildings; a one-down, two-up back-to-back stone terraced house in Batley Carr;

1947 – 1952: Woodsome Estate, on the edge of Victorian Batley; a three-bed council house;

1952 – 1970: 77 Chapel Fold, Staincliffe Estate; a 4-bed council house, even further on the edge of Batley than Woodsome;

1970 – 1993: 6 Russel Close. A three-bed council house at Central Estate, very near the town centre and the area where Bob was born and brought up.

With Bob's connivance, one of his sons, Malcolm, bought the Russell Close house in the 1980s, when Margaret Thatcher liberated the working classes of Britain from bondage and embraced them into her home-owning democracy. Mary and Bob were never part of the material progress made by many in Britain after the war and into the first years of the twenty-first century. But they did make progress in their housing conditions: from a two-up-one-down-back-to-back, to a three-bed former council house, eventually owned by one of their nine sons: a house where Mary lived for another ten years after Bob died.

For Bob, going to live at Russell Close when he was nearing sixty was like going back to the Batley of his childhood. The Batley Town Centre of 1912, the year Bob was born, was much changed by 1970, but for Bob, Russell Close was not very far from where he and James grew up with Winnie, before he moved to "far-away" Batley Carr after marrying Mary. (Batley Carr is, in fact, about a mile from Batley town centre, down the Bradford Road, going toward Dewsbury.) When he was not brooding darkly in his easy chairs in the three front rooms of his post-war houses, often entirely on his own, with the rest of his family escaping his moodiness by packing themselves into the back rooms, Bob was a worrier and a nagger and Mary took the brunt of his nagging.

"Mary. Ave yeh sin them bluddy wet towels thrown all ovver bathroom floo-er? Can't yeh geh them bluddy lads teh side em away in t'immersion cubberd after thiv ad a bath?"

"Or, feh God's sake Bob. Stop yeh bluddy moanin. Why dooern't yeh tell em yersen, if yeh that bothered?"

"Ah wish thad tek moo-er care washin them pans up, Mary. Look! Look at this wun. Thes bits er bluddy owd tatie and God knaws wot in corners. Just tek a look at it. It's no bluddy wunder my stummak's like it is. Thes bluddy gerrms all ovver these pans."

"Oo aye! Is the? Yeh see that theer? It's called a dish cloth. Why dooern't y'ave a gu at usin it if yeh doo-ern't like way ah wash up? An as foh yer bluddy poorly stummak. Yer knaw full well whah tha's wi."

"Woh'si wi?"

"Bluddy beer. If tha stopped suppin that stuff, yeh stummak'd bi better i noo-er time."

If Mary was not on hand to receive his complaints, Bob sometimes exploded with temper at his children, threatening to kill them or belt them black and blue but rarely even touching them physically. Except for Brian, all of Bob's sons, and his oldest daughter Shirley, shared his love of sports, both as spectators and participants. Through sport there was a thread of bonding between Bob and them. Brian had no interest in sport as a child and no confidence in his physical abilities and so the potential thread of contact, of bonding through sport, did not exist between him and Bob. But there were rare occasions in Brian's childhood when Bob snapped out of his customary taciturnity. Usually, his sudden cheerfulness was a preliminary sign of his intention "teh slope off teh Nash" (as Mary put it) for a few pints of beer, after several days of abstemiousness. When he was in a good mood he liked to tease from his armchair, calling his children pet names; "fishface" and "buggerlugs" were two of his favourites. In this mood, he liked to be served by Mary and the bairns:

"Mary, lass. Mek me a cuppa tee-er."

"Oy, fishface. Pass mi them cigs ovver ere."

Bob loved animals and there was always a pet in the house which was always his pet first and a family pet second. Mary had little time for pets, saying she had more than enough to do looking after Bob and her bairns let alone a cat or a dog. Blackie the cat lived with the family for seventeen years at Woodsome and Chapel Fold. She was a mangy, skinny creature in her later years with large balding patches on her black fur. She was a prolific breeder which pleased Bob but made Mary demented with anger when she discovered Blackie's latest nest of offspring – in the clean blanket cupboard, or behind the shoes under the staircase. Sam, a black half-corgi, half-everything-else, lived for fourteen years at Chapel Fold. He was a wilful, surly dog and nobody could control him when he decided to chase a car, or a cat, or when he just ran off out of sheer defiance. Sam used to pester Mary in her scullery, especially if she was cooking meat. He had a habit of standing right behind her, sniffing avidly as she tested the meat in the oven, causing her to fall over him as she moved around.

"Ger aht-er me roo-ed, floo-wer claat," she would yell, kneeing him up his arse, away from her cooker, after he ignored several of her more patient demands.

In his more affable, reflective moods, Bob spent hours stroking and grooming his current pet. He would kiss and stroke animals – and pre-walking-talking babies – but he was incapable of showing physical affection otherwise. In front of the children, he never kissed or touched Mary, or indeed any of them, once they started walking and talking. Sometimes Bob linked arms with Mary on the rare occasions that they went off teh Nash or to a pub together for a night of drinking and socialising with friends. Sometimes Bob appeared by the side of the bed Brian and David shared when they were young, waking them from sleep, touching their faces and rubbing his bristly jaw against their cheeks, murmering affectionate words, his breath reeking of beer. It was something he never did when sober, no matter how good his mood.

Bob often showed contempt for his younger brother James. The relationship between them was that of the older responsible brother dominating the younger weaker

13

one. James intermittently turned up late at night at Chapel Fold, or Russell Close, drunk out of his mind; shouting in the street; showing everybody up; making a nuisance of himself.

"Jesus, Jimmy. What's tha think thas doin? Terr-nin up ere et this time er neet in this bluddy state. Ah'm bluddy ashamed er thi. I am that. Ger off owme wi yeh."

"Aw get shifted, Bob. As if you nivver goh bluddy drunk! E's yer brutther. Wi can't tern im away. Cum in, Jimmy lad, an stop yeh shartin. Tha'll wek bairns up wi yeh noise. That's it, owd lad. In yeh cum."

When James arrived out of the blue in a drunken state it was because he was homeless and had been on a long drinking spree and he needed somewhere to kip down for a few days and nights, before sobering up and finding somewhere new to live, and then starting another building job. Bob and James adopted the roles they probably had as boys whenever James came to stay. Uncle James would hang his head in shame on the morning following his drunken arrival.

"Mary, owd lass. Ah'm reight sorry feh last neet. Ah'd got now call cummin ere i that state. Ah'm fair ashamed er missen. I am that."

"Nay owd lad. Nivver eed. Cum an geh sum brekfest."

"Nivver eed? Nivver eed? What yeh bluddy talkin abaht? An so you *shud* be bluddy ashamed. When's thar bahner grow up'n geh thissen settled dahn, an stop yeh bluddy boozin?"…

Until eventually James found somewhere new to live and work. Then he left, until his next drunken spree. Inbetween drinking sessions James worked hard in the building trade for many years but in his late-fifties he had a serious accident at work which left him with severe head injuries and blindness, forcing him to stop work. After the accident, James became a more settled presence in the family. Before, no one knew where James lived. He

14

just turned up occasionally at the current Hirst house, completely intoxicated, from "sumweer-er-uther." But eventually he lived in a council flat in nearby Birstall which he shared with John; a heavy-drinking compatriot of his.

There was something about Uncle James's abject shame after a drinking spree, about his obsequiousness toward Bob, and his grovelling apologies to Mary, that repelled Brian. When he became blind he used to ask who was in the room on his visits to Chapel Fold. He liked to trace the shape of his nephews' faces with his hands as they told him their names, which Brian also found repellent. Moira, John and Michael were all close to James; they knew and understood his lifestyle and when he settled into the council flat at Birstall they helped him with cleaning, shopping and decorating. During his years in Birstall, followed by some months in sheltered housing back in Cross Bank, James continued drinking heavily, until he died in his middle sixties. He left all his fortune of a couple of thousand pounds in cash in his sheltered flat when he died. It was to go to Bob. Picture Bob: in the living room at Russell Close just after James died, frantically counting his legacy up, into piles of a hundred pound:

"Afoo-er bluddy tax-man finnds aht an teks it all off us. Ere wi gu. Wun pownd, two pownds, ninety nine powds, a bluddy undred: one pownd, two pounds, ninety nine – an two undred" …

Bob's excitement over James's legacy was a rare thing. Toward his children he was usually silent, withdrawn. Sometimes for weeks at a time he moodily hunched himself up in his armchair, barely saying a word to anyone, in a house that was almost always full of people. At other times his silence denoted complete absorption; it was the silence of an indefatigable letter writer. For many years he wrote dozens of letters to whom it concerned, outlining his case for compensation pensions: from the army, for his contracting malaria during the war, which he swore was the sole culprit behind his stomach problems, and from the mining authorities, for his eye and knee injuries, incurred when he hewed underground. He spent hours and hours, drafting and re-drafting the letters before writing up a beautiful copperplate final copy to put in the post, until "them lot" (the army and mining compensation review boards) were forced to take account of his case. Eventually, and entirely due to his dogged persistence, he was awarded both army and mining disability pensions, which enabled him to enjoy some quality of life in later years through travel and buying items for himself, for Mary and for the house; things he would not have been able to afford on sick pay and the basic old age pension.

Bob's spelling, punctuation and grammar standards were good and his letters demonstrated his wide vocabulary. The idiom of his letters was highly elaborate and ornamented by modern standards:

"Dearest Sir,

I am writing to you, an honourable and learned member of the medical profession, as a mere working man, seeking compensation for the injuries and illnesses which have bedevilled my life over numerous years ..."

The teenage Brian once took a sneaky look at one of these letters and it struck him as strange and impressive that this silent, withdrawn, mute man had so many long words, phrases and sentences; frothing away inside his head.

Although Bob could be critical of Mary's cooking and housework, they were activities he had nothing to do with for most of his life. Bob and Mary came from a generation where it was an incontrovertible fact that the woman did the cooking and housework, not the man of the house. But Mary did sometimes doughtily grumble over Bob treating her as his cook and maid, especially when they were arguing over his sloping off teh Nash. It was a little lever of power she had over Bob: his dependence on her for his domestic needs. During the early 1960s, Bob's domestic dependence on Mary was temporarily broken when she enjoyed a spell in hospital, leaving him to cope with looking after the five youngest children. David and Brian – the oldest two bairns – were able to cook simple meals by this time. But to their astonishment and dismay, on the first day of Mary's absence from home, Bob insisted on being fully in charge of the house and the cooking. It was extraordinary to the two boys: the man who normally expected even a cup of tea to be mashed for him and served at his armchair by Mary or one of his children, was now planning to take on the domestic regime. Fifteen-year-old Brian and fourteen-year-old David suspected Bob was using the occasion as an opportunity of getting closer to them; to prove he could be a proper Dad. He perhaps had some idea of how alien and distant he had become and he saw Mary's absence as a chance of filling the void between himself and his middle sons.

The day Bob took over the cooking was a complete disaster. An hour or so before dinnertime, David suggested they could all have egg and chips.

"Bugger yeh bluddy egg-n-chips. Thi naw good feh yer at all. Thas bahner ave a proper meal terdee, an ahm doin it."

Bob ushered David and Brian away from the gas cooker and bent down to get one of the meat roasting tins from the compartment at the bottom of the gas oven. They watched him in astonishment from the scullery doorway. It seemed he really meant it when he said he was cooking dinner. He reached into the pantry and brought out onions, cheese and tinned tomatoes. He chopped the onions roughly and layered them in the roasting tin. He poured a tin of tomatoes over the onions and topped it with thick slices of cheddar cheese. He put the roasting tin in the gas oven at far too high a temperaturte for far too long. He snapped at David and Brian, who were by now rooted in fascination; pulling faces at what was happening.

"An yow tow can stop pullin them funny faces. This is bahner be a gran dinner, is this. Better fer yeh than bluddy egg-n-chips. Nah then. Ah think thah's dun."

The finished result was awful. The cheese and onions were badly burned in parts and hardly cooked in others, while the tomatoes were dried-out husks of rusty looking stuff, scattered amongst the burnt cheese and onions. By this time, Richard, Stephen and Lynne had smelled the food from out in the garden where they had been playing and they came inside, eager for dinner.

"Brian, mek thissen users-ful. Geh sum bread buttered fer us t'ave wi this ere cheese-n-unyen."

He served the concoction onto plates, with a mountain of bread in the middle of the table, layered in Stork margarine. Everyone sat or stood round the table to eat. David and Brian giggled and made a few stabs at the mess. Richard went into a furious temper at the very idea of eating this stuff. Stephen and Lynne cried. They did not recognise it as food. Bob's first day of taking over Mary's regime was his last. It was David and Brian who ended up soaking and cleaning the blackened roasting tin. The next day, Bob sulked in his armchair in the front room as the two oldest boys cooked and served up beans and chips for themselves and the young-uns.

Pizza was completely unknown in Batley in 1960, except perhaps among a few "posh fowk." Maybe Bob tasted it in Malta and Gibraltar in the war and his cheese, onion and tomato concoction was his version, from memory, of that then exotic dish. Although Bob never spoke of it, the basic ingredients of Mediterranean cuisine must have lodged themselves in his taste bud memory, from his wartime experiences and his mess was an attempt to re-create those flavours. In his sixties and seventies, Bob periodically became convinced it was Mary's cooking that was poisoning his stomach. Mary's protests that alcohol might also have something to do with it were dismissed as preposterous and he would suddenly decide to boycot her meals for a few days and prepare his own food instead. His favourite recipe was a distant relative of another great Mediterranean dish: minestrone soup. He took the biggest boiling pan he could find in Mary's scullery and poured tins of tomatoes into it, adding roughly chopped onions, celery, carrot, potatoes and water. He then left the mixture in the pan to simmer, for hours and hours. And once it was thoroughly cooked to a soup consistency, he ate his "muckment," as Mary called it, for days at a time, dipping and soaking bread into it. Bob's weird ideas about food were a joke amongst the rest of the family in those days before celebrity TV chefs but his dishes had the basic concept of healthy food at heart. He had good ideas about healthy eating but lacked the skills to implement them.

When Bob moved "back" to Russell Close, he was fully ill-health retired and from then, his life slotted into regular patterns of behaviour. The worst pattern was when he went on a several-day drinking spree, down at the Nash. As he grew older he became less and less able to hold his beer and he would roll up the hill to Russell Close after closing time, when the rest of the family had gone to bed, talking and chuntering gibberish, all to himself. Once inside the house he sat in his armchair all alone: talking, singing and calling out to Mary, who was upstairs in bed, trying to sleep, along with the bairns. His solitary drunken racket often went on until three or four in the morning, until sleep finally overtook him, in the middle of a rambling monologue, and silence descended upon Russell Close.

After a few days on the booze Bob was forced to temporarily stop drinking beer by his poorly stomach. Coming off the booze always plunged him into a foul mood and he skulked in bed for several days, only coming downstairs at night when everyone else was asleep. During the day, Mary took invalid snacks upstairs to him: a banana sandwich, a bowl of tinned soup, and the like. Sooner or later he would tire of staying in bed and he sulked all day and most of the night in his chair by the fireplace at Russell Close, watching day and night television, disregarding what anyone else might want to watch. Or he moodily read through the claims letters he had written years earlier, or looked at old photographs, which he kept in a ramshackle cupboard in the fireplace corner by his chair, along with other sundry memorabilia, such as his old army boot cleaning brushes and rags, and his and his Dad's war medals.

After a few days of moody TV watching and going through his things, he cheered up a little, especially if the weather was good. On a hot sunny day he loved to strip down to his swimming trunks and lie all day in the sun on the back garden grass at Russell Close, just outside the kitchen door. Perhaps he thought of happier times, lying in the sun; remembering hot sunny Egypt, with Paddy Mac and Tommy Tighe. Perhaps it was on one of those sunny days that he started to think about building a back garden path, prompted by Mary's complaints over how steep the back garden was, making it difficult for her to find her balance to hang out the washing. Bob spent years, on-and-off, building a stepped path from the kitchen door to the highest level of the garden. His building method was unusual. First, he nagged and nattered Mary.

"What yeh bluddy doin? Throwin them tins in bin? Ah've towd yer. Ahm savin em. Give us em ere."

He grabbed every empty tin he could get hold of from Mary, for weeks and weeks, peeling off the labels then swilling the tins under the kitchen tap, before throwing them underneath the kitchen window outside. Mary looked on with a mixture of bemusement and annoyance.

"What the bluddy ell ah you lakin at, Bob? Thes a bin aht theer feh waste. What yeh doin? Throwin tins in garden?"

Bob flashed a sly grin at her.

"Nivver thee mind. Mek sure tha dooern't throw now moo-er tins in bin. Ahm savin em. Tha'll soon finnd aht why."

When a pile of tins had accumulated in the garden corner outside the kitchen door, he then spent hours patiently flattening them with a heavy hammer and when he thought there were enough, he dug out the foundation for the first step of his new garden path. It was only then that he revealed his secret: the tins were to form the hard core for the path.

"Why the bluddy ell do ah nee-erd teh spend time an munny on ardcore, when wiv gor all thee-ers tins gooin spare? It's a shame teh waste 'em, an norarf."

He spent hours hammering and flattening the hundreds of tins. Then he "borrowed" sand and cement, and bricks for the low side walls, from his oldest son Barry, who by that time had his own building business, until eventually a rickety and precarious path, on a tin can foundation, was built. Later in life, he lost interest in the garden and his second son Robert (young Bob) removed the tin-can foundation and built a more conventional, long-lasting, safer path, for Mary's ease in hanging out her everlasting washing.

Long before the tin can path episode, when the family lived at Chapel Fold and Brian was around fifteen or sixteen, there was a rare – and brief – incident when Bob made an effort to reach out to him; to make the contact of a father to his son, and not through sport. By that age Brian was an avid reader. He was beginning to develop a love of words. He loved the sound of words just for their own sake and he loved collecting new words to add to his expanding vocabulary. Normally his father barely even acknowledged his existence but on this occasion he did. Brian was sitting in the sun in the back garden and Mary was there, hanging out the washing. Bob was in the garden, too: in one of his lecturing moods. He pointed at a pile of old rubbish – bits of ironwork, old worn out footballs, discarded toys and dog bones – built up under the back room window.

"Look-et it, Mary! Look-et all this bluddy rubbish. It'll bi attracting rats an all soo-erts. It's time thah got rid on it, instead a lerrin it pile up ere. It's just. It's just... *accumulating*."

"Theer's bluddy coil shuvvle, ovver theer. If yeh thah bothered abaht it, why doo-ern't *yoo* shuvvle it up, an throw it in bin yersen?"

As usual Bob ignored Mary's riposte. Instead, he looked directly at Brian hard when he said that lovely word: accumulating. He was trying to reach out to his son, through a word. Brian did not respond directly, although a look of recognition passed between him and Bob. Later, he looked the word up in a school dictionary and added it to his vocabulary.

There was a small bookcase in the front room at Chapel Fold. As well as other books, the shelves held the complete works of Charles Dickens, which Brian steadily read his way through over a period of six years, starting with *Pickwick Papers*, aged ten in 1957, and ending with *David Copperfield*, at the age of sixteen. The Second World War was more than ten years over in 1957 but it was only then that some of its darker aspects were becoming part of widespread public knowledge in Britain. It was around this time that Bob bought a set of *Illustrated History Of The Second World War* volumes. The Dickens volumes were old and musty with faded blue cloth covers, making the brand new war books stand out on the bookshelves, with their bright red covers, large gold front-cover lettering and glue-smelling glossy pages. Bob never spoke directly of his war experiences to his younger children, born after the war. Occasionally, the "younger-end" might hear him obliquely referring to the war when he was talking to Mary, or to one of the "older-end," or to an adult visitor. Sometimes he angrily hectored Mary while she was cooking in the Chapel Fold scullery.

"An thah bluddy bastard Monty. What did e knaw? E kept issen well beyind lines, wi all them uther bluddy bastard genrals."

"Aw, feh God's sake, Bob. War's ovver wi. Why can't yeh jus feh-gerit?"

In reply, he would shoot a hopeless stricken look at Mary and moodily leave her with her cooking, shuffling off to the front room to browse through one of the shiny new war books. He was oblivious of everyone and anything as he pored silently over those illustrated volumes, sitting in the big easy chair, reading every word, brooding over the photographs. One day he went out of the front room, leaving a war book lying open on the arm of the chair where he had been sitting. Brian was reading Dickens, inbetween gazing at the Boz cartoons, lying on the floor behind the sofa, while Bob read his war book. He was curious over Bob's new reading material and went to look at the open book on the chair arm, taking advantage of Bob's absence from the room. He saw a photograph of human corpses piled high, at a place called Belsen. The photograph filled the page and the printed words on the opposite page told him how and why the corpses were there. Bob returned and caught him looking at the picture of the corpses. Brian was deeply troubled and perturbed by the photograph and he wanted to understand the words telling him about Belsen and what the Nazis did to the Jews. He wanted to ask Bob about "Belsen" and "Jews" and "Nazis." But Bob was too remote, too far away in another world, and he dared not ask. He returned to Dickens, lying on the floor behind the sofa.

For just a moment, Bob looked as if he might say something, but changed his mind. Instead, he sat down, took the book from the chair arm and resumed his brooding silent reading. Did he want Brian to ask about

Belsen? And if he had asked, would he have been able to explain? It seemed he could not bring himself to even try, but the way he pored over the war volumes in 1957 was a clear sign that even though the war was ten years over, it still filled his head.

The only time Brian ever saw the war spill out of Bob's head and become externally manifest was some twenty five years after he first saw the photograph of the Belsen corpses. Brian was in his thirties and Bob was nearing seventy. It was thirty five years since the end of the Second World War. Brian was staying at Russell Close during a holiday from his schoolteaching post in Derbyshire. By then Bob and Mary had the house to themselves, as all their twelve surviving children were married or living elsewhere. Bob had been out on a night's drinking spree down at the Nash and Mary and Brian were both in bed when he returned, mumbling to himself. Instead of the usual hours of talking to himself downstairs in his chair, he came up to bed within a few minutes. As he was falling asleep, Brian heard Bob muttering as he changed into his pyjamas in the bathroom, before stumbling across the landing to his and Mary's bedroom. A second or two later – so it seemed – Brian was suddenly awoken by a voice calling out in fear. It was Bob, on the unlit dark landing outside the bedroom door. He was making a terrible noise. It was a mixture of moaning, growling and crying. The noises were building up into an awful, roaring crisis. Disturbed, Brian got out of bed, opened the bedroom door, and switched on the landing light. Bob was standing on the landing dressed in pyjamas. He was holding a sweeping brush left by Mary on the landing. He held it as if it were a bayonet or a long-handled weapon and he was staring, wide-eyed and terrified, straight ahead at the closed door of the airing cupboard. He was a few feet away from the cupboard but he looked as if he was staring across a huge empty distance. He made a jabbing motion with the brush and aimed it at the cupboard door. He was groaning and was about to charge at the door and smash the brush into it.

"Dad. What's the matter? Come on, give me the brush."

Brian reached out to take the brush from Bob's hands and the sound of his son's voice seemed to pull him out of the nightmare. He meekly let Brian take the brush before shuffling back to bed. After returning to bed himself, Brian stayed awake, musing over what had happened and he realised, for the first time, how War had dominated Bob's life: from the death of his father in the First World War, to his own front-line experience of the Second World War. Bob was just one of hundreds of thousands of the inter-war generation, across the world, whose mental life was damaged by the two World Wars of the twentieth century. And still, in our own century, our world leaders play the war game.

Despite the mental wounds that war inflicted on Bob, there were happier times in his later years. As he grew older and less mobile he loved to watch television, especially re-showings of American popular movies from the 1930s to the 1950s, and all the big sporting events. For months before colour television became widely available in Britain in the early 1960s, the three terrestrial TV channels then available were constantly giving out trailers:

"From such-and-such a day, you can watch such-and-such a programme in your very own front room – IN COLOUR!"

Bob and Mary still had their old monochrome set the day colour TV came to Britain. That evening, Mary noticed Bob seemed particularly keen to settle himself comfortably in his armchair facing the TV, with a pot of tea and biscuits to hand. She was puzzled, as no old American movies or big sporting events were showing on the telly. From the comfort of his armchair Bob gave his order to Mary:

"Mary, owd lass. Switch telly on."

Mary was pleased Bob was staying-in, so she played the good little wife and walked over and switched on the telly. (There were no remote controls in those days.) The TV image came on after a few seconds of fuzz. The picture was monochrome, of course.

"What the buddy ell's up wi this telly?" Grumbles Bob, shooting an angry look at Mary, now curled up on the settee, picking her toe nails, engrossed in reading a Woman's Own story, or a love book, or in completing a newspaper crossword.

"Whas up wi you? Yeh bluddy owd misery. Wor ave ah dun this time?" Snaps Mary, irritated and annoyed by Bob's interruption.

"Thas dun nowt. It's that. Thah bugger ovver theer. Tha's whasup," says Bob, angrily gesturing at the TV.

"Telly? Whasup wi it? It looks orreight teh me."

"Bloody thing's ser-poo-ersd ter bi i culler. Tha's whasup, yer dozy mare. Look at it. Look. It's still in black-n-white."

As far as Bob was concerned it was always Mary's fault if anything went wrong. At first he refused to believe her when she told him you actually had to buy or rent a colour TV and not all black and white ones were to magically transform into colour that night. But eventually he accepted his mistake and a shadow of a smile flickered across his face when he was teased over the colour telly episode later, by his oldest son Barry. He soon rented a colour set which he enjoyed for the rest of his life but his misunderstanding was typical of his lifelong ignorance of anything electrical or technological.

Until he reached his early-sixties Bob never went away on holiday. The most he might do was join the Nash Annual Day Trip in August to Blackpool, Morecombe or Scarborough, or spend a day at York Races. Mary was in her fifties before she could eventually afford to go away to the coast for a week in a B&B, or in a rented caravan. Before that, she had only ever been away from Batley on day trips – and not even on day trips before the war. But whenever she tried to persuade Bob to accompany her on a holiday he would only say he had enough of "bluddy away" in the war. And he would sulk at home for a week while Mary went off with her sister Louie, or with Barry's and Shirley's families, taking her youngest bairn Michael with her. To Mary's astonishment Bob came home quite sober from the Nash one day with his old army pal Paddy Mac. She was astonished because Bob never came home sober after drinking with Paddy and because of what Paddy was saying.

"Nah then, Mary owd lass. Me an thar Bob's bin talkin abaht this feh months nah. Yeh knaws it's cummin up teh winter soo-in, an all them cowd bluddy Ba'ley winds? Well ower Dave – an is missis an bairns – wants thee an Bob teh gu an spend three months wi em this winter. Ah canna gu missen this year, cos er thar operation ahm avin. It's summer tha knaws, in Australia, when it's winter ere."

"Nay Paddy, luv. Me an Bob can't affoo-werd teh fly ter Australia – can wi?"

Mary looked across at Bob for confirmation of what she had said but Paddy answered for him.

"Coo-ers yer can. Ahve bin inter it wi Bob. All yeh need is money feh tairfares. Ower Dave an is missis'll pay ferowt else. An yeh can affoo-erd tair fairs. Can't yeh, Bob?"

Bob nodded. Mary was flabbergasted. She was amazed by the very idea of travelling all the way round the world to Australia to stay with Paddy's Dave, who she hadn't seen since he was nowt but a little lad, afore he went off and emigrated. And she was amazed that Bob was so casually confirming they could afford the air fares: it was the first time *she* knew he had that much money to spare.

"Nay Paddy, owd lad. Ah can't bi gaddin off ter Australia feh three months. Worrif summat appened teh wun-er mi granbairns, while ah worraway? Ah'd nivver fergive missen. But gu on, Bob. You gu. Ah can see yeh wants-ter. Yow gu an enjoy yersen, owd lad. As'll be reight on me own ere, wi'art yoo-er luvly cheerful face arahnd."

Thus it was that in his sixties Bob went on a long-haul Qantas flight from Manchester to Sydney to stay in New South Wales for three months. The last time he had been away from home for more than a day was nearly forty years earlier, in the war. A few days after Bob returned from Australia Brian telephoned Mary.

"Ee d'yer knaw, Brian luv, yeh Dad's as brown as a berry! Last time ah saw him that brown wah when e cem ome on lee-erve, in war. E's browt loo-erds er-photers back wi im. Dave's gorra bewtiful garden theer – an a swimmin pool, yer knaw. By! Dave wor oney a slip on a bairn last time ah saw im. Oo, aye. An pichers er Dave's bairns, an all. All-on-em – yer Dad inclewded – avin a whale on a time, suppin beer rahnd swimmin pool. Aye. Pity e aster gu all way round world teh finnd imsen a family. Ah doo-ern't knaw what's wrong wi family e's gor ere. Still. T'owd lad. E enjoyed issen. An I enjoyed them few weeks wi'out im, an all. I expect e'll bi bluddy owd misery e allus is, afoor weeks aht."

Bob repeated his three month stays with his adoptive family in New South Wales the following two or three winters. After what was to prove Bob's final Australia trip, one of his middle sons, Malcolm, picked him up at Manchester Airport and was shocked to see him being pushed into Arrivals in a wheel chair, ashen-faced and exhausted, by a concerned Qantas stewardess. On the drive back to Batley from Manchester Malcolm gradually realised: yes, Bob was thoroughly exhausted but he also discovered he had not helped matters by drinking himself into a stupor during the long flight home. He was over seventy. It took him several weeks to recover from the long, alcohol-filled flight from Sydney and he never went again. But in those last few years of reasonable health and an awakening of his old self, he did persuade Mary to accompany him on a holiday organised by the British Legion; to Malta, where he was stationed in the war. They went to Yugoslavia, too, when there still was a Yugoslavia, in its last days before the going of Tito and the terrible near-total disintegration that followed.

On his trips to Malta and Yugoslavia Bob proudly wore his British Legion beret and blazer with his war medals decorating his chest. It pleased both him and Mary how well they were treated, and with such respect, by both the Maltese and the Yugoslavs when they saw Bob was a war veteran. When he reached his middle-seventies, Bob joined a British Legion trip he had wanted to make all his life: to the war cemeteries of France. He laid a wreath at the Menin Gate Memorial in Ypres, where he saw the name of the father he never knew, listed on panel 47. And when they were both nearing eighty, Mary agreed to marry Bob "properly" (as he thought of it) and a small RC wedding, with just themselves, the priest, and Paddy as witness, took place at St Mary's. Through these symbolic acts perhaps Bob at last found peace; recognition of his own worth; and reconciliation and amelioration inside his head of the bitternesses that had festered there so long.

From his late seventies Bob's health grew worse. He became a wizened, shrunken, grey-haired old man who ate little and spent most of his time in clear discomfort in bed. Being the faithful Roman Catholic he had always been, when he knew he was dying he returned to his Church. In his last months he attended Mass when he could at St Mary's, and when he was too weak to attend, a young, modern, warm Irish priest – quite different from that old bigot, Father Shine, who refused to marry Bob and heathen Mary sixty years earlier – came to the house, to talk, pray and give Bob the Church's blessing. It was a deep comfort to him.

Bob reached his 80th birthday in October 1992. He was too ill to enjoy a celebratory night down at the Nash. He died, after a long grinding illness, in July 1993. For some time before Bob's death, Mary slept in a separate bedroom from the one she and Bob had always shared at Russell Close and some weeks after his death she told Brian about the night Bob died.

"Ah woke up at two, like allus, an ah went teh see if e wor orreight. See if e wanted a cuppertea, or a sanwige."

"Like you always do. As if he can't make a cup of tea or a sandwich for himself."

"Aye, ah knaw, luv. Ah'm a daft owd bugger. Bur e'd ad nowt t'eat all day. An when ah oppened doo-er, bed wor empty. Nubdy theer! Yer cud er knocked me dahn wi a feather. Ah went dahnstairs an looked all ovver for im. He wah noo-weer. It wah thah weird. So ah went back up an ah saw all pillers an blankets'd gone frum bed. Brian, luv. E wah lying on floor, inbetween bed an winder. Ee'd med is bed up fer hissen. On floor. Eh. T'owd lad. He did look peaceful, lyin theer!"

The young priest, who had grown to know Bob well by the time of his death, expressed it movingly in his homily at the full Requiem Mass at St Mary's.

"He died like the old soldier he was – more comfortable on hard ground than in a soft bed."

On the night Bob died, Brian was marking GCSE coursework until nearly midnight in his flat in Derby. It was a busy and hectic time in the build-up to his year eleven class taking exams. After marking the last script he made a mug of tea before going to bed and sat on the big easy sofa to drink it. What happened then is easy to explain on a rational level. At the back of his mind he had known for months that Bob was nearing death. But suddenly, after a long day absorbed in teaching, he began mulling over Bob's life. He was thinking about his life in Bob's own Yorkshire miner's voice, as if it were Bob – talking inside his head. He thought of those early days with Winnie, James, Auntie Mary, Uncle Bill, Granma Hirst and the spectre of his dead father. Then meeting Mary, to the next war, to the long arid years after, to trips to Australia; and The Menin Gate. There was something unutterably sad about Bob's voice inside Brian's head telling his life story. It was not the story that made him sad. It was the fact that he knew the story so well already. All Brian's life, from being very young to that moment, his Dad's tragic life story was passed down to him, by Mary and his older siblings mainly and by guesswork and putting two and two together on his own part. Why, he asked Bob in his head, did he not talk about his life himself: in the flesh: while he was still alive?

Brian looked at his watch. It was after two. He had been listening to Bob's life story for two hours. He had another busy day at school coming up. He went to bed and fell asleep immediately. The bedside telephone rang at five o' clock. It was his brother John, telling him of Bob's death. John lived only a few streets away from Mary and she had telephoned, just after two, to tell him of finding Bob's body on the bedroom floor. Brian, in his sleepy state, was baffled as to why John was telling him this "news." He already "knew" Bob was dead. He did not need to be told.

A para-normal experience? Or something that can easily be explained, using reason? Did Bob's dying spirit come down from Yorkshire to Derby to make his peace with Brian, before going? Or was Bob's impending death somewhere at the back of his mind in any case? Who knows? But peace and reconciliation there has always been between Brian and Bob since he died.

In those last fairly contented years of his life Bob was in the habit of mulling over junk- mail catalogues. He loved musing over the pictures and the details and prices of the items being advertised, deciding whether or not to buy, just as he used to muse over his letters to the mining and army compensation claim boards and the horse racing pages of the Daily Herald, in earlier years. He made some good purchases from the junk-mail, such as the power shower fixed over the bath at Russell Close which Mary much preferred to a bath. He also bought "a loo-erd'n owd rubbish," according to Mary; rubbish that was never used.

A final word from Mary, who wanted to talk to Brian about more important things than the load of old rubbish.

"Brian, luv. Yeh knaw. Yeh Dad want allus the bluddy owd misery yow knew feh moo-erst-er yoo-er life. Ee wor a luvli man when ah first knew him an e stayed a luvli man, and a luvli Dad, reight up teh war. It wah war ruined im. Ah want yeh t'ave summat teh remember him by."

She offered Brian a pair of Bob's British Legion cuff links and was delighted when she saw he was touched and happy to take the keepsake.

"Look," she said, opening a drawer in the sideboard. "Look et all this bluddy stuff e bowt – an nivver used."

The drawer was stuffed with miscellaneous items of clothing still in factory packaging: string vests, long johns, thick woollen winter socks.

"D'yeh know. Ah cud do with some long johns an thick socks when ah go over to France at New Year. Yeh wouldn't believe how cowd it gets there."

Mam's face lit up in delight.

"'Ere, lad. Gu on. Tek-em, tek-em," she said, selecting some dark blue long johns and two pairs of thick woollen socks, thrusting them into his hands.

Brian still has the keepsakes Mary gave him that day and he still occasionally wears them: the cuff links, the long johns, the thick woollen socks: his material inheritance from Bob.

*Bob's Granma Hirst:
1900s*

Bob's Dad: 1914

Winnie, Bob and James:
1916

Swimming Champs:
James on left,
Bob on right: 1920s.

Left to right: Paddy, Bob, Tommy: Egypt 1939

Winnie on left with neighbours: 1910

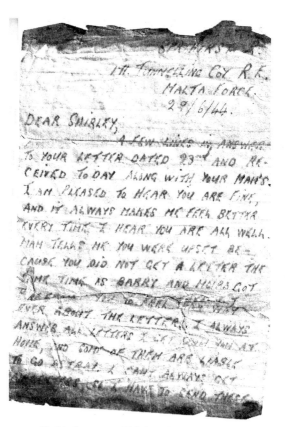

Bob's letter to Shirley: Malta 1944

Bob in Australia: 1980s

MARY

Mary Wolstenholme was born on April 30th 1915. She grew up in Batley Carr. Her parents worked in manual jobs in the woollen mills. Granma Elsie Wolstenholme (née Poskett) came from a rough Wakefield lower working class family. Grandad Wolstenholme's family were better-off. His parents rented a three-bedroom detached house with its own bathroom at the top of Warwick Road in Batley Carr. Elsie's family, on the other hand, were the sort of fowk who performed midnight flits from one house to another, when they could not pay rent arrears. John and Elsie met around 1912 when they both worked in the same Batley Carr woollen mill, to which Elsie walked seven miles from Wakefield every morning, beginning her shift at 7.00am. As far as his parents were concerned, John went down in the world when he married Elsie and moved into a one-down, two-up, back-to-back house at Batley Carr, just down the hill from the detached house at the top of Warwick Road.

Grandad Wolstenholme died when Brian was ten but an abiding image of him remains. He sits in an upright easy chair, smoking a strong-smelling Woodie, engrossed in the Daily Herald horse-racing pages. He faces the black-leaded fire range in the musky damp-smelling downstairs room in the house at Batley Carr while Granma makes tea, or is busy with household chores. Grandad was never unfriendly but he rarely spoke to Brian directly. He was lame from birth and his disability prevented him from joining the armed forces in the First World War. He had hanging-flesh, a wrinkled face, huge ears and he looked a little like the poet W.H. Auden in his later years. He seemed ancient to Brian but he was not much more than seventy when he died. In his twenties, Brian learned from Auntie Louie (Mary's sister) that Grandad was quite a lad in his younger days.

"Oo aye, owd flower. Ee liked a laff, did mi Dad – an his cigs an beer. Ee used teh bi social secret'ry et Batley Carr Club an all, yeh knaw."

Granma Elsie Wolstenholme died in her mid-seventies. The last time Brian saw her was a few weeks before her death, when he was nearing nineteen. It was at his brother David's wedding. She was sitting in the pew behind and, while the solemn marriage vows were being intoned, she nudged Brian in the back and held out a little package for him to take:

"Ere y'are, luv. Feh yeh bethdi."

Brian whispered his thanks and turned back to the service, surreptitiously pulling back the soft paper packaging. Inside he found three pristine white handkerchiefs, which he kept for years afterwards. The incident at David's wedding was typical of Granma's stiff-lipped Victorian love for her family. She was a small woman, below five foot tall and no more than six stone in weight, but she could be blunt and fearless. After her grandson John's birth, when Mary was still confined to bed, Elsie was helping in the house. There was a knock on the door and to Elsie's astonishment it was Winnie, calling to see her latest granbairn, or so she said. Winnie stayed a few minutes, watching Elsie busy with the chores. When Elsie stopped for a rest, Winnie spoke.

"Are yer cummin fur a drink then? Teh wet babby's ed?"

Elsie was furious at this irresponsibility and did not hide it:

"Ah'm bluddy not cummin fer a drink wi thee, when my lass as on'y just ad new babby. Thar can goo-er bi thissen."

And that was that.

After Grandad died, for what seemed like a lifetime, Brian was sent down to Granma's house at Batley Carr every Friday after school to pass on the Thrift money from Mary, for Granma to pass on to the Thrift man when he came to collect it later in the evening. The money built up into an account over the year and at Whitsuntide it was spent on new clothes for the bairns. It was a few months before Brian worked out the subterfuge involved in being sent down to Granma's with the money. It was a "bit of brass" kept secret from Bob by Mary. If Bob found out about the money she had scrimped and saved, "Teh pur on side foh Thrift Club," he would have wanted it back to spend on beer. The Thrift Club worked like a bank or a building society where the money saved gathered interest until the time came to spend it on needed items of clothing for the bairns.

It was a tradition for working class children in 1950s Batley to be dressed in brand new clothes at Whitsuntide and on Whit Sunday, after Sunday School, the bairns visited neighbours and relations to show-off their new Whitsun outfits and, if they were in luck, they were given a few special Whitsun pennies at the houses they visited. The Whitsun outfits were among the few brand-new clothes the post-war Hirst children had. Their everyday clothes were invariably hand-me-downs from older siblings, or they came from the "rag-oyle." Some time before Whitsun, when enough money had accumulated in the Thrift Club with interest added-on, Mary took her children to a room right at the top of a big posh house on the Bradford Road overlooking Batley Park, to try on and then buy the Whitsun outfits. The clothes were cheaper purchased directly from the house of the clothes seller, rather than from a shop. When Brian showed his new clothes off to women neighbours and relatives on Whit Sunday, they gave him a few pennies and ooh-ed and ah-ed.

"Ee, nah then, owd flower. Down't yow look luvli in them noo cloo-ers? Them cullers fair su-it thi. By eck, e's a gran lookin bairn, int e?"

After Grandad died, Granma took to smoking Woodies (a habit she had not indulged in before then), sitting in what used to be Grandad's chair on those Friday evenings, and gazing in silence into the coal fire. Brian sat in the easy chair at the other side of the dining table from Granma and his memories of her are all in profile. She was tiny and slim with a large white birth mark on her left cheek and she was always wrapped in a full-length pinny. The brief conversation between them on Friday nights was more like interrogator and collaborator.

"Is yeh Mam still not talkin ter ower Moira? Did yeh Dad gu teh club on Sundi dinner? As ower Barry bin round teh yoo-er ouse this wee-erk?"

"Yeh. Thi started talkin on Wensdi. Yeh, an mi Mam wah ded mad wi im. No. E's cummin rownd on Sundi."

Then they sat for long periods in silence, Granma puffing on her Woodie, Brian gazing around the room, with just the sound of the spitting fire and the ticking of the mantel shelf clock. If Granma was in a good mood and feeling flush, she sent Brian to the chip shop nearby to fetch a fish cake for her and chips for him. On his return she would be waiting with a glass of Mackeson Stout which she warmed with the end of a red hot poker heated on the coal fire. Then she would drink the mulled stout and eat her fishcake, wedged inside a soft white margarined teacake.

Granma lived in a soot-blackened stone terraced house built on a steep hillside. Thousands of terraces were built in the Heavy Woollen District in Victorian times, to house the shoddy and woollen mill workers. The terrace was both split-level and back-to-back. Walking down the hill on Friday afternoons to Granma's house at Batley Carr from the new council estate at Staincliffe was like walking from one period of history into another. Staincliffe Estate was made up of brand new red-brick houses, all having ample gardens bordered by red brick walls and neat pathways leading to the front and back doors. The "causas" were made of mass-produced, symmetrical concrete slabs, usually laid in alternate rows of two slabs, followed by three. These were important details for a child who loved playing hopscotch, as Brian did, because the squares of the game were already set out in the pattern of the slabs, which meant there was no need to chalk them on the causa.

The walk seemed endless but eventually you reached Granma's terrace. It was at the "top-end" of Batley Carr and as he walked down from Purlwell, Brian could see more rows of houses below, gradually dropping down to the woollen and shoddy mills lined along the Bradford Road in the valley bottom, each mill with its own high chimney constantly releasing billowing thick smoke into the sky. The houses at the front end of the terrace lined a proper, made-up road. Here, the paving slabs varied in size and were made of old dark Yorkshire stone. On wet days, rainwater gathered in pockets on their uneven surfaces, providing endlessly varied mini-puddles for Brian to stamp his feet in, creating spectacular fountains of spray. The front doors were situated right next to the old stone causa. Each house front consisted of just a door and a downstairs window, with two windows above, the same pattern of front door and window repeated for ten or twelve houses. Below the downstairs window of each house, at causa level, were two interesting iron grills set side by side in the house wall. The grills gave access to the coyle-oyles of the front house in the terrace, and of the house behind and below.

Everybody seemed to know you down at Granma's. On a warm Friday evening most of the front doors were open and women were gossiping in the doorways, with the men standing behind, smoking Woodies or Capstan Full Strength, "Waitin feh Club ter oppen," anticipating their Friday night beer intake.

"Nah then, young Esti. Ow's tha bahn?" the men might call.

Or, "Ey up Brian, owd cock. Off to see thi Granma?" from the women.

Elsie Wainwright was a close friend of Brian's big sister Shirley and so the greetings were especially warm and friendly as he walked past the Wainwright house on the top-row, on his way down to Granma's on the bottom-row. Between the first terrace and the next was a wide gap with a ginnel inbetween the two gable-end walls. The ginnel led down steep stone steps to the lower back terraces. Granma lived in the fourth or fifth house to the right on the back terrace ("bottom row"), behind and below the Wainwright's house. The bottom row faced an unmade cindery yard with outside lavs opposite, built against a high brick wall. Downstairs at Granma's there was just the door and the living room window facing straight on to the cinder yard.

Just inside Granma's house was a tiny lobby and a door that led upstairs. In wintertime, a tin pail stood in a corner of the lobby. This was the piss pot which Grandad and Granma and any visitors all used. No one seemed to mind that you could hear people pissing into the pail and sometimes you heard them farting. It saved fowk having to make the cold trek across the yard to the outside lav and that was all that mattered. In summertime, the outside lavs attracted hundreds of flies which invaded the house and so there was always a sticky fly paper hanging from the lobby ceiling, full of writhing dying flies. To the left of the lobby hung a dark heavy grey blanket attached to a solid iron rail above. In winter, you had to pull back the blanket and close it again quickly, once you stepped inside the main living room, to keep out the cold from the lobby.

The downstairs room was sparse. To the left was the window looking out over the yard, the outside lavs and the high brick wall opposite. In front of the window was a sideboard with ornaments and doilies on top. Facing you, with the window and sideboard to the left, was the sink corner. There was a huge off-white pot sink with two gas rings to the side and cupboards underneath. Next to the sink and gas rings was the black-leaded coal fireplace and range, with an iron-doored oven to the side of the fire. In addition, two iron trivets could be swung over the fire, to boil water or cook food. The big dining table, with the two easy chairs at either side, faced the fire range and sink. Beyond the dining table to the right were steps which led to another doorway, with another heavy blanket draped in front. This doorway led into the dank, windowless cellar-pantry-coiloyle, combined. A big marble slab stood on a table in a corner of the pantry on which milk and perishables were kept cool. In the far right corner was the "coyle pile." The coyle was emptied from sacks by the coyle-men and thrown down the shoot behind the removable grill below the front window of the Wainwright house on the front top terrace.

The Batley Carr terraces and yards were almost entirely demolished in the late-1950s and early-1960s. They were declared slums by central and local government and the people in them were re-housed to new council estates. Granma spent the last few years of her life in a one-bedroom council flat on a new estate at Purlwell, just further up the hill from where her old terraced house used to be at Batley Carr. If the Batley Carr terraces had stayed, and restored and refurbished, no doubt they would be part of heritage England now, with gawping tourists and heritage-strollers coming to ooh and aah, as they do at the terraces of Holmfirth, in *Last Of The Summer Wine* country, which are just like those of long-gone old Batley Carr, although now much gentrified.

Granma Wolstenholme died after suffering a stroke in her seventies. She loved all her granbairns but she adored the eldest, Barry. She was rushing for the bus from Batley Carr to Park Street in Batley where Barry lived, to visit him and his wife Sheila for tea. As she was hurrying across the "piece" – a rubble-strewn empty piece of land where houses had been demolished after being hit by stray bombs in the war – she stumbled and fell and the fall caused the stroke. She lived only a few weeks after her stroke, with her daughters Louie and Mary nursing her at her new flat, where she died.

Mary had one sister, Louie, two years younger than her. Louie left school at fourteen and worked at Burroughs Shoddy Mills on the Bradford Road as a rag-sorter for most of her long working life. She married Horace Chadwick quite late in life for those days, in her late-twenties. Uncle Horace was a miner, originally from Barnsley. He worked in the West Yorkshire mines continuously from the age of fourteen to sixty five. He died not long after leaving the mines: lung disease ("miners lung") killed him, of course. Louie and Horace had one son, Glynne, three days younger than Brian. Glynne was killed by a lorry while out riding his bike at the age of eighteen in 1965. Auntie Louie also had a daughter, Ann, six years younger than Glynne.

When Brian heard of Louie's death in her late-eighties, the news brought wonderful loving memories of her in his early childhood flooding back into his mind. She was a marvellous Auntie to all her nephews and nieces. One of Brian's sisters-in-law, Pat, discussing Louie not long after her funeral, described her beautifully and poetically as a "reight easy woman," which is to say, she was open; giving; relaxed. She was at ease with herself and with life, and although she did not know it, from this ease she gave huge doses of unqualified love to her family and friends. The ease which she carried with her had the capacity to bring so much out of those who knew her. Her ease was a two-way quality; she gave it to others unconditionally and this made others give themselves back to her. You could not be anyone but yourself with Auntie Louie. Dissimulation did not come into her world.

One of Brian's earliest memories of Auntie Louie involves him and David arriving in their Whit Sunday clothes at her prefab at Healey, after Sunday School. Glynne, solid, intensely shy and quiet, bigger than David and Brian, is standing on the doorstep. There is a pent up excitement waiting to be released in the chemistry of the three boys meeting again. They are bursting: with the excitement of being together: with the thrill of wearing the new clothes: with anticipating Louie's response to them, dressed in their Whitsun finery. A front door and a lock did not seem to exist at Auntie Louie's prefab. One minute you were outside and the next minute you were inside. Louie soon appeared, standing in the kitchen doorway, surrounded by steam from the Sunday dinner cooking pans, amazed to see her nephews looking so beautiful in their Whitsun clothes. Her face lit in a smile and she advanced upon them, peering through her steamy glasses at their beauty. The hug, the squeeze of the shoulder, the stroke of the hair, all happened in a second and then she held them at arm's length to admire them anew.

"Ey up, owd cock. Down't yow look luvly. Thah's a bootiful coit. Nah then. Weer's mi perse? Ah've got summat teh gi thi."

And the Whitsun pennies passed from her to the boys. She had a loud raucous voice which partly came from her early deafness and which was also characteristic of the mill and rag- oyle women in Batley. The machinery in the mills made a tremendous racket and the workers had to shout to be heard over the noise. Granma Wolstenholme could be stiff-lipped and Victorian at times; inclined to tut disapprovingly at naughtiness in both adults and children. Grandad Wolstenholme liked his Club, women, beer and betting on the horses. It is a crude generalisation but Mary tended to follow in Granma's footsteps, whereas Louie followed in Grandad's. Louie had a liberated time as a single young woman during the war years, working in munitions. Mary meanwhile was already bringing up four young children and Bob away in the war most of the time. Louie smoked heavily until her sixties but she became worse than any Taliban, in what she wanted to do to sinful smokers after she stopped the habit. She loved Club life, bingo and drinking. Brian once went to the Nash with his older brother John when he was in his twenties. It was a midweek bingo evening and there was the customary reverential silence as the numbers were called.

"'OWSE!" yelled Auntie Louie, delighted to win after a long losing streak. The numbers were called again to double-check. Auntie Louie had misheard a number.

"AW. FUCKIN' 'ELL," she yelled at top mill-floor volume – and instantly clapped her hand over her mouth in laughing shock when she realised what she had said – for all the Club to hear. But the embarrassment did not last long. That was her. Open, easy. Full of life and enjoyment.

Glynne's death was a nightmare which never ended for Louie. For years she suffered depression but despite this dark shadow Auntie Louie never lost her love of life. She loved her whisky even at the end. When Mary was in her eighties, her daughter-in-law Pat drove her to visit Louie at her house in Purlwell, at Christmas-time. Mary and Louie sat for hours shouting at each other, trying to overcome their mutual deafness, with Pat looking on. The room grew darker and darker. The lights stayed off and Louie continued to sup her whisky until eventually Pat suggested putting on the light. After a while, Mary and Pat left Louie in her lit-up sitting room, happy with her drink. Louie gave all her family and friends a great gift. She gave unconditional love, laughter, a simple joy for living and being with other people. It did not matter if the lights were on, or not. It was being with you, being there for you, that mattered in her world. It was only with her death that Brian came to fully appreciate Louie and understand how her zest for life rubbed off on all her nephews and nieces. She was a model of how to be simply happy and at ease with life.

Mary's life took a different course from Louie's, in some respects. She left school at fourteen and went to work in a rug-making mill, "brodding" the rugs.

"Ah ated it theer. Ah were nowt burra slip on a lass, wi all them owd wimmin lookin dahn ther noses at mi. So, ah soo-in left, an went teh wek in rags, wi yer Auntie Louie, at Burroughs. By, we ad sum laffs theer. Yer knaw what yer Auntie Louie wah like. Gi'in as good as shi got, from ware'ouse men. By ell. She warra bugger but yer ad teh laff."

At eighteen Mary met Bob and only months after they met they married. And less than nine months after their marriage came their first child Barry, just a few days after Mary's nineteenth birthday. Bob and Mary came from small families compared with most of their generation. Yet they themselves went on to have thirteen children over a period of twenty three years. They never said why they had so many children. Probably no one ever asked. It was the sort of Family Silence all families have over something or other, all of their twelve surviving bairns keeping any opinions they might have over their parents productivity to themselves. But it happened: from the age of just nineteen in 1934, to the age of forty three in 1958, Mary was an almost non-stop child-bearer and mother.

Mary often talks about what a "luvli man" Bob was – "afoo-wer war."

"Wi ad a reight good time after wi wah married, yeh knaw. Yeh Dad wor on good pay, in pit, an then int army. An he used teh luv elpin mi wi dressin Ower Barry, an Shirley, an Margret n Moira. An gi'in em a bath an all. E used teh read em bedtime stories, an e wrote all them luvli letters – when he wor away in war. Ee wah shattered though, after war. Ee wah nivver same agen. An it want easy, wi all on us cooped up i Wainwright's Buildings."

Life became a little easier for Mary just a few months after Brian was born when she moved in 1947 to a three bedroom council house at Woodsome Estate on the spreading post-war edges of Batley: a house with a bathroom and front and back gardens. But in spite of the bigger house, life must have just become harder and harder for her and that hardship continued unremittingly well into the 1970s when her life, at last, became a little easier. Some vignettes of Mary. First, as a ninety-year-old responding to Brian when he asks her the name of the street in which he was born at Batley Carr.

"It wah called Wainwrights Buildings, luv. Wi dint ave a cot feh yeh, yeh knaw. Not many fowk did i them days. We med up a cot in top er chest a drawers. Lined it wi towils-n-blankits. That wah yeh fest bed after yeh wah born. Yeh dint see-erm teh mind it. The was a wumman lived in yard. Nah then, wot wa shi called? Can I ell as remember. Anyway, she were a reight ard wumman. Dint ave much time feh wimmin's talk. Shi fair serprised mi after you wah born. Shi kept cummin rahnd an mekkin a reight fuss on yer. Owdin yer in er arms an cooin ovver yeh, in front er fire. Coo-erse, that winter you was born luv, was an ard un. Snow an cowd an ice fer wee-erks. Shi dint cum teh see yow, yer knaw. Shi cem teh sit bi fire. We ad coyle, yeh see, wi yeh Dad werkin dahn pit. She dint ave none."

Typical of Mary. No value judgments made about the neighbour. No preaching points made about how hard life was then. Just the anecdote. Just a telling of how it was and a deep intrinsic acceptance of things as you find them in life. There is a real toughness, a real capacity to endure anything, in the way Mary tells the story. There is an acceptance of the hardness of life, as well as an entirely unjudgmental understanding of the neighbour, so desperate to catch a little warmth.

And now to Woodsome Estate. Mary is in her pinny, her hands and all of her smelling of Fairy Household Soap. She is rubbing mountains of dirty clothes on a soapy rubbing board then squeezing them through a hand-held mangle. She runs into the garden with the washing tray and a wooden peg in her mouth, and hangs endless clothes on the line. On a good day she sings the latest popular song while doing the washing: "Ow-much-is-that-dor-gi-in-the-wind-ow..." And she has time to hug her children, always clinging onto her pinny. On a bad day she is utterly weighed down by the mountain of physical work, weeping over the frustration of never seeming to complete it and irritable, dismissive, over the bairns' demands for attention. This was her life at Woodsome: endless washing, cleaning, cooking, looking after eight children and a ninth on the way, with none of the household appliances of today. And she had still not reached the age of forty. Was she happy then? Was she contented? Did she accept her lot in life? Did she ever look back to the eighteen year old Mary and wonder how she had arrived where she was, at forty? It is doubtful. She got on with life. She endured hardship, penury and a difficult, self-absorbed husband. And on the whole she did so successfully. She kept a clean house and made sure her bairns were cleaned, clothed and fed. And even though there were times when she wept with misery and rage at the endless drudgery of her life, there were far more more times when she was happy; when she sang those popular songs while doing the household chores during the day and avidly read love books and magazines in the evening, mouthing out the words she read, curled up in her chair with her legs beneath her, picking her toe nails while absorbed in her book.

Most of the time Mary was loving, kind and encouraging to all her children. But there was a sharp and dismissive side to her tongue. She was always busy managing a household, with a husband and children constantly threatening to swamp her, and somehow, her bairns always seemed to choose to nag her when she was at her busiest.

"Mam, Mam. Can ah ave a penny teh buy sum spanish?"

"Mam. Mam. Can ah -"

– "Aw, feh God's sake, Brian. Gu ter ell an pick mint, will yeh?"

"Mam, Mam. Weer's mi coit?"

"Mam, Mam. Weer's mi socks?" -

– "Weer d'yeh think, Brian? Ther up mi bluddy arse, on a nail!"

Or on a really exhausted day:

"Aw, gu an *shite*, Brian, will yeh!"

There were times when Mary hugged her children or laughed and gossiped with neighbours and the "older-end" of her bairns. Woodsome Estate was a rough place where some of the poorest of the poor and some of the toughest of the tough were re-housed from the old back-to-back demolished areas of Batley. There was one family living a few houses down the road with several sons who were constantly in trouble with the law, some of them regularly banged-up for petty crimes of stealing, brawling or drunkenness. The Hirsts were more respectable, more law-abiding, but Mary was always intrigued, fascinated by the goings-on of this troublesome neighbouring family. And always sympathetic. Never judgmental.

"Eh, poor Mrs. S. Er Fred's i trubble agen. Eh, poo-wer Fred. Ee's nowt burra big daft lad."

There was another family at Woodsome, mainly made up of girls, who all seemed to have dirty blonde hair; black fingernails; thin ragged dresses; dirt tide marks round their necks; a smell of pee. One day Brian followed one of the girls into her house, when she was called in for tea from playing outside. The house inside smelt of urine, dirt and poverty. He recognised the essence of the place for what it was, even as a six-year-old: it was destitution. Nothing on the floor, just wooden boards. And sheets of newspaper spread out across the tea table in place of a table cloth. The girls stood around the table – there were not enough chairs for them all to sit on – drinking weak milky tea from old jam jars and eating bread, spread with a thin smear of Stork margarine and jam.

When Brian returned home he noticed the lino and rugs on the floors – the rugs brodded by Mary. Yes, like the girls down the street, the younger-end of the Hirst bairns had to stand at the dining table; there were only enough chairs for the older-end. But the Hirst family had an oil cloth cover on the table and they drank tea out of white pots, some chipped or with broken handles. (Mugs were then called pots. Mary bought them from the pot stall on Dewsbury Market.) And they had Tate and Lyle Golden Syrup treacle, or jam, spread thickly over the Stork margarine on their tea-time bread.

"Mam, Mam! Yeh shud see J's owse. S'ded mucki."

"Dooern't talk about poo-er Mrs H's owse like that, Brian. Shurrup! An geh yoo-er tea ettn will yeh!"."

What was Mary's anger about? Was it about the injustice of the family up the road having to live like that? Yes, probably. But anger too at the thought that she herself was only a few pennies a week ahead of "poor Mrs. H." It was anger at the struggle to survive and keep her dignity in circumstances which constantly wore her down.

The family moved from Woodsome to Staincliffe Estate in the winter of 1952-1953. Woodsome was established as rough. Staincliffe was brand new, with no reputation to live up to. Woodsome was still in the country and retained some links to the rural past of Batley. At Woodsome, the Hirst lads only had to walk through the gap in the privet hedge at the top of the back garden and they were in a farmer's field. The field sparkled with ice puddles in winter, which Brian and David loved to crack, and was criss-crossed in hard black earth ruts. In summer it was full of dark golden wheat, where they made paths and dens and Malcolm and John never tired of catching field mice which they doggedly but unsuccessfully tried to tame. Staincliffe was more hemmed-in, surrounded as it was by the back gardens of other neighbours. In spite of the beautiful rustic name of the street at Staincliffe, Chapel Fold, the countryside was in retreat. New estate houses stood where grazing land and sheep folds used to be. The Woodsome house had three bedrooms; the Staincliffe house had four. When Mary and Bob moved to Woodsome from Wainwright Buildings there were seven children; when they moved to Staincliffe there were nine.

The day they moved was cold and snowy. Mary, Shirley, Moira and Louie were in a frenzy of scrubbing-down the Woodsome house, trying to leave it decent for the next tenants to move in, as well as working on the Chapel Fold house which also needed a scrub-down after the mess left by builders, plasterers and decorators. Bob and the oldest brothers moved the furniture entirely by hand and Uncle James made one of his rare appearances to help. It was half a mile between the two houses but the expense of a paid remover was out of the question. The morning of the move was a huge anarchic adventure for David and Brian. They were sent out to play in the snowy back garden at Woodsome, before everyone proceeded on foot to Chapel Fold. The garden was full of incongruously dumped furniture waiting to be hauled across to the new house. Chests of drawers, wardrobes and chairs were defamiliarised, with drawers and cushions and other loose fittings removed and stacked indoors, leaving just skeletons of furniture weirdly dumped on the snow in the garden. The two boys went wild with the strangeness; playing hide-and-seek in the furniture; slopping wet snow and mud inside the skeletal frames. They were not normally so badly behaved when adults were around but moving day was different. The adults were too busy to notice their behaviour, except Uncle James, who seemed to be in charge of the the garden and of them, but Jimmy had only the dimmest idea of disciplining children. The boys knew his warnings never came to anything but he lost patience over their anarchic naughtiness that day:

"Reight! That's it. If thar wee-ern't tek neh gawm en me, ah'm off inside teh tell thi Mam what thar two's up teh."

He marched inside and a few seconds later Mary emerged from the house:

"What the? – Ooo, jus look at this bluddy mess thar two ev med. Let mi get mi bluddy ands on yeh. As'll tan yoo-er bluddy arses, an nor arf!"

What had begun as a riotous hilarious morning ended in tears and stinging arms and legs from Mary's furious slaps. The boys cheered up later in the day, however, when they were each given cooking pans to carry on the trip from Woodsome to Chapel Fold. Walking through the streets wearing a pan on your head was the funniest thing in the world and slapping the palms of hands on the bases of frying pans made glorious sounds, at a time just before Jamaican steel bands became known in Yorkshire.

Batley scored very badly in a late-1940s government survey into housing conditions in England. The survey found that most of the town's population lived in overcrowded back-to-back terraced houses, with no bathroom, inside toilet, separate kitchen, or garden. The post-war Labour government was determined to create a better Britain, free of the ills, meanness and degradation which many of the the lower working class suffered before the war. Poor fowk were to have the same rights and benefits that posh fowk already enjoyed: ready access to a doctor and a good health service; a broader wider education for children, in contrast to the narrow utilitarian three Rs education which poorer children tended to receive before the war and, not least, decent housing for those living in slum dwellings. For Mary, Bob and their children – and millions more people like them – these post-war benefits were real and tangible. The Hirst family now had their own family doctor, Alan Hinchcliffe, who came to the house when they were sick to administer potions, pills or common sense advice. Batley General Hospital and Leeds teaching hospitals were also readily available, providing more specialist medical needs. The children went to nursery, infant, junior and secondary schools which aimed to nurture the whole child: schools which did not just dole out a narrow – and often brutally inculcated – diet of the three Rs. Schools which came under the leadership of the inspirational, idealistic, Alec Clegg, Chief Education Officer for the West Riding County Council. In addition to a liberal child-centred education, pupils also had one third of a pint of whole milk each day completely free, as well as free nutritious dinners for those (such as the Hirst children) whose parents could not afford to pay. Free cod liver oil tablets were also given to children such as Brian and his brothers, who were seen to be in danger of vitamin deficiency and rickets. (Brian was only dimly aware of this: he knew the capsules he swallowed with the morning playtime milk had something to do with his family being "poor.")

The new council house at 77 Chapel Fold was a world away from the back-to-back at Wainwright Buildings. It was built in the early 1950s, a good ten years before the Parker

Morris Housing Standards were introduced in England in 1961, but it easily met, and indeed exceeded, those standards. (The Parker Morris scheme was abandoned in the early 1980s during Thatcher's reign – for both private and council housing – on the grounds that its standards were "too expensive." So much for a "progressive" government.) Downstairs at the back of the house was a kitchen, with fully-fitted cupboards and drawers – and a shelved pantry with air-bricks to keep fresh food cool. (It was several years more before a fridge was bought.) A dining-sitting room, called the "back room," with a tiled fire place, fireside oven and a back water burner, and more fitted cupboards, led off from the kitchen, with the back room window overlooking the back garden. Another door led to the front of the house where there was a spacious hall and large front room, with another tiled fireplace. Upstairs were four bedrooms leading off a small landing; the two larger bedrooms to the right each having a tiled fire place. The bathroom was fitted with bath, toilet, hand wash basin and a large built-in airing cupboard. Outside was a small front garden. The house was in the middle of a terrace of four and a shared passageway between the Hirst house and the house next door led up to the back doors and back gardens. Separate from the house, to the side of the back garden, was a solid brick single-story building, divided into an outside toilet, coil-oyle and outhouse.

Chapel Fold was a vast improvement on the houses Bob and Mary lived in until the end of the war. It is a pity though that so many of the old stone terraces were bulldozed to make way for the new red brick estates. A more enlightened policy would have kept the best of the old houses and restored and refurbished them, alongside building new dwellings to house an expanding population. Apart from the loss of the sheer visual beauty of the old stone terraces climbing the hills of the Pennine landscape, which we can still see in towns such as Holmfirth, the heart and harmony of Batley was decimated in the ripping down of so many of its buildings. The new sprawling estates on the town's outskirts never acquired that deep-knit sense of community and identity found in the pre-war districts of Batley Carr and Cross Bank, where Bob and Mary grew up betweeen the two World Wars. But none of this bothered the family on that first exciting day in the new home. The younger boys chased and ran over the echoing new floorboards. Fires were lit for the first and last time in all four fireplaces to air and warm the new house. Mary, Shirley and Moira dealt with the layout of the furniture.

"Cum on, then, Shirley lass. An Moi. Le's geh this finished, so's wi can ave a sit dahn, wi a nice pot a tea."

"Mam! Mam! Weer's mi Dad – an Uncle Jimmy – an Ower Barry?"

"Pher. Yer knaw wee-er thev goo-ern, dooern't yeh? Sloped off teh Nash, them three. Come on David, owd flower. An you Brian, luv. It's well past yoor bedtime. Up wi goo-er. That's reight. In ere. In yer noo bedroom. Nite-nite. Mind the rats dooern't bite."

Mary did not complain or criticise Bob that first night at Chapel Fold when he sloped off with James and Barry down teh Nash. But there were many times later when his sloping-off roused her temper. Bob could not stop himself sloping-off and Mary could not stand it. As the man of the house Bob felt he had an inviolable right to spend his nights at the Nash downing copious pints of cheap beer. It was Mary who was left to fume and natter about the irresponsible waste of money spent on beer when there was precious little coming in for the essential needs of a large, ever-expanding family.

There were evenings when the house at Chapel Fold was full of rage and conflict between Mary and Bob. Bob would begin to get ready for a night down at the Nash. He always washed, shaved and changed from his indoor working clothes into a suit, tie and militarily polished shoes when he went out drinking. He was a handsome man, having his mother's good looks. He was small, dark, slim, vain and proud of his appearance, when out of the house socialising. While Bob prepared to go out, Mary prepared to protest. After tea was over the atmosphere in the house became tense with the expectation of impending strife. Mary waited for the slightest sign from Bob of his intention to slope off. If he stayed sitting in his chair still dressed in his work clothes after a certain time then it meant he was staying in and Mary relaxed, happily curling herself up on a chair in the back room with a love book, or she listened to the radio, or gossiped for hours with her daughters, or with women neighbours who had "bobbed round for a natter," standing at the back doorway. On those occasions the house itself, let alone its occupants, breathed a sigh of relief: war was postponed. If, however, Bob showed signs of going out then battle commenced. The signals from Bob were always the same. He suddenly became cheerful, teasing Mary and his children:

"Ey up, fish face. Goo an get mi shoo-ers frum upsteers."

"Brian, owd cock, pass me that black polish frum yonder cubberd."

"Mary, lass. Aster ironed mi shet?"

Mary's lips pursed.

"Dooern't you bluddy 'Mary lass' *me*. Weer d'yeh think *yoor* gooin?"

Sometimes the argument just simmered, with Bob turning on his charm and humour and Mary sniffing, snapping back at him until Bob, having washed, shaved and changed, sloped off. At the worst end of the scale, the argument took on a frightening intensity of rage on both sides. Bob and Mary swore profusely at each other though their swearing repertoire was limited by today's standard. Mary's swearing was more or less limited to: piss, shit, shite, bloody, bugger. Bob's swearwords were similarly limited – in the house, although not when talking to other men, with no women or children present. If he was really riled, "bastard" was used – it sounded terrible to the children – or his own curious swear word "cowing."

"Ah'm cowin gooin teh Nash whither tha leeks it er noo-en. That bastard, bluddy Churchill. Look wor e did teh miners in Genral Strike."

"What the bluddy ell's Churchill got teh doo wi thee slopin off teh Nash agee-en?"

"Bastard ad Uncle Bill locked up i prison. Tha's what."

"Goo an shite, Bob. It's got nowt teh do wi thee gooin teh Nash..."

Doors were ferociously slammed as Mary and Bob paced and circled each other between the front room and the back rooms. When really riled and pushed beyond endurance, Mary would throw a shoe cleaning brush, or whatever other object might be at hand, at Bob. There was one terrible occasion when an iron frying pan was involved in a battle. The bairns were keeping out of the way in the big front room while war raged in the back rooms. Suddenly the front room door flew open and Mary ran in, clutching a pan in one hand. With the other hand she slammed the door shut on Bob who was chasing close behind. There was a violent struggle: Mary on the inside pushing the door shut against Bob and Bob outside, furiously pushing to get inside. Eventually Bob forced the door open. Mary made to hit him with the pan. He grabbed the pan and, in the ensuing struggle, accidentally hit her on the face. She had a swollen black eye for days afterwards.

But the worst thing, for Brian, was not the fighting and door-slamming. Apart from anything else, Mary was not a physical fighter and Bob never used the full force he was capable of. Mary's throws, slaps and wild lashings out at Bob – and sometimes at her children – lacked the true force of intention to hurt and were usually way off-target in any case. Her throws, slaps and attempted blows were manifestations of the extreme end of her patience. They were acts of pain, of utter frustration at what life was doing to her, rather than calculated intentions to hurt. Bob's black moods, scowls and verbal warnings were almost always enough to subdue both Mary and his bairns. A violent anger with the world, with the turn his life had taken, often simmered in Bob's facial expressions and body language but he was not a physically violent man toward either Mary or his children. He never hit Mary – except by accident defending himself against her attack – and there was only one occasion when he hit Brian, and his blows were far from vicious or with intent to hurt. No. The worst thing was Mary's sobs and tears after Bob sloped off. No matter how many times he did it, she was inconsolable for hours after he left. And her sobs and tears broke Brian's heart, every time, no matter how often they were repeated over those twelve formative years of his life at Chapel Fold.

During the six week summer holiday at the end of year nine, Brian and David were taught by Mary how to cook simple basic midday meals for themselves and the younger bairns. (They had already acquired these skills when Bob made that one botched effort to cook his pizza-like meal.) By now there were twelve Hirst children. Barry, the oldest, was 27 and married with two children. Shirley was 25, and married with one child and another expected. Moira was 24, still single and working in London. Young Bob was 20, and working. John was 18, Malcolm 16, and both were working. That left Brian, at 14 the oldest still at school, followed by David, 13; Richard, 10; Stephen, 8; Lynne, 7 and Michael, 3.

Being shown how to cook bacon and eggs, or chips and beans, or corned beef hash, and how to make tea and prepare bread and margarine, was not something Mary thought her boys should learn on feminist grounds. It was a matter of necessity. Bob was often out of work at that time on sick pay or the jobs he was doing were on subsistence pay. In spite of his sickness and low pay, his thirst for beer did not diminish and some of the limited cash he earned went on drink. There were many times when Mary emptied her purse onto the dining table in the back room at the end of the financial week, before the allowances and the "keep" of the children who were working came in, when the purse might contain a couple of pennies, or just a threpni bit and an aipni. Mary sobbed or at best fretted over the lack of money. How was she going to pay for the end-of-week top-ups she needed for the table with threppence aipney? Because of the desperate money situation, she decided she would herself have to find a job, as if she did not already have enough to do, with a four bedroom house to run and a semi-invalid husband and nine children still living at home. When she found herself a job, someone had to share the burden of carrying out the household chores, as it was now impossible for her to do them all herself. In that long school holiday of 1961, sharing the burden fell on Brian and David, the two oldest bairns still at home and not yet working.

Mary returned to work as a rag-sorter, this time not at Burroughs but at the nearby "Percy Walker Company Limited: Shoddy and Flock Manufacturers," as it mellifluously said on the side of the warehouse lorry and on the mill gates. But Walkers was more commonly known by Batley fowk as a "rag-oyle." Batley was full of rag-oyles and mellifluous slogans sign-painted on mill gates or on the sides of lorries and buses in those days. The red buses serving Batley and surrounding towns had a grandiloquent title painted in gold on their sides: "The West Riding Of Yorkshire Heavy Woollen District Transport Company Limited." The toilet paper at junior and secondary schools was embossed with the words: "West Riding County Council Education Committee. Please wash your hands," printed in elegant green on every shiny slippery sheet. (The toilet paper at Chapel Fold, right up to the early-

1960s, consisted of torn up pieces of newspaper hung on a nail on the indoor side of the outside lav and newspaper in a corner on the floor of the indoor toilet.)

A regular street sight of the time was the rag'n'bone man with horse and cart and those calls: "Any owd raaaa-gs? Any owd raaaa-gs?" Most of the rags collected by rag men across the length and breadth of England in the 1950s-60s ended up in the rag-oyles of Batley and Dewsbury. The street-callers' rags were bundled into huge sackcloth bales and the shoddy mill lorries collected the rag bales and took them back to Batley and Dewsbury. You could see the Percy Walker lorry struggling to the rag-oyle all year round, grinding its way through the gears up the steep Halifax Road with mountains of wobbling rag bales piled on its platform, emiting a strong stale smell of damp decaying cloth. When the Percy Walker lorry arrived at the mill the warehousemen unloaded the bales onto the floor of the sorting shed behind. This was where Mary and the other rag-sorters (all women) worked. Their job was to sort the rags into separate piles: a pile for woollens, a pile for cottons, a pile for synthetics, piles of good quality rags and piles of rags that were "noo-er good feh nowt neh nubdi." The rag-sorters took a capacious bag to work. One of the unofficial perks of the job was to "slip" good quality items of clothes into the bags as they sorted through the rags, when the foreman just happened not to be watching.

"Ee, this shirt'll just fit Ower David."

"Ey up, Mary lass. Slip this luvli jumper i thi bag. It'll reight soo-it thar Malcolm."

The sorted rags that did not end up in Mary's and the other women's big bags were taken to be washed, shaken and dried in another part of the mill and finally the cleaned rags were shredded on huge machines and made into flock which was then taken away in fresh-smelling new bales and used to stuff mattresses, pillows and furniture. Brian always knew when rag-washing was going on at

Percy Walkers because when he walked by, the vents in the mill walls let out clouds of steam which had the unique damp mouldy smell of the rag-oyle.

When Mary returned from work she thoroughly washed and ironed the shirts, jumpers, trousers, jackets, skirts, blouses, dresses and socks which had slipped into her bag from the rag-oyle. Then a bairn was told to try on the jacket, or shirt, or trousers. Sometimes David, Malcolm, John and Brian took a liking to the item brought from the rags and they tried it on without demur and adopted it as their own. If they did not like an item of clothing, they protested, usually to the smell. The clothes from the rag-oyle never quite lost that special smell of stale dampness no matter how good their quality or how much Mary washed, scrubbed and ironed. Some of Brian's middle class friends in adult life who had childhoods far distant from the shoddy mills of Batley, would sometimes proudly show off a suit bought in an Oxfam charity shop, or a coat from Help The Aged. But to Brian, today's charity shop clothes have that never forgotten whiff of the rag-oyle about them and buying his own new clothes is still, at the back of his mind, a real privilege, not an axiomatic right. It still hurts today, remembering the sly taunts of children at junior and lower secondary school, sidling over to him in the playground; sniffing ostentatiously:

"Ey up, Bri. Dus thi Mam wek in rags then?"

"Nice coit, Esti. Did it cum frum rags?"

In some ways working at Percy Walker's was a liberating experience for Mary. It took her out of the house for a few hours each weekday, away from the constant demands of her children and a brooding, sulking Bob. She loved the mill gossip and the cheek and brazenness of some of the more hardened rag-sorters toward the warehousemen and foremen. She always returned home exhausted from the work at Walkers but later, when she had cooked a meal and performed another dozen necessary jobs, and it was time for a sit-down, her eyes glittered with mischief and humour and she regaled her grown-up daughters with the shocking but thrilling backchat and all the goings-on at the mill, while the younger bairns hovered in the backround, hoping to catch snippets of rudenesses beyond their understanding.

"Goo on, geraht an play, Brian. Goo on, David."

And they were ushered out of the room into the back garden where, from an open window, they heard Mam's voice:

"Eee, yer'll nivver gess wor Edie Ides sed this mornin..."

"Ooo, yer should've erd wha Nelly Arkins said teh Wilf on loading bay this aft."

And her voice dropped to a whisper and she and her daughters laughed and laughed.

Mary suffered from chronic bronchitic asthma. On a bad day it completely took her breath away. After her shift in the rag-oyle she sometimes struggled to walk the five minutes on the level from Percy Walkers to Chapel Fold and climbing the four steps from the pavement to the back door path was a monumental effort. Once inside the house she dropped her work bag on the scullery floor and flopped down on the nearest dining chair in the back room, wheezing mightily and gasping for breath. Sometimes for an hour she feebly waved away anyone who attempted to talk to her. She could not speak until she had rested, slumped on the upright chair, and regained her breath.

For work, she wore a headscarf, scuffed slip-on shoes and an old coat hid her neck-to-knee work pinafore. Her work clothes absorbed the very essence of the stink of the rags and were black with rag-grease and grime, as were her hands, and other parts of her body not protected by her clothes. The work the women rag-sorters did in the shoddy mills now seems tough and the conditions of work filthy. Mary did not do the full-time forty-eight hour week, with added overtime, that the likes of her workmates, Edie Hydes and Nelly Harkins, did. The full-time sorters, inbetween raucous joking and flirting with the warehousemen, worked fast and hard. It was piecework pay and so the more rags you sorted and had weighed the more pay you got. Mary did not work full-time. Her work hours were centred around the school day but during the hours she did work, in order to earn the money and keep up with the demanding schedules, she had to work fast and hard. Because of her asthma and the massive job she was already doing as a housewife, mother and husband-carer, she was physically incapable of doing a full-time week at the mill. A full-time job there, week after week, might well have killed her.

Edie and Nelly were kind to Mary. As well as filling her working hours with all the fun and humour they could milk from the job, they slipped extra items onto her sorted piles of rags when she was flagging, ensuring she kept up with the schedules, or they slipped the best of the rags to her to slip into her bag and often they gave Mary small presents of sweets and chocolates to give to her bairns: bairns they had never seen. They had smaller families, more income and more supportive spouses than Mary, and they knew it. But Edie and Nelly also had hearts of gold underneath the toughness they acquired to survive in the job of rag sorter.

Relations between Mary and each one of her children were often strained and stretched to the limit. By the age of fourteen Brian understood the lack of money in the household but it still galled that he seemed to have so much less than his friends, or the posh fowk he read about in books and magazines. Sometimes he pushed Mary beyond endurance for something he wanted: a polo neck shirt, a Parker pen, a school trip. He pushed with words. He pushed until Mary raged over her inability to deliver the wanted thing. He did this one night in the scullery at Chapel Fold while Mary was "brillowing" a mountain of pans at the big pot sink. He was pushing and pushing. He wanted a black polo neck shirt. He was goading and goading, standing in the doorway between the scullery and back room.

"No, Brian," Mary was repeating quietly, again and again. "Yer knaw wi can't affoo-erd it. An that's all ther is territ."

But he pushed and pushed, and pushed too far. In a sudden surrender to the rage that was boiling inside her over Brian being so persistent with his pleas, rage at what she could not do for him, Mary grabbed the big bread knife from the drainer and turned and threw it in his direction. It was a bungled throw. Instead of sinking into Brian it sank into the cupboard door beside him and wobbled a second or two before it fell to the floor. There was a short shocked pause between them and then they laughed at what had happened, and at what might have happened. And after that night, Brian tried his best not to goad his Mam too far.

Mary supported Brian unstintingly in becoming the first of her bairns to stay on at school after the age of fifteen, in spite of initial uncomprehending opposition from Bob and the very real sacrifice of having to "keep him," without him giving any "keep" money back to her. She supported him from the age of fifteen to eighteen, when he gained a place at a teacher training college in September 1965. She shocked Brian the day he left Chapel Fold to catch the bus to Dewbury on the first stage of his journey to Bingley College of Education. She discarded her pinny and slippers, put on her coat and outdoor shoes and walked with him to the bus stop to see him off, leaving Bob and all the children and all her many chores. Cuddles and kisses from Mary for her bairns stopped well before the onset of adolescence. Making a fuss over the bairns was something there simply was not the time to do and, once the bairns were grown, it was seen as affected in the family way of doing things. For Mam to go out of her way to see a grown man off to college (wherever and whatever that might be) was a phenomenon. But walk with Brian she did to the bus stop on Halifax Road, with Percy Walkers Mill frowning at this frivolity, just a hundred yards away on the other side of the Halifax Road.

Mary stayed at the bus stop, nattering about what he had packed, and possibly had not packed, until the bus came. They did not kiss before Brian caught the bus. Instead she stood at the stop, watching him climb aboard, and store his suitcase, and find a seat. She stood, trying to smile encouragingly. And then she waved him off. He realised only then how much she loved him and what a wrench it was for her, his going away and leaving her to do this mysterious thing: become a student and then a teacher. She had already seen four of his older brothers and two older sisters grow up and leave home and four younger brothers and a younger sister were still at home, demanding her time and attention. But the wrench for her of Brian's leaving was as strong as that of a mother of an only child. It is forty years and more since Mary stood at the Halifax Road bus stop; a fifty year old mother of twelve children watching the bus depart, taking the middle one of her nine sons away from her. It is an abiding image for Brian of Mary's unfailing constancy and love as a mother.

Children stayed at the centre of Mary's life for many more years after Brian left for college. In 1965 Michael was seven years old and Linda and Christopher, Mary's oldest two grandchildren, were eight and seven. It was not until Michael left home, after his marriage to a girl called Sandra in 1977, that Mary ceased to be the full-time mother she had been since 1934. She was sixty two when Michael married. You might expect that she would grab the chance of finally putting her feet up but she did not. Apart from regularly nannying grandchildren, she continued to do paid work throughout her sixties and into her seventies.

For a short time she cleaned at the Nash and her last job, which she finally gave up at the age of seventy five, was again in cleaning, at The Black Bull, just down the hill from Russell Close, going toward Cross Bank.

Why did Mary choose to continue doing paid work so long? Or did she choose? Was she forced to continue working out of economic necessity? On the negative side, working as a rag-sorter at Percy Walkers in her forties and fifties knocked the hell out of her physically. On the positive side it gave her an income, and a measure of financial independence from Bob – and it took her out into the world. It was the same all over again with her cleaning jobs at the Nash and the Bull, in her sixties and seventies. The work was hard but it kept her in touch with the world outside Russell Close.

The Black Bull was one of the roughest pubs in Batley when Mary cleaned there. In its layout it was typical of West Yorkshire town centre pubs then. There were four main drinking areas leading off a long central passage as you came into the pub from the street. The passage was a popular drinking area in its own right for solitary men who were just "bobbing-in" for a quick pint, and with others who were not staying the night but doing a round of pubs. There was a small serving counter in the passage for these passing-through drinkers and it was also where customers from the lounge ordered and collected drinks.

To the left of the main front entrance was the public bar. Women were not banned from the "public" but it was understood it was a male-only bar. It was bare and sparse with a long bar, stools, a wooden floor and a few iron-framed tables and chairs for those who wanted to sit down, play dominoes, or read a newspaper. At the end of the night the wooden plank floor was covered in hundreds of tab ends and ground-in cigarette ash. Ash trays were provided but they soon overflowed or were ignored. Much business was done in the public bar among the labourers and skilled workers frequenting it. A builder might put a joiner onto a job up Birstall; a plumber might tell a brickie about a new extension at Healey, and so on. It was a place where workmen escaped in their leisure hours to talk and banter, to put each other onto jobs, or to seriously discuss the form at York races, or Batley Rugby League team's chances of beating Wakefield Trinity up Mount Pleasant that weekend. Rugby League was a religion and Mount Pleasant, where Batley RL team played, was ranked alongside heaven on match days.

Occasionally arguments or hard physical fights erupted in the Bull. Though infrequent the fights could be bloody and vicious. But David Foster, or his wife Joan, the Bull landlord and landlady during Mary's time there, soon intervened. David studied at Batley Grammar School with Mary's oldest lad Barry, where they both played in the school rugby team. And later, in his twenties, David played rugby professionally for Batley. He had a reputation for hardness and fearlessness. He was a stocky cock bantam of a man whose technique when a fight broke out in his pub was to wade straight into the thick of it no matter if the fighters were twice his size. He thought nothing of leaping over the bar counter to get at the troublemakers quickly. He swore, cursed, kicked, punched and dragged the fighters out of the bar into the street and barred them from his pub – for life. Often the fight continued and became more bloody in the street outside. David "didn't give a fuck," so long as the fight was not taking place in his pub. The disruption sometimes put him in a vile temper and he snapped and bit the head off anyone who dared talk to him after the outburst of fighting. Sometimes he was so furious he closed the pub early and ordered everyone out, like an angry schoolteacher putting the whole class in detention, due to the misdemeanour of one or two pupils. He had a soft side too. The miscreants knew he would admit them into his pub again after the rumpus had cooled down and then all they had to do was keep a low profile for a few weeks, before the next fight erupted.

Joan Foster was as fearless as David in her own way and she seemed unimpressed and unintimidated by David's occasional extreme displays of macho aggression. She was a large untidy woman with a greasy complexion and dark hair. She had a deeply sardonic and sceptical look on her face at the way the rest of the world was behaving and she stayed calm and relaxed, no matter how frantic the atmosphere in the pub became. The expression was not used during the 1970s, the heyday of her life as a pub landlady, but Joan seemed the epitome of "laid-backness."

The back room, on the other side of the serving area from the public bar, was where the younger set gathered to listen to music on the juke box, and impress each other with their knowledge of the latest rock idols. It was generally a peaceful bar but later in the night at weekends, when it was packed with people well into their tenth, eleventh or twelfth drink, it could become tense. Volence suddenly flared up and then all hell was let loose throughout the pub. Glasses were thrown and smashed everywhere. Brian witnessed just one of those Saturday night explosions. It was enough. He was sitting in the back room with his brother John and sister-in-law Pat, in the middle of a long, spongy, red velvety bench. There were perhaps thirty people packed inside the room; mainly courting couples, a few single fowk and single-sex groups. Everyone was drinking heavily. Suddenly two young men sitting a few spaces down the bench started angrily eye-balling each other, making threats to do each other in. In his drunken haze Brian thought nothing of it until his stupor was shattered by the screams of a girl. In less than a second, one of the men had grabbed an empty beer bottle from the table, smashed off the top and rammed the jagged glass bottle neck into the other man's face, causing a huge flow of blood to erupt from his victim.

There was a tidal surge of bodies on the long bench as everyone tried to break away from a burgeoning mass fight. It was like a cartoon show: bodies were rippling and falling away from the two young men and their supporters and detractors. Brian found himself on the floor among other bodies all around before Pat pulled him from the scrum and out into the relative safety of the passage while John staggered to a seat in the corner, where he stayed sitting upright and grinning, totally unperturbed by the violence escalating and spreading around as the rival sides started seriously laying into each other. Pat and Brian huddled in the passage listening to the screams, thuds, thumps and more shattering glass as the fight grew in numbers and intensity. Eventually David broke the fighters up with the help of some of the more sober regulars from the public bar and then John emerged, after the fighters had been brutally ejected, smiling dopily, quite unscathed by the violence that had just occurred.

The Black Bull had a pot man, Sid, who was in his sixties when Mary worked there. When the pub closed at night it was Sid who cleared up the worst of the detritus from the fights, as well as sweeping away the fag ends and mess on the floors. In return for his work Sid was given a small wage, and a room of his own at the pub, with his own TV, and free meals which he mostly cooked himself. Nowadays, Sid might well be one of those homeless people we all too often see huddled in shabby corners of our towns and city centres, known to the authorities but swept out of sight like valueless litter. Out of sight, out of mind, seems to be the attitude today toward those such as Sid. Not so at the time when Mary cleaned at the Bull. It was at times a rough pub, frequented by men and women who ranged from skilled, respectable and financially comfortable, to those at the absolute bottom of the social pile. But there was a community then. Successful people, on the whole, did not sweep failures under the carpet. They tolerated and helped those in financial, social, personal trouble if they could, by small acts of giving. They might buy them a meal when they were hungry, or find them a place to live in return for work: sometimes filthy, bottom-of-the-ladder work, but work which had to be done. There was a mutual respect then in working class communities such as the Batley Black Bull clientele, where even the most destitute were accorded what humans most need after the fundamental necessities of food, clothing and shelter: a sense of their own dignity and worth, given through small kind gestures and helping hands from better-off fowk. The ability to behave and fuction as a community, as a collective group with a larger responsibility for its individual members, especially the weak and vulnerable, seems to have disappeared from society today at all levels. Instead, the weak and vulnerable are marginalised, swept aside from the mainstream, or worse still demonised and punished for their failure to keep up with the majority. Or they are treated as objects, as statistics, allocated to a new government tsar to meddle with, or they are made into a government target, trumpeted by the latest government Minister given the task of sorting out "the problem." What happened to the real working class communities we used to have in England? How did they disappear, somewhere around the end of the 1970s, never to return?

In the early 1970s, when communities still existed in places such as working class Batley, as far as Mary was concerned, Sid was a nice, gentle man who was always glad to let her in when she arrived at the pub to set about the cleaning early on a Sunday morning, after a lively Saturday night. It was invariably Sid who was up and about in the morning, allowing David and Joan to have a lie-in. Mary knew Sid had severe problems with alcohol at times and he could easily slip from his delicate position in the mainstream into marginalisation and homelessness. But she never judged him, just as she never judged those "criminal" families she had known years before at Woodsome Estate. From Mary, it was always:

"Eh, poor Mrs. H. All them lasses teh look after an no munny cummin in at all."

"Eh, poor Fred S. E's gone an gor hissen locked up agee-en, feh walloping a copper."

Now, in her more comfortable sixties and seventies, it was:

"Eh, poow-er Sid. E wor up till fow-er this mornin, cleanin up mess after that feight las neet."

Just like the rag-sorting at Percy Walkers all those years before, cleaning at the Bull was hard work for Mary. No matter how much Sid worked at clearing the worst of the mess, she still cut her hands on pieces of broken glass wedged in hidden corners, or there was vomit on the lounge carpet, or sticky remains of drinks spilled over backs of chairs, waiting to be cleaned-up. Mary left Chapel Fold early four mornings each week to be at work for eight, to get the cleaning done before opening time at eleven. By ten the worst of the work was done and David and Joan appeared, bleary-eyed from their private quarters upstairs. Often Sid cooked a full fried breakfast for everyone, including Mary, and if there was time they all sat down and laughed over the events of the night-before. Just as she loved the gossip at Percy Walker's many years earlier, Mary loved these breakfast natters. She was rarely shocked by what she heard. Sometimes she was titillated. At other times she was saddened by the circumstances that led to fights and disputes. Often, in such a close-knit community, she knew the culprits by name or sight, or she knew their Mams and Dads and spouses, and she fretted over the shame and trouble they were causing their families. Cleaning at the Bull kept Mary in touch with the world. It kept her alert, alive and aware, at the onset of old age.

Mary got back to Russell Close one morning after a cleaning shift at the Bull.

"Ee, ah wah fair tickled pink this mornin. Thid all ad a reight good drinkin session las neet – Sid, David, Joan – an all reglers. Ah dooern't knaw whah time thi stopped, bur a ber it want afoor two this mornin, frum look on em all. Ahm not kiddin yow, ah must a banged on that side dooer feh ten minits, afoower Joan kem down an oppnd it. Sid wah too far gone teh cum dahn this mornin. Shi looked like bluddy dee-eth, warmed up. Ah ses, 'Ger in that kitchin, Joan. Down't werry abaht me. As'll soo-in ger everything clee-ernd up. Goo on. Gerroff wi yeh.' Well, ah thowt ad berra start in public. Eh, do yow knaw, ah cudn't believe my bluddy ees wen I oppend that doo-wer. Yeh'll nivver believe it. Peter Arkins an Alan Watson, boo-eth on em, laid aht on chairs, wi nowt on but tunderpants – an socks. Fast er bluddy slee-erp. Snoorin ther eds off. Ah din't knaw wot teh doo-er at fest, but then ah thowt 'bugger it.' Ah shook bowth on em as ard as ah cud an towd em teh gerroff owme. As ses to em, ah ses: 'Ah dooern't knaw what thy Mam'll atter seh teh thee, Peter – an whah yoor miss'll think, Alan. Sleepin on a pub bench on a Satdi neet, when yeh bowth shud be oo-erm, in yeh nice warm beds.' By, did they slink ahta that pub when thi'd gor emsens dressed. Ah bet boo-eth on em gor a reight rollickin wen thi gor oo-em. Laff! Ah cudn't stop!"

After Mary finally gave up paid work she remained young in outlook and active until well into her eighties and it is only in recent years, as she moves into her nineties, that she has started to slow down. Her first trip abroad took place in her sixties. She had been in hospital for a thyroid problem and her doctors recommended she take life easy for a week or two. Malcolm at that time was living in a house near Lillehammer in Norway with his wife Caroline and their three small children. It was decided: Mary would stay with Malcolm and his family for several weeks to convalesce: in the middle of the Norwegian winter. Just days after her operation she departed for Norway. She loved the rough ferry crossing over a wintry North Sea from Newcastle to Bergen. While other passengers struggled to cope with the crossing, Mary enjoyed the food on board, tasting her first smorgasbord and other new dishes. She accompanied Bob on those trips to Malta and Yugoslavia, during her middle and late sixties. And from their early-sixties to their middle-eighties, Mary and Louie set off once a year on a week-long coach tour, somewhere in Britain: usually a seaside resort: somewhere "on the flat" as they both grew older, more breathless and slower at walking. Mary's last holidays were spent with her oldest daughter Shirley at her grandaughter Linda's apartment in the Algarve. But as she neared ninety, with her usual down-to-earth pragmatism, she decided taking holidays was too much of an effort. Travel became a burden. She decided she was better off staying at home. Mary still enjoys an occasional day trip with Shirley from Batley to Scarborough to spend a day with Brian, or a few days spent in Bridlington with her youngest bairn Michael and his family. If you ask her, a holiday is always "luvli," the accommodation "bew-tiful" and the weather "gor-gess."

In 2004, eleven years after Bob died, when Mary was nearing ninety, she decided to move from the three-bedroom council house at Russell Close to a small ground floor one-bedroom flat not far away at Centenary Way, Down Cross Bank. Characteristically she has shown no sentiment or nostalgia for those thirty years of living at Russell Close. She only sees the advantages of living in her flat: it is compact and easy to manage; it is warm and, above all else, it is "on the flat." No more of the steep climb up the hill to Russell Close; no more climbing them bluddy steep steps to the steep front garden path and then more steep steps to the front door. Her grandaughter Michelle cleans for her and Mary pays, using her attendance allowance. Ower John brings meals cooked by Pat three or four times a week which are re-heated in the microwave. Mary is now very deaf and her walking is slower than it was but recently a small operation was carried out on her arthritic hands and to her delight she can once again bake and cook some of her own meals, without her hands seizing up.

On April 30th 2005, a Saturday, Mary reached her ninetieth birthday. Whenever anyone asked her what present she wanted for her birthday the answer was always "nothing," until her eldest grandson Christopher came up with an idea she liked: a photograph of her, on her birthday, surrounded by her ten surviving bairns, her thirty grandbairns, her nearly forty great grandbairns and a handful of her great, great grandbairns. And so a Community Centre Hall, adjacent to the Nash, was duly hired and the entire extended family of over eighty turned up, apart from one grandson living in Amsterdam and a grandaughter who had given birth the day before. The final photograph is not the best quality and it is difficult to discern both individuals and generations but if you look closely, you can just identify Mary, seated in the middle, peering over the head of the great grandchild she is holding on her lap.

Brian drove Mary the short distance to the community hall from her flat on her birthday. She looked sprightly and well. Her hair had been permed by a hairdresser grandaughter and she was wearing a long green skirt, a floral blouse and "sensible" flat shoes. One of the great pleasures of Mary's old age is that she has been able to indulge in buying new clothes whenever she wants: within reason, of course! She was a little apprehensive about having the whole family gathered together, including some family members with whom she had little contact over recent years and some with whom there were tensions.

"Everything'll be fine. Fowk know you don't want a fuss. All you've got to do is go there, have the photo tekkn, an then come back here an put your feet up."

"Ah knaw, owd lad. Ah'm mekkin a fuss abaht nowt. Come on then. Les gerr off."

It was an impressive sight when Mary arrived at the hall, with all the family gathered together, including the spouses and partners of her children, and the spouses and partners of some of her grandchildren and great grandchildren. The twenty and more under-fives were happily running around the hall, making new friends and meeting old ones. The adolescents were huddled with their own immediate family group, shyly staring around the hall, amazed that all these people were relatives. Meanwhile, the younger parents fussed and tidied-up their young ones, to look their best for the camera. Mary's oldest daughter-in-law Sheila, now in her early seventies, ever the organiser, brought cakes, biscuits, tea and coffee, all spread out at a serving hatch. Mary did what she always does when she is with her family: she made a bee line for the babies and infants. Her hands were troubling her that day and so at first she did not attempt to hold any of the bairns.

All who know Mary now marvel at how well preserved, forward-looking and optimistic she still is as she comes nearer to the end of her long, hard life. Has it been a lifetime of never smoking and rarely drinking alcohol – and rarely taking drugs and pharmaceuticals other than her sworn-by Beechams Powders – that has kept her so well? Is it the pressures and strains of having such a large family and never being able to stop to take breath that has kept her going so resolutely? Maybe the great grandchild on her lap, and all her descendents around her in the birthday photograph, are the clue to her good health and longevity. In a lifetime surrounded by children, you do not have time to grow old.

The photograph party went well. In a low-key Yorkshire way the whole gathering enjoyed it. By two o' clock it was over and people were leaving. Tradition dies hard in the hard drinking, Nash Members, Catholic side of the family and a group of Brian's nieces – and Ower John – persuaded him to join them for a drink at the Nash after the abstemious photo session in the Community Hall. For many years, from her early sixties to her mid-eighties, Mary became an institution along with Louie, at the Nash. The highlight of their week was to go down there on a Saturday night to sing along with a top class turn, or to tut over a lousy one, and to catch up with the ins-and-outs of the Nash community.

Mary stopped going to the Nash in her late-eighties and initially appeared uninterested in joining the Nash-going party. But when Brian chivvied her to hurry, so he could drop her off at her flat and get back teh Nash for a drink before closing time, her face lit up, realising he was not returning straightaway to his flat in Scarborough and she decided to join the Nash party. It was curiosity – nosiness if you like – that propelled her. She wanted to see who was there and look at all the changes inside, since her last visit a couple of years earlier. She stayed at the Nash for an hour, sipping an orange juice and holding on to her grandaughter Kate's arm as she was taken on a tour of the club. The newly decorated lounge bar was pronounced "luvli" and the concert hall "bew-tiful." It was a good end to her 90th birthday: spending an hour with some of her family in the community she has always known and lived among, in a place she loves.

*Grandad Wolstenholme,
1950s*

*Granma Wolstenholme,
with Barry 1930s*

Mary and Louie, 1920.

Mary and Louie at Nash, 1990s

Mary Holding Young Bob, 1940

Bob, Michael, Sandra, Mary, 1977

Left to Right standing: Rachel (Ann's Daughter); Dot; Anne; David's Mary; Maggie; Lynne's Mick; Donna, Christine (Christopher's wife). Seated: Pat, Mary, Sheila. April 2005

Auntie Louie and Uncle Horace, 1970s?

Mary's whole family. Seated: Michael, Bob, Malcolm, Brian, Shirley, Mary, Lynne, Stephen, Richard, David, John. April 2005

BARRY

Barry was born in May 1934, just days after Mary's nineteenth birthday. He died of liver cancer at the age of fifty nine in October 1993, a few weeks after Bob's death in July of the same year. Mary sometimes talks of Barry's "bewtiful" treble singing voice as a boy and proudly tells how he performed solo in church and school concerts. He had a confident, purposeful and ambitious personality from the start, according to Mary, and he passed the scholarship exam to enter Batley Grammar School at the age of eleven: a real achievement for a lower working class boy at that time.

"Yeh Dad din't want Ower Barry teh gu teh grammar school. Yeh knaw wor e wah like. E nattered issen silly abaht ow we cuddnt affoo-erd teh keep im at school after fowteen. Bur ah towd im. E'd passed scholarship, an we was just gooin ter ave teh *cope* wi im stayin on at school longer. An so thahs whah wi did."

Barry excelled in sports. He was a good swimmer, trained by Bob from a very early age, and he also played in the Grammar School rugby team. Barry was one of the last to sit the School Certificate, before O and A levels started, in which pupils had to pass exams in a range of arts and science subjects. He gained his School Certificate at the age of fifteen and his formal academic education ended there. Bob hoped Barry would go into mining safety work when he left school but he rejected that idea and followed in Uncle James's footsteps, taking an apprenticeship to become a master builder instead.

Some people might consider it a waste that an intelligent School Certificate boy should choose to work in the building trade instead of going on to A Levels and university. But higher education was never considered: by Barry himself, by his parents, or by his school. Higher education was something posh fowk went in for at that time. The Grammar School did not push working class boys such as Barry to go into further or higher education, particularly those working class boys whose parents lacked clear educational aspirations for their sons and those who had no knowledge of the further and higher education opportunities then available: and more importantly, parents who had no idea how to milk the education system, as posh fowk and more aspirational working class fowk did. Staying on for sixth form and going to university was beyond the orbit of possibility at that time for the vast majority of bright, grammar school, lower working class children. It was beyond the mindset of all but the most fiercely aspirational parents – which Bob and Mary were not. It was largely beyond the mindset of the grammar school teachers of the time. And it was beyond the aspirations of many of the children themselves.

Barry completed his apprenticeship and became a master builder in his early twenties. There was a two-year break in his apprenticeship for National Service at the Yeadon RAF base (now Leeds-Bradford Airport). By this time he was a handsome, stocky young man with thick golden hair, which he never lost until near the end of his life, when he had intensive cancer treatment. He kept that direct confident manner throughout his life. He enjoyed the social and sporting life in the RAF and it was during his National Service that he met Sheila Monahan, who soon became his wife. When Brian was at infant school, Barry occasionally arrived at Chapel Fold on some mysterious thing called "leave," dressed in his light bluey-grey RAF uniform, the beret neatly tucked into a strap at the shoulder. On one of his leaves he brought a large tin of RAF blue gloss paint home which he said had "fallen off the back of a lorry." It was used to paint the walls of the two smaller bedrooms at Chapel Fold.

Not long after Barry finished National Service he brought Sheila home to be introduced to Bob and Mary and all the family. There was tremendous excitement over the visit. Never before had the Hirst family experienced a complete stranger – Barry's girlfriend – coming for Sunday tea. Mary took huge care preparing the ham, egg, tinned salmon salad and cakes. Bob dressed up in his best clothes and stayed off the Sunday lunch time booze at the Nash in order to meet this girl-friend phenomenon. Shirley and Moira speculated endlessly over Sheila.

"What soort on a skirt is shi wearin on Sundi? What culler mascara dus she ave? Dus she like stilettos? Is er air boo-font-style?"

"Ow the ell do I know, Sis? Shi's a lass. Shi weers close – an shoes – an paints er face – an shi's gorra grand ed on air on er. Satisfied?"

"Oo, or reet then. Now need teh bi seh sarki."

Brian was fascinated to find that Sheila lived in Bradford (about six miles distant from Batley) and wondered what she would sound like, coming from this foreign place. As her Irish surname suggests, she was from another Yorkshire Irish Catholic family but her Bradford-speak was different from Batley-speak, which pleased Brian when he first heard her voice. Her accent was edgier, sharper, snappier.

Batley-speak: "Ey up! Gerr im, ovver yonder. In teddy boy soo-it. Oo's e think e is? Smaart aarse!"

Bradford-speak: "Nah then! Ge im ovver theer. In is teddy boy soot. Oo's e think e is? Sma ah'se!"

Sheila disappointed no one when she came to Sunday tea. She was natural, polite and friendly toward Bob and Mary. She was attractive and smartly dressed, but not overly so, for Shirley and Moira and she happily chatted to everyone: in Bradford-speak. She became a regular visitor and before too long she and Barry were married at a Catholic Church in Bradford and six months or so after the wedding their first child Linda was born, followed by Christopher eighteen months later. Seven months after Christopher's birth, Mary and Bob had their last surprise child, Michael: Linda's and Christopher's younger uncle.

Brian has a photograph taken at Barry's wedding. It shows the bride and groom standing in a formal pose outside a Yorkshire stone church, with Bob and Mary and all of Barry's then seven brothers and three sisters. Mary was forty at the time and Bob forty two. Mary looks younger than her actual age; it is difficult to believe she is the mother of eleven of the fourteen people in the photograph. The younger-end have been given gob-stoppers – to keep them happy during the tedium of photograph-taking. The gob stopper can just be seen in Lynne's left cheek and a youthful looking Bob holds her in his arms for the camera. Mary holds Stephen's shoulders and his left cheek is also bulging. Richard hides his face from the camera, standing in front of Malcolm, who holds on to his arms. Shirley and Moira are bridesmaids and all of the boys, except the youngest two, and John, are dressed in suits and ties. Brian adored Sheila from the start and he stands as close as he can next to her, a shy smile on his face, coyly looking to the side.

The photograph was taken in 1955 before Mary worked at Percy Walkers, about the time Brian took the Thrift money to Granma's every Friday teatime. It is resonant of its time. It is clearly a working class family group but there is no evidence at all of the family's often near-perilous lack of money. Everyone is dressed smartly and simply. The children are wearing newly-bought Whitsun clothes. There is no sign of fat or obesity on any of the bairns (or adults) but nor could any of them be described as looking malnourished or underweight. Everyone's hair looks glossily clean and all seem to have healthy clear skin. (Thanks to Fairy Household Soap, which served then as an all-purpose cleaner, for hair and bodies, as well as for cleaning the house.) Self-deprecation, an attitude of, "Well, you just have to get on with it," fostered by Mary, is a family characteristic and the photograph projects that attitude to life. To Brian, it tells a story of a working class family doing modestly well: a family with a sense of their own worth and dignity, in spite of the material and emotional difficulties they often faced.

Barry did well in the building trade, from leaving national service right up to his early death. He was the first in the family to own a car. His first car was an old, tinny, black Austin Seven, soon followed by a brand new grey upright Ford Popular. Riding in his early cars was one of the thrilling joys of Brian's childhood. There was no one else he knew well off enough to own a car. He was the first in the family to take out a mortgage to buy his own house and the first to have those posh fowk's luxuries: a television and telephone. It was not too long before Barry became the first self-employed person in the family. His building business never became large-scale but there were many years when he sub-contracted other builders, before he worked on his own in later years. Sheila played a full part in their success and prosperity. She managed Barry's papers and worked full and part-time virtually all her married life – and for some years after Barry's death. Mary helped, child-minding Linda and Christopher during their infant years when Sheila was at work. Like Barry, Sheila was grammar school educated, at St. Joseph's Convent School in Bradford. For many years she was full-time secretary, personal assistant and invaluable solo employee to an eccentric, Oxford-educated, one-man-business solicitor in Batley. Later she worked as office manager of a large firm of lawyers in Leeds.

In the early years of their marriage, Barry and Sheila socialised with a fast, successful, self-employed, entrepreneurial group, most of them Barry's friends through rugby and grammar school. Barry's best friends, George Harwood and Bernard Lee, were as well known to his younger siblings as their own friends were. George was a handsome blond rugby player who always seemed to have an endless line-up of girlfriends. From an early age, he ran his own painting and decorationg business which grew as the years went by. Bernard was a witty, fast talking card, a con-man who wore flashy clothes and dangerously drove a throaty Jowett Javelin.

Barry and Sheila's first house was a small back-to-back down Mount Pleasant but they soon graduated to a bigger house on Park Road, just off the main valley-bottom Bradford Road, not all that far from Granma's at Batley Carr. The Park Road house was superficially a similar stone terraced house to Granma's but it was a "through" house with a proper indoor bathroom and even a strip of garden at the front. The contrast in lifestyles between Granma and her oldest grandchild was vast. Granma still lived the life of a poor retired Victorian mill worker, whereas Barry and Sheila were sophisticated and successful and very much of the moment. Brian sometimes babysat for Barry and Sheila and the highlights of his visits included: the rides in Barry's car from Chapel Fold to Park Road and back, waving to the imagined crowds of peasants lining the streets to cheer him: the two shilling payment – and not least, Sheila's fascinating tales of war-time in Bradford, and her convent girl's schooling.

"One day, ah was the most popular girl in junior school. No kiddin, Brian luv. Mi Dad worra ri un. If there was sumthin gooin on the black market, e noo ow te ge old on it. Ee goh me two oranges once – an oranges were like gowd dust durin war. Ah'm not kiddin you, Brian, ah shared them oranges with *fifteen* other kids! We all ad a segment each. We devoured em. Yer couldn't foh the life of yeh geh oranges then. Mi Dad wen mad wen e found I adn't charged for them segments! Oo, an Sister Bernadette, at St. Joseph's. Shi took us feh Latin. Cud she remember my first name? No, she couldn. Shi called me Mona – short feh Monahan. Never Sheila. Mona! Feh five ole years!"

Barry's and Sheila's lifestyle came to an abrupt end in the early 1970s when Barry found himself up in the magistrates court on a criminal charge. It was to do with "tickets" which he and his sub-contractors should have filled in for the Inland Revenue. He was accused of fiddling the system and tax avoidance. To everybody's horror he was found guilty and sent down for a short spell. The tax tickets avoidance dodge was becoming a problem in the building trade and Barry was made an example of: a warning of what could happen to people who tried to dodge taxes, never mind the fiddles of the corporates and the wealthy at the time. Unlike the wealthy, Barry could not afford expensive barristers to plead his case.

What happened to Barry was a shocking and traumatic thing: for Barry himself, for Sheila, Bob and Mary, and all his family and friends. He was a thinking intelligent man who more than likely was harshly judged and punished – by a legal system which regularly turned a blind eye on the tax avoidance strategies of the very rich and influential. Barry never seemed to bear a grudge over what happened to him. Instead he became a more thoughtful and considerate person who changed his lifestyle and working patterns after he came out from his time in an open prison. First he worked for a year in Saudi Arabia, supervising the building works of a vast development. He returned home leaner and fitter and with a small fortune in earnings. After Saudi Arabia he worked on smaller jobs, involving minimum sub-contracting.

Barry inherited Bob's liking for alcohol but he seemed more in control of his drinking than Bob ever was. There was always that tint of wrongness about Bob's drinking, perhaps caused by shameful memories of Winnie, slipping out for a jug of beer or gin, leaving her boys alone at home. Barry's drinking was more social, more a matter of genuine bonhomie. He followed Grandad Wolstenholme in that respect. After his time spent away he began socialising again in local pubs and clubs. He was invariably alone and could usually be found leaning against the passage wall near the bar, a pint of beer in hand, in any one of several pubs and clubs around Batley and Dewsbury. In an unobtrusive way, he loved those weekend drinking and socialising sessions. He loved the beer, the company and the banter. He had a sardonic, knowing smile and he was an expert at winding people up, adding to the around-the-bar entertainment. There was no malice in his teasing: winding up and verbal repartee were much loved aspects of standing around a bar in the West Riding in those days. He was an expert at witty repartee and was popular and well liked for his bar room social skills. In spite of his popularity and sharp wit, he rarely stayed at one venue for long, preferring instead to roam from bar to bar. There was something a little detached about his bonhomie; something a little sceptical. Perhaps he never quite trusted people again, after his experience with English "justice."

Brian has another photograph, taken at his younger brother Stephen's wedding in the 1970s. Stephen and several of his friends and brothers (and Bob) are lined up in front of a bar, beer glasses in hand, smiling at the camera, with just one female, Mary, poking her nose in at the side. Barry is in his favourite position: leaning against the wall to the side of the bar just on the edge of the group, a sardonic sceptical smile on his face. He is smiling at Brian, at something he is saying which appeals to his sense of humour. Or perhaps he is smiling at the fact that Brian is relaxed, happy and drunkenly grinning at the camera. It was only at this time, when Brian was in his early-thirties and Barry in his mid-forties, that the big age and experience gap between them began to close and they became brothers, on an equal relaxed footing, and they grew to like and respect each other.

By the time he reached his forties Barry was a mellower more philosophical person than the sporty dynamo he had been in his younger days. He often called-in at Russell Close before Sunday dinner on his way back home to Sheila, with presents of wonderful vegetables freshly dug from his allotment, where he had just spent the morning. He rarely sat down to drink the tea Mary made, preferring to stand in the back kitchen doorway, looking out on the garden or leaning against the kitchen cupboards with a tea mug clutched in his hand, much as he stood with his pint glass in the bars and clubs he frequented. He was different then from his young self. He was kind and considerate to both Mary and Bob and pleased to see any others in the family who dropped in for a Sunday morning chat. He never lost that sardonic smile and dry sense of humour.

"Ow's Ower Christopher gerrin on et collidge?" Mary might ask.

"Oo?" Barry replies, raising his eyebrows quizzically and hitching up his glasses. "Oh, im. Bluddy Peter Pan, that lad. The boy oo nivver grew up."

To an outsider it might seem a cold unfeeling thing to reply to a grandmother asking her oldest son about her oldest grandson. But it was not. It was warm, loving and affectionate. It was Barry's way of expressing his feelings for his son. He knew how to make the family laugh and family laughter is a joyous and bonding thing. In the last

91

few years of Barry's life his sardonic distance melted away when he spoke of his first grandchild Louise. He adored her. Every small action she took, every word she said, was a miracle, a wonder of nature. To some in the family it was extraordinary, and touching, to see this dry sceptic transformed into a doting grandfather.

During Brian's weekly phone calls to Mary at this time she often mentioned how much Barry's back was bothering him. She nattered over the fact that he was still working in the building trade: fetching, stretching, lifting and carrying: not a physically easy job for a fifty nine year-old. He would not see a doctor, even though the back pains became worse and more persistent. Seeing doctors was something he had never needed to do. When Bob died in June 1993, Barry and Sheila were taking a spur-of-the-moment holiday in Cyprus. It was something of a surprise, not to say a miracle, as Sheila, who is deeply phobic about aeroplanes, had agreed to travel to Cyprus – on an aeroplane. Barry enjoyed several long-haul holidays abroad with friends over the later years of his marriage, while Sheila preferred to holiday at Butlins, Blackpool or Scarborough, with the children and her Bradford family. One of Barry's holidays abroad involved a long and wide-ranging tour of the USA. He loved every minute of it, revelling in the sights, sounds and voices which so reminded him of the American jazz musicians he worshipped, and the much admired Hollywood films of his youth.

Barry and Sheila were staying in a telephone-less villa in Cyprus, owned by one of their friends and contacting them to tell them of Bob's death took some time. It was touch-and-go whether they would return in time for the funeral but they made it. Bob's funeral was the last time most of the family saw Barry. He knew by then that he himself had cancer of the liver and had only months to live. It was unspoken but the family later assumed the sudden Cyprus trip was taken to enable Barry and Sheila to absorb the terrible and unexpected prognosis he had been given. The family gathered at Russell Close before Bob's funeral. Barry was at first among a crowd, huddled in the scullery. He was red faced, which everyone took to be sunburn. It was the only time Brian saw him lose his customary detachment and composure. He was devastated and sobbing and Sheila had to lead him outside like a child, to calm him down with strokes, murmurs and kisses. Barry was close to his Dad and the tears were for Bob, but they were for himself too, and for Mary, to whom he was going to have to break the news of his own impending death, once Bob's funeral was over.

A few days after Bob's funeral, the telephone rang in Brian's Derby flat one evening. Unusually it was Mary. Normally Brian rang her. In a frail but steady voice Mary told Brian of Barry's condition. He died a few weeks later, in October 1993. The last weeks of his life are a story to be told by Shirley.

Sheila and Barry, 1960s.

Shirley, Moira, Sheila and young bridesmaid, 1955

*Barry's Wedding. Left to right: Shirley, John, Mary,
Stephen, Barry, Sheila, Lynne, Brian, Bob, David, Moira,
Malcolm, Richard, Young Bob. 1955*

*Stephen's Wedding. Front: Bob, Brian (seated), Michael,
Mary. Back: John, Stephen (centre) Mick, Barry leaning
against wall with Christopher. Seven of Stephen's friends.
1970s*

SHIRLEY

Shirley was born eighteen months after Barry in November 1935. Like Barry, she has ginger hair which has barely changed colour as she nears her seventieth birthday. In keeping with her red hair, Mary says Shirley was a fiery-tempered child, a temper she has never quite lost although the fire has dimmed a little with age. During the war when Bob was far away on active service in Malta, Shirley's stormy temperament was sometimes too much for Mary to handle, cooped up as she was with four small children inside the claustrophobic little house at Wainwright's Buildings.

"Oo, aye. Shi cud be a reight stubborn little bugger, cud Ower Shirley. Ah med er sit aht on front step all neet once, yer knaw. When war were on. Shi just drove mi demented an ah cudn't stand avin er defyin mi any moo-wer. Course, mi Mam-n-Dad on'y lived just rahnd corner. An ah knew what'd appen after ah sat er ont outside step. Mi Dad saw er sittin theer, din't e? An so, a course, e took er down to theer ouse feh neet. Much good *that* punishment did!"

Bob taught Shirley to swim at an early age and by the time she reached her teenage years she was a fast and powerful swimmer. Her swimmimg teacher spoke of her reaching Olympic standard but although she won trophies she never went further. At age eleven, Shirley attended

Foxcroft Girls Secondary Modern, up the hill from Batley Carr and after spending one year there, she passed the twelve-plus exam to enter Batley Technical School, where the girls studied domestic, office and secretarial skills and the boys took building, metalwork and engineering. Shirley left technical school at fifteen to work in the offices of a factory in Birstall. A year later she moved to a better paid job at Taylor's Mill in Batley to work as a mender and not long after that, she left Taylors to work as a weaver at Smiths Mill in Batley Carr. She loved working at Smiths. It was a family mill, with granmas, dowters and grandowters – all working in the same place. Shirley had known many of the women at Smiths since growing up in Batley Carr. She worked at Smiths for eight years, until shortly before the birth of her first child Julie.

One of Brian's earliest memories of Shirley is when he was around the age of six and she was eighteen. In this memory, Bob and Shirley are physically fighting, angrily grappling with each other. It ended with slamming doors: Bob storming off out into the garden and Shirley stomping up to the bedroom. Perhaps the fight was to do with Shirley's smoking habit, or Bob's drinking, or his disregard for Mary? Shirley began smoking early, around the age of thirteen. Mary disapproved of the habit but Louie mischievously slipped her a cig whenever Shirley asked, both of them smirking behind Mary's back.

In her early-twenties, Shirley took David and Brian for a five day holiday to New Brighton. It was Brian's and David's first holiday away from home, apart from day trips to northern seaside towns. Brian was nine and David eight. Richard, Stephen and Lynne were pre-school toddlers and Michael was only a few months old. Shirley probably paid for the holiday and no doubt its purpose, as much as anything, was to give Mary a short break from two of her children, at least. In spite of her youth Shirley was more than capable of looking after and controlling her two excitable younger brothers. They responded far more quickly to a sharp word from her than they did to Mary's threats. They had seen Shirley's temper erupt often enough to know it was dangerous to challenge her or goad her too far and so they "did as they were towd." It was a cold and windy week. It was not a beach holiday; it was more about walking-around and taking-short-trips. There was an exciting windy trip on a ferry to Liverpool, sitting on a slatted bench on the open deck with the water foaming, the wind blowing and buildings in the distance coming closer to the lurching boat. There was a bus ride, too, through the Mersey Tunnel, which excited and terrified Brian simultaneously.

One evening Shirley and the two boys were sitting in the dining room at the New Brighton B&B eating dinner. Some older people at an adjacent table questioned Shirley about their ages. They congratulated her on her competence in looking after her younger brothers and complimented the boys on their good behaviour and manners. Brian stiffened with pride but he was a little uncomfortable, and he saw Shirley was too. There was something just a little skincrawlingly patronising in the tone of the people at the next table. It was as if, for a reason Brian did not yet understand, they thought he should not somehow be so polite and well mannered. It would be a few years before he understood the tribal and class shades of England and people's ability to tell by the way others spoke and dressed from which class they originated. It was a world where the inhabitants of a private semi-detached house considered themselves to exist on a higher plane than the people living in the council estate, just round the corner from them.

Not long after the New Brighton holiday, Shirley suddenly decided one afternoon to take David and Brian all the way to a cinema in Leeds, a good forty minute bus journey in those days on the slow old Huddersfield-Leeds Road. The film was completely unsuitable for two small boys and possibly also for a late-teenage girl who had travelled little and knew no languages other than her own. It was a Polish film with English sub-titles which, being a good reader, Brian could follow. Brian would recognise the film's genre now as socialist-realist but he did not then. It was a terrifying story, which took place underground in a narrow claustrophobic seam of a coal mine, where a number of miners were trapped and injured after a pit prop collapse. David, realising the film was not *Lassie* or *Roy Rogers*, sensibly hunkered down in the cinema seat and quickly fell asleep. Being more highly strung than David, Brian was both riveted and repelled by this dark story taking place in a strange foreign language on the screen. At first he snivelled. No effect on Shirley. He whimpered. No effect. He cried and sobbed.

"Shirley, Shirley! Ah don't like it. Ah'm scared. Ah want teh gu ome!"

Sudden galvanisation of Shirley. She yanked his arm and shook David awake and dragged them outside.

"An thes gunner be NO lollipops feh yow tow on bus back ome. Showin me up in front er all them fowk like that!"

Another day around that time. They had been to the park, or the pictures, or to Barry's house, or maybe to the shops. Shirley, David and Brian are on the Staincliffe Estate bus from the town centre, going back home. It is a hot day: tea time: the bus is packed with people. They find seats downstairs at the back. The seats face each other near the luggage space and the open boarding platform, from where they can catch some fresh air. The nasty conductor everyone hates is on duty. He is more irritable and impatient than usual on the hot, packed bus, growling and snarling at the passengers as he collects money and snaps out tickets from a machine hanging on a long leather strap from his shoulder. He smells sweaty and there are wet patches under the armpits of his dark blue conductor's shirt. Shirley glares and mutters, becoming more and more incensed at every crass utterance the conductor makes to other passengers. David and Brian sink in their seats, waiting for an explosion. Mr. Nasty completes the fare collection and comes to stand on the platform near their seats, to get some air as the tired old bus grinds its slow ascent up the interminable Clerk Green Hill. Shirley by now has worked herself into a lather of fury against Sweaty Jim. She and the conductor glare at each other all the way up Clerk Green and along Manor Way. He silently dares her to say a word and he will chuck her off the bus. Shirley stays silent but she is boiling inside. They reach their stop at the top of Pine Grove. Shirley makes eye-to-eye contact with the conductor as she stands to get off.

"An you. YOU BLUDDY LITTLE HITLER," she hisses, right into his sweaty face. "YOU don't deserve teh bih a bus conductor. You shud bih in GESTAPO, you shud."

And off she marches, brothers in tow, leaving the conductor gaping.

"That's reight, lass. You bluddy tell im," shouts an elderly man.

"By! Thar towd that bugger, Shirley lass. E's a bastard, e is," from someone else.

"Yer did reight, lass. E's ad that coming ter im feh donkey's years, as that one," another concurs.

Shirley, Brian and David march victoriously now, down Pine Grove. Brian is marvelling and musing as they turn the corner into Chapel Fold, not so much at his sister's brave stance but more at her powerful words.

"Where did she get them?" He wonders. "I want some of those, too."

Another early memory of Shirley. Brian is ten: at Granma Wolstenholme's house. Consternation.Worry. Fluster.

"Aw, bluddy ell! Look wor Ower Shirley's gone an dun. Shi's left er purse on table. Shi'll need it afore er shift's ovver."

"Granma. Ah can tek er purse. Ah noo weer shi weks: ah *do!*"

"Nay, owd cock. Ah'm not seh shoo-er. It's dayn-ger-es feh bairns, is yon mill yard. Aw, gu on then. Tek it. But, Brian: BE CAREFUL. DOO-EN'T RUN. WALK!"

Brian is excited and scared going through the big gates into Smiths Mill yard clutching Shirley's purse. There is a racket coming from the weaving shed floor and a mill smell. It is not the stale damp smell of the rag-oyle. It is more an oily waxy smell. A foreman comes over and asks him what he wants and he explains. He takes Brian to the main door of the weaving shed and tells him to wait there until he fetches Shirley. It is amazing inside the mill. There is a fantastic overwhelming noise of powerful machinery and rows of machines with string things above and bobbing things bouncing up and down, pulling threads of yarn into a pattern along the strings. There are dozens of women standing at the benches. They are all incredibly busy, their hands doing rapid operations on the weaving apparatus. Some wear headscarves, some tied into turbans, and colourful overalls cover them from their necks to below their knees. A radio is playing dance band music faintly under the clatter of machinery and some of the women are singing to the tune, or they are laughing and mouthing messages to each other across the high machinery. Shirley suddenly emerges from all of this. She is strange and distant: not Brian's usual sister. The turban and overall hide the young woman he knows. He holds the purse out to her and she takes it quickly. She seems to find him as strange as he finds her in this place and she ushers him into the yard.

"Thanks feh bringin mi purse, luv. Gu on, urry back teh mi Granma's. Ah'll see yeh later."

In her seventies Shirley had forgotten the purse episode but she vividly recalled Smiths as a "lovely family" mill to work in, where mothers worked with daughters and where older women treated Shirley like a daughter. The women had fun in the mill, competing with each other to see who could finish a job fastest. It made Shirley's day, when she finally beat a much older, more experienced woman, but they still kept their "mother-daughter" relationship. Shirley also recalled Granma cooking her midday meals when she worked at Smiths. She knew what the meal was going to consist of well before arriving at Granma's house as she could smell the cooking odours coming through the coiloyle grill on the top front row as she walked past Elsie Wainwright's house, before going down the ginnel to Granma's on the bottom-back-row.

During their late teens and early twenties, Shirley and Moira used to doll themselves up on a Saturday night and off they would go with Elsie Wainwright, Doreen Barraclough and other friends, for a night of Babycham and dancing at the Gaiety Dance Hall (above Woolworths) on Commercial Street, Down Batley. Perhaps it was at the Saturday night Gaiety that Shirley met Jimmy Colleran; another Yorkshire-Irish-Catholic. There was nothing like a formal introduction of Jimmy into the Hirst family as there had been with Sheila. Jimmy met the family more obliquely.

There were no supermarkets in Batley around the time Shirley met Jimmy. There were shops in the middle of Staincliffe Estate and more along the Halifax Road, down from Percy Walkers Mill. Some of the shops were expensive, and besides, it was a trail to get to them and then you had to carry heavy bags of shopping all the way back home. At Woodsome and later at Staincliffe, people were out on the edges of town and traders came to the home, saving customers the long traipse to the shops.

In the early years at Chapel Fold – the early-to-mid 1950s – Benjamin Hick arrived once a week to sell fruit and vegetables. Mr. Hick was like someone from the nineteenth century. He had a beautiful great brown horse which pulled a fruit and vegetable cart around the estate, stopping at every few houses. Benjamin himself was dressed like a country gamekeeper with his feathered deerstalker hat, thick tweed jacket, mustard waistcoat, checked shirt, heavy wool tie, leather gaitered boots – and a whip with which he would prod the horse to "goo-er" or "woo-er." The cart was high and had a covered top to protect the produce from the weather. Underneath were tiered planks covered in bright green artificial grass on which fruits and vegetables were displayed in trays. Green painted wooden shutters could be rattled down from the top and fastened so the produce would not fall from the cart when it was in motion. The back of the cart was made up of a solid green painted board with words (which Brian loved reading aloud to himself) painted in elaborate gold lettering across the background green: "Benjamin Hick. Family Greengrocer, Fruiterer and Poulterer. Established since —" Co-op milk was delivered to the door too, by horse and cart, before Batley Co-operative Society modernised to hissing electric vans. Bob, the red-cheeked Co-op breadman, delivered big loaves of white unsliced bread and, if times were flush, a few currant teacakes as well, from an electric cart – green again, with "Batley Co-operative Society Bakery" written along the sides. Nelson Hirst the butcher was very modern. His mid-week meat delivery came in a small Baby Austin motor van.

When Benjamin Hick retired and disappeared from the streets of Batley, Jimmy Colleran briefly took his place. Instead of a horse and cart, Jimmy delivered from a second-hand lorry, an Austin, with an open platform at the back where the fruits and vegetables were ranged not quite so beautifully as Hick's. Jimmy looked like a countryman too but he was younger, more modern, noisier and cheekier than Mr. Hick. He dressed in a working tweed jacket, heavy serge trousers, an open necked shirt and solid working shoes. He was a tall man with a broad handsome face, black hair, swarthy tanned skin and a solid build. He was forever whistling, singing, laughing, talking and joking. He spoke broad old-fashioned Yorkshire as he weighed out taties, onions and carrots for his customers. Suddenly Jimmy the fruit n' veg man became Shirley's boyfriend and not long after that he became her husband and a few months later Shirley and Jimmy had their first child, Julie.

Brian was appointed Shirley's and Jimmy's regular babysitter from Julie's birth, when he was aged thirteen. He continued babysitting almost every weekend to the age of eighteen, by which time Linda and Stephen had also arrived. Over those five babysitting years, the eleven- year gap between older sister and younger brother narrowed and Shirley and Brian became close friends. They talked about everything: the family, Jimmy's family, Brian's friends, Shirley's friends, neighbours, what she was reading, what he was reading, who was the best singer in the world, who the best actor, which was the greatest film ever, and on and on, subliminally vying with each other to see who could use the most extensive vocabulary and range of expression.

Brian also grew close to Jimmy. But the friendships were kept separate. His "feminine" conversations with Shirley took place when Jimmy was not around. And similarly, "masculine" conversations with Jimmy occurred when Shirley was busy elsewhere. Brian was never as open and at ease talking with men as he was with women and conversations with Jimmy tended to take the form of him listening and Jimmy talking. He did not mind the one-sidedness. Jimmy respected the fact that Brian was becoming an "educated" person and he wanted to test out his ideas and bestow him with all the knowledge he had gleaned from his daily reading of public library books. Jimmy talked simply, within a narrow range of vocabulary and expression, in broad West Yorkshire dialect: "Nah then, Brian. Are's tah bahn?" (Now then, Brian. How are you?) was a typical greeting from him. But his monologues were invariably fascinating. He talked big universal ideas in a simple but profound way. He talked politics, economics, philosophy. He analysed the nature of society, class, religion, history and historical figures.

"Sithee, Brian owd lad. Nivver trust a Tory. All them lot's int'rested in is angin on teh ther munny, what thi call ther in-eri-tens. An bugger us werk-es – born wi nowt ter ower names…

… Ee, dustah knaw. Ah sometimes cum aht ere at neet an look at that sky full er stars up yonder. An tha knaw, owd lad, it fair meks yeh wunder weer it's all cum fro…

… Ey up! That bluddy Marx! Ee dint arf knaw a thing er two abaht fowk. Ahve bin readin a good libr'y book on im. Up wi werk-es, an dahn wi rulers, wi Marx. An fair distribewshen fer all. Aye, owd lad. That'd soo-in soo-ert things aht. An nor arf! …"

After a talk with Shirley, Brian felt satisfied; perhaps some understanding of one of her neighbours had been talked through and resolved. After listening to Jimmy, he was fired-up; angry at the injustices of the class system in England; deeply regretful that the Cromwell years ended with the restoration of the monarchy; furious with the worst excesses of the capitalist system. Later in life Brian learned the Socratic dialogic method of coming to an understanding of the world. He learned structuralist analysis, where you take a whole object or idea and break it down into its smaller parts in order to understand the whole thing better. He read all of Montaigne's essays in which that wonderful thinker teaches you to know the world by knowing yourself. Jimmy instinctively understood and pursued these approaches, without any formal education after the age of fifteen. Often though, after Jimmy's long disquisitions, both he and Brian were left baffled, inchoate, wondering why the world never operated in the way they thought it should.

Shirley became a different person after she married Jimmy. She was less dominant, less aggressive, more in the shadow of Jimmy's larger-than-life personality. Even though Jimmy could be profoundly serious in one-to-one conversation, laughter and entertainment were rarely far from the surface when he was around. Like Grandad Wolstenholme at Batley Carr Club, Jimmy was Social Secretary for several years at White Lee Club and Birstall Nash and he was often the star "turn" in his own right on Saturday entertainment nights. (White Lee and Birstall are villages outlying Batley where Jimmy lived all his life.) He had a good strong baritone voice and loved nothing more than singing his favourite ballads in his own house, accompanying himself on his own one-man-band contraption: an hilarious combination of guitar/banjo/mouth-organ/drum which, to his delight, occasionally came out right, though more often than not he failed to master the complex mixture of simultaneously singing, strumming, blowing and hitting. Shirley cringed and complained when Jimmy decided to shower everyone with his gifts as an entertainer at full volume in their small front room. Her grumbles, however, failed to deter or deflate him: he knew how to stop her complaints and make her laugh. "Dowis," said the way someone unable to pronounce the letter R would say Doris, was his pet name for Shirley.

"Stop tha moanin, Dowis, an ger inter that kitchen, weer yeh belong," he would retort to her grumbles and in spite of her incipient feminism, Shirley would sink into helpless laughter. In his act at the Club, Jimmy was as much a comedian as a singer. Frequent verbal sparring went on between Shirley and Jimmy. They had their differences in values and aspirations. When they differed, Shirley drew on her vocabulary and tongue to win an argument. Jimmy drew on native wit and his subtle, deep sense of humour – his sense of the absurdity of existence. And win he usually did, with Shirley collapsing in exasperated laughter.

At other times the old fiery Shirley re-emerged. One Saturday babysitting night, to Brian's surprise, Jimmy returned from a night out at Birstall Nash – alone. He said nothing about the missing Shirley, greeting Brian cheerfully and making a pot of tea before sitting down to put the world to rights once again. Just as they were becoming interested in their topic, the door burst open and Shirley appeared, a look of fury directed at Jimmy. She marched over and stood behind his chair, willing him to notice her but Jimmy continued talking to Brian as if she were not there, hovering menacingly behind him. Suddenly she raised her arm and smashed her handbag down on his head:

"Don't you EVER bluddy do that agen. Showin me up like that."

Jimmy was bigger and stronger than Shirley and held her off from attacking him further. A long argument ensued, mainly from Shirley with Jimmy dismissing her fury as "summat-abaht-nowt." The something-about-nothing was that Jimmy had tired of Shirley gossiping and lingering among friends and he had left her to walk home alone. In those days, in that community, a couple stayed together in public and it was the man's role to escort the woman home through the dark Saturday night streets. Eventually they made it up, largely through Jimmy laughing the episode off. The following morning before Brian left for Chapel Fold, Shirley ordered him not to say a word to Mary about the argument. He did not understand why Mam should not know but he could see it was hugely important to her and so the order was obeyed.

Shirley and Jimmy eventually became a double act. Shirley played the practical pragmatic one, quietly getting things done in the background while Jimmy sang, joked, philosophised and dreamed. Jimmy made a huge sacrifice when he married. He gave up his mobile greengrocery business, sold the lorry and took a job cutting and shaping carpets in The Briar, a huge carpet factory in Birstall. He stuck at the Briar job for over twenty years until compulsory redundancy struck in his early-fifties. When he knew he was to be married he decided the greengrocer enterprise was too risky financially for a man who was soon to become a husband and father. But he longed for the freedom of the outdoor life and being his own man and throughout his time of working at The Briar he sought ways of re-creating his semi-rural upbringing and the carefree outdoors entrepreneurialism of his pre-married life. He kept rabbits (for eating) and hens and bantams (for eggs) in the back garden. He grew vegetables and flowers in profusion and sold them to passers-by on the street, from boxes displayed on the front garden steps. Every year he made jars and jars of wonderful pickles: onions, red cabbage and beetroot, which he sold at the factory and clubs, just through word-of-mouth as to their excellence. At one stage he took to buying unpainted garden gnomes in bulk and painted them up to re-sell. (Years later Eddie Grundy, in BBC Radio 4's "The Archers," did the same.) He did it with his usual mixture of seriousness and humour: he wanted to be his own man and he wanted to be an entrepreneur but he milked the humorous side of the gnomes for all it was worth. Shirley meanwhile stayed on the sidelines of Jimmy's enterprises, grumpy and sceptical, but seduced too by his enthusiasm and ambition.

In the early years of their marriage Jimmy's passions were outside the house. Shirley's passion, apart from her children, was the house itself. She became obsessively dedicated to decorating and furnishing her houses to her own exacting standards. Shirley's and Jimmy's interests differed to begin with but gradually they infected each other. Ideally in his leisure time Jimmy preferred to stay in his shed musing or working in his garden but he would traipse around the shops for hours with Shirley, choosing just the right sort of wallpaper for the little bedroom, or fabric for the new front room curtains. And Shirley compromised too, leaving Jimmy to the garden or to his latest enterprise while she herself stayed indoors, climbing ladders, painting, cutting, pasting and wallpaper-hanging.

Once the children were at school, Shirley's ambitions grew and she decided to add to the family income by returning to work. Jimmy was not comfortable with this decision; he had traditional notions of the place of husband and wife: the husband should go out to work and the wife stay at home. But he knew he could not fight an irresistible force and Shirley's first job as a married woman was "home help," to the elderly fowk living in the bungalows on the small council estate at Howden Clough in Birstall where she lived at that time. Later she became an ancillary nurse in the geriatric wards of local hospitals and she remained in this taxing job until her mid-sixties. To an outside observer, the work she did might seem unskilled, low paid and below her intelligence level. Shirley no doubt felt this herself. She sometimes dimissed the foolishnesses and incompetence of the doctors and nurses she worked with, clearly frustrated she was on a lower rank than them. But in spite of her occasional frustration she took her work seriously and became an expert in looking after the aged and in understanding their emotional and physical needs.

As the years went by, it was Shirley's horizons that seemed to expand while Jimmy's stayed the same. Not only did she find work to which she was committed, she also learnt to drive and bought a car in her late-forties. Jimmy never drove again after selling his greengrocery lorry. Shirley stopped smoking in her early forties but she could not persuade Jimmy to do the same. She made a wider circle of friends through her work and it was she who pushed Jimmy to take holidays abroad, once the children had left home to lead their own lives. Jimmy's horizons contracted when he left Briar Carpets. Redundancy hit him hard. He felt diminished, as a person, without paid work. But eventually he found a job which he enjoyed and to which he was suited, selling specially adapted furniture for the elderly and disabled at a Birstall outlet.

Jimmy died of lung cancer in 1991, just before he reached his sixtieth birthday. The last time Brian saw him was a few months before he died: where else but in his garden? He was a shadow of his former self. He had shrunk, his hair was white and his strong baritone voice was now just a whisper. Jimmy and Brian sat on two old kitchen chairs outside the greenhouse in the back garden: both of them baffled: baffled this time not by history, religion, the follies of leaders, or other great issues, but by cancer: by its cruelty and what it does to your body.

Jimmy's funeral at St Patrick's RC Church in Birstall was a packed affair. Hundreds of people – family, friends, club members, workmates – came to see him off at the full Requiem Mass. After the Mass, everyone trooped the long trek through the Protestant Birstall Parish Churchyard to the very end, where an area of land was reserved for RC burials. They followed a wobbling bier pushed by the undertakers along a precarious path. Brian walked with Sheila and his oldest niece Linda. They were giggling together, remembering Sheila's granma's funeral on a freezing winter's day in Bradford.

"Brian, kid. Honist. I am *not* kiddin *you*. Mi granma's bier slipped on tice an just went off on its own momentum. Ah cud just ear er in er coffin: 'Thatll teach yow buggers: thinking thas bahner berry me!' Laff! Ah nearly died."

Shirley was smiling too as people gathered around the burial plot for Last Rites. Brian stood beside her. She pointed to the bier:

"Eh, it dus mek me smile. That bier. He loved is beer an e's on another kind right a tend. E'd ave liked that idea. An e loved the ride, Brian. Ah cud ear im, yeh know: 'By ell, Shirley lass, it's a grand contraption, is this ere bier!'"

Jimmy was buried in a lovely spot in the Pennine industrial-rural landscape he so loved, with green fields for rabbiting and a mill dam for fishing nearby. Brian still sometimes recalls Jimmy, sitting by the fireplace at Howden Clough, clearing his throat before singing his favourite ballad:

"I peeped in to say good night... Scar-let ri-bbons for her hair..."

The last time Shirley saw Jimmy was in his hospital bed. The Consultant and nursing team were there and his progress after the radiotherapy treatment was discussed, with some optimism for his future. Shirley left the hospital convinced Jimmy would survive for some time to come but on arriving home the hospital telephoned: Jimmy died just after she left. She described to Brian many months later how she raged over Jimmy's death. She felt he had cheated her; he could have stayed with her, but chose to go. And worse than that; he chose to leave when she was not with him. For years after his death, tears of rage-filled grief overwhelmed her whenever she drove near the route of visiting him during his final hospital days. Rage is just an intrinsic quality in Shirley's personality, from that small girl in war-time Batley Carr, to the mother and grandmother she had become when Jimmy died. Rage is how Shirley has sometimes dealt with the difficulties of life. But it was the rage also of a woman left by the man she had come to love deeply. It was rage against the future, against a world empty of Jimmy's solid presence.

When Barry died not long after Jimmy, Shirley was determined to see him through to the end. As soon as Barry knew he was going to die he made it clear he wanted to spend the last weeks of his life at home, with Sheila, Linda, Christopher – and the hospice Macmillan nurses, when necessary. He wanted no one else in the house. He wanted to save his wider family and friends seeing him experiencing what he knew would be a painful and searing time up to his death. But Shirley wanted, needed, on a visceral level deeper than words, to be with her brother in his dying days. She insisted on seeing him. Sheila wanted Shirley to be there too, but he had made his wants clear. And so, as Barry lay on his bed, sleeping and drugged on painkillers constantly pumping through his body, Shirley arrived at the house one day and persuaded Sheila to let her in. Once inside, she crouched on hands and knees and crept across the bedroom floor: to be near to her brother: to be close to him: during his last days.

After that, Sheila and Barry let Shirley and Mary into the house to share in Barry's dying days and in his death. Those three strong women were with him every last moment. They shared moments of agony and joy. They gave Barry strength and each other strength. After the funeral, Shirley related to Brian those last days spent with Barry. It was terrible and wonderful for all of them: for Sheila, losing the man she had married and lived with for almost forty years: for Mary, at nearly eighty, losing the first child she had borne at nineteen: and for Shirley, losing her closest brother and still grieving over the recent deaths of Jimmy and Bob. But she was with her brother until his end and being there mitigated some of the rage she still felt at not being with Jimmy in his dying moments.

Initial rage has always been a feature of the way Shirley deals with the world but after the rage the pattern of her behaviour is to find new dimensions in life. After Jimmy died she continued to work on geriatric wards until she retired. She worked because she felt she needed the money but also the work gave her satisfaction and it kept her in the wider world. She joined a local Ramblers group and made new friends as well as keeping closely in touch with her former workmates and neighbourhood friends. Houses remained of immense importance to Shirley, from the first small back-to-back at Blackburn Road in Birstall, which she and Jimmy rented after their marriage, to the two council houses at Howden Clough, on the high Pennine edges of Birstall, to their first owned house down in the valley near Birstall Smithies crossroads. To everybody's surprise, not long after Jimmy died, Shirley sold the private semi and moved to a house on the small council development at Howden Clough where she had lived before, but this time as an owner. She is passionate about her house and its decor and furnishings; making it to her liking gives her endless pleasure. The view from her small conservatory across Howden Clough Cricket Club field to the rolling high Pennines to the west is one she loves and one Jimmy loved. Much of the story of her's and Jimmy's lives are in that view. Birstall is down below in the valley where Briar Carpets used to be and where Birstall Nash is still. And across the valley is White Lee, where Jimmy grew up and where he courted Shirley at the White Lee Club. Shirley lost Jimmy early but she now has a large family of her own with grandchildren and great grandchildren who keep her active and busy.

Jimmy must be smiling in his plot at the cemetery, watching the progress of his wife and children. Julie is a social worker dealing with difficult children. Stephen is self-employed and has worked as a carpenter as far away as Israel, inbetween travelling the world three times over on long backpacking tours. Linda is a businesswoman and an entrepreneur in her own right, from running a sandwich bar to investing in property. Shirley, in a small and cautious way, has become a businesswoman also, sharing with Linda in the ownership of a buy-to-let house. When not caring for her own large family, Shirley now regularly stays at Linda's property in the Algarve, either with friends, or alone.

David, Shirley, Brian. New Brighton, 1950s.

Shirley and Jimmy, 1950s

MOIRA

Moira was born one year after Shirley in November 1936. From birth she had chronic bronchitic asthma and there were times throughout her life when her hold on survival was tenuous. She was small, thin and underweight, in contrast to Barry's and Shirley's strong stockiness. By the time she reached twelve, her bronchitis was so bad she spent several months in a home for delicate children at Lynmouth in Devon. It was the 1940s and the doctors said the Devon air was sweeter and purer than the air of industrial West Yorkshire, with its hundreds of polluting chimneys, both industrial and residential. According to Mary, Moira returned from Lynmouth a little plumper than before but still delicate – and with a Devon burr to her accent. She soon lost the burr but she was never to be rid of her breathing difficulties, which plagued her all her life.

Moira was ten years older than Brian. She was always there in his childhood and early adolescence. Much more than Barry and Shirley, her delicate health tied her to the house and family. There was a distance between Barry and to a certain extent Shirley, and the middle and younger siblings. Not so with Moira. She was a pivotal part of the family and she took an intense, loving and bossy interest in all her brothers and sisters. She cared for them deeply and became as involved as they would allow, in both the minutiae and big moments of their lives. When her siblings were successful she was overjoyed by their success. When they were depressed and despondent she shared their misery and sorrow, doing everything she could to alleviate it. When they were stupid or badly behaved she was furious and vented her anger on them without inhibition. For a time, her health problems curtailed her capacity to develop her own life-interests fully and she lived vicariously through the lives of her family and closest friends. She was a natural, compulsive giver, unreservedly doling out care and involvement in the lives of those she loved. Her passion for her own blood family never left her, even after she married and had three children of her own.

Not long after returning from Devon, Moira attended Foxcroft Girls Secondary Modern School. Had her early education not been interrupted by illness and convalescence she would almost certainly have passed the eleven-plus and gone to grammar school. She was one of the high flyers at Foxcroft but in common with most girls attending secondary modern schools at that time she left school at fifteen. Her first job was as general office girl in a solicitors' practice at Batley Carr. As we already know from Barry's Grammar School experience, lower working class secondary modern boys and girls in the early 1950s were not considered able enough to take O and A levels, or to go on to higher education, except for the lucky few with inspirational teachers, or highly aspirational parents who were prepared to negotiate their children through a higher education system built for the middle and upper classes. In spite of the fact that her secondary education was not up to her potential, Moira often reminisced enthusiastically about her schooldays and remembered and treasured much of what she learned.

Moira threw herself enthusiastically into her first job and regaled Mary and Shirley with tales of the work she did, and the characters she worked with, when the three of them settled down for a nightly gossip at Chapel Fold, after tea was over and the chores were done. Her office was a fusty, prim, rigidly hierarchical place, where a skirt only an inch shorter that the regulation length was observed with a censuring tut and a cold eye by the spinster senior clerical staff. It was a sheltered place. Due to her poor health, both as a child and adolescent, Moira was sheltered from the rougher edges of lower working class life in 1940s-50s Batley and that sheltering continued into her late teens. In her middle teens, she became passionate about clothes, fashion, hairdos and cosmetics, but unlike Shirley and Barry she rarely went out on the town, often being too ill and frail to cope with teenage socialising. She must have been aware of how sheltered she was and how narrow her experiences were, especially when listening to Barry's and Shirley's stories of the worldly fast set they mixed with in the clubs and pubs of the West Riding.

When she reached twenty, Moira shocked Mary to the core by suddenly resigning from the stuffy little solicitors office to become a wages clerk at Rest Assured, a local bed manufacturer on the Bradford Road at Birstall. (Rest Assured took over the same factory buildings where Shirley worked immediately after leaving school.) The office staff at Rest Assured were a more modern crowd than the spinsters at Batley Carr. At Rest Assured Moira saw more of life, in the office and on the factory floor, and it thrilled and delighted her. It was only then that she began to go out on the town with Shirley and their mutual group of friends. The names of those friends; how they evoke the time: Elsie Wainwright, Doreen Barraclough, Mavis Fryer. And, ah, the whispered stories – never quite fully overheard by the younger-end – of their exploits on Saturday nights at The Gaiety Dance Club Down Batley! All of this came before Mary escaped from the confines of housewifery to Percy Walkers and she was shocked, primly disapproving and concerned for Moira's safety and moral integrity when she came home after a day at work and enthusiastically recounted the latest scandal at Rest Assured. "Rest Assured" Mary certainly was not, in the face of her frail, delicate daughter becoming a knowing woman of the world.

In her early-twenties Moira dropped an even bigger bombshell: she had found a job in the head offices of Jaeger Knitware, in that distant and dangerous city – London. Her bombshell shattered Mary. How was her delicate daughter going to cope with life in the Big City? Mary was saddened also. She was about to lose the company of a best friend as well as a daughter. There was a twenty one year gap between Mary and Moira but they became close friends as Moira grew into a young woman. They gossiped and shared confidences endlessly. Occasionally they seriously fell out. One of their fallings-out went on for weeks and they only communicated with each other through a third person. The stand-off between them was like a heavy fire blanket, suffocating the house at Chapel Fold and everyone in it. It was a nasty neighbour put an end to the Cold War between Mam and Moira, although she did not know it. The neighbour lived in a house on Hawthorne Avenue, round the back from Chapel Fold. The Hirst back garden and the neighbour's garden bordered each other. Mrs. Nasty was surrounded by people like the Hirsts who had little interest in gardens; people who were non-territorial over property. The back gardens were criss-crossed by short-cut paths which "Chapel Fold fowk used teh get teh shops an bus stop on Manor Way, an which Awthorne Avenue fowk used as a short-cut teh Dowsbry bus stop on Alifax Roo-ed." Mrs. Nasty hated all this *laissez-faire* informality over territory and she barricaded her back garden against intruders with high privet hedges and wire netting, and woe betide any children caught trying to penetrate her defences. The Hirst boys were careful to avoid balls landing in her garden, knowing getting them back would involve intricate, delicate negotiations.

The Cold War lasted weeks, until the day the neighbour exploded with anger and called the Hirst boys every bad name she could think of when their football just happened to land in her garden. Mary was angry with her boys and did her best to propitiate Mrs. Nasty, who was having none of it. Enter Moira, brooding in her bedroom upstairs, from where she overheard the dragon's tirade through the partly opened window. In the middle of the tirade the bedroom window flew fully open and Moira appeared: all five foot of her: all six stone.

"Oo, you are a *nasty* owd cow, Missis Nasty. Oo de'ye think *you* are. Callin' *my* Mam, an *my* brutthers, them names? Lady Muck? Yeh shud ger inside an draw yeh curtains, if yeh don't like avin neighbours. Cum inside, Mam. Now! Ignoo-wer that *vile owd bat*, n'let's ave a cupper tea."

Within minutes Moira and Mary were back on normal relations and both of them, after that long stand-off, remembered in future to hold their tongues when they did not see eye-to-eye. Mary's and Moira's lives were inextricably intertwined, notwithstanding the occasional Cold War. And here was Moira; leaving the nest to live in London. It was a huge wrench for both of them but more for Mary, who was going to be left with an often morose and uncommunicative husband and a house full of boys – and baby Lynne. Mary's life was an endless line of children and chores at that time. She visited pubs and clubs with Bob occasionally but she was mostly tied to the house and it was Moira who was her main link with the social world of Batley, beyond the four walls of the house at Chapel Fold.

Shortly before applying for the London job, Moira spent a summer season working in the offices of Butlins Holiday Camp at Filey on the Yorkshire Coast. Perhaps it was working and living away from home at Butlins that gave her the taste for some independence from family ties, and perhaps also it was the experience as a ten-year-old of living away from Batley in Devon for those few months that gave her the desire to venture beyond her home town. While living in London, Moira returned home often. The thrills of living in the big city did not break her strong links to her community and family. She loved the bedsitter life in Paddington and was full of stories of her glamorous flatmate Maureen, who originated from that exotic city, Birmingham, and Maureen's East End Jewish Cockney taxi-driver boyfriend, Jud. In London, Moira enthusiastically took up all the latest styles and fashions in clothes and hairdos. She had naturally lustrous, deep red hair, much fierier and redder than Shirley's and Barry's lighter ginger hues. On her first visit home from London her hair was piled high in a mountainous bouffant. It was magnificent: all that tiered red gold rising above her small face. Her clothes too were immensely fashionable: a Jaeger winter coat bought at a knockdown perk-of-the-job price, and lethal-looking black stiletto shoes. She brought interesting things from London; things you simply did not see in Batley in those days, such as a tiered set of wooden Russian peasant women dolls which you could unscrew and unscrew, only to find smaller and smaller dolls inside the larger ones. In early-1960s Batley, the Russian dolls were a real novelty. Moira gave her younger siblings a taste for the "different" and some of them were to have different lifestyles from Batley lower working class, later in life. It was Moira's example which partly enabled them to do that.

In her mid-twenties Moira returned to Batley for good. During her trips home she occasionally dated a handsome young man bearing exactly the same name as Shirley's husband: Jimmy Colleran. The dating developed into a more serious relationship and eventually she and Jimmy were married – at St. Mary's, Down Cross Bank. And less than nine months after the wedding, the first of their three children, Timothy, was born. The Batley News had the title "A Bride And Seven Brothers" in its report of Moira's and Jimmy's wedding. Jimmy was the oldest of seven brothers and there were sisters, too. Moira's and Shirley's Jimmys were distantly related but apart from their family name, and good looks, they had little else in common. Moira's Jimmy came from a hard-drinking, rigidly Roman Catholic Batley-Irish family. He was a serious drinker by the time he met Moira and his drinking hardened even more as he grew older.

Moira's Jimmy was quite different from Shirley's. Shirley's Jimmy made you feel comfortable and welcome. There was something embracing and enfolding about his natural friendliness. Brian always felt safe, at ease, with him. Moira's Jimmy was less naturally warm. When Brian arrived at Shirley's to babysit, Jimmy's greeting would go something like:

"Nah then, Brian, owd cock. Dusta want a cupper tee-er?"

He made Brian feel valued and welcomed. Not so with Moira's Jimmy. He had a satirical way of looking Brian up-and-down, as if he were a rival and indeed Moira's brothers *were* his rivals: it must have been galling for him having a wife so wrapped-up in the lives of her parents and siblings. A typical greeting to Brian from this Jimmy might go:

"Nah then, young Esti. Ow yeh doin?" Or. "Ello, Brian Est. Young Est. Yeh sister's upsteers, gerrin ersen dressed up."

Brian did not understand Jimmy's distancing technique, his way of referring to him and his family as "Esties," third-personing them, but he dimly apprehended there was something dynastic about it. Jimmy was "A Colleran" and he was not going to be put down by "A Younger Est" no matter how much Moira eulogised her family. In spite of the distancing, Jimmy sometimes tried to like and get to know Brian. His approaches were mainly physical and he only managed to repel and frighten Brian, when he grabbed hold of his arm and squeezed tight, or gave him a hard-knotted "friendly" punch in the chest. It just did not work. They did not click. Brian found Jimmy's physical power intimidating, and Brian's verbal nature was alien to Jimmy. Sometimes when Brian chatted with Moira about what he was reading, or about school, or the latest gossip at Chapel Fold, Jimmy put on an earnest interested look and tried his best to listen and join in. But he was uncomfortable in that role, sitting stiffly in the easy chair by the fireplace, clutching a mug of tea. His hands often shook: a morning-after-the-night-before phenomenon. Sometimes you could see, in the heavy droop of his eyelids and the slackness of his jaw as he tried to concentrate on listening, that he was still full of alcohol from his last drinking session. Sometimes you could smell the alcohol on his breath. But beside this, Jimmy did not partake in gossip. His world consisted of hard bricklaying and hard drinking and his relationships were more about power; about keeping ascendency over the other. He was not *au fait* with the subtle negotiation of power relationships which often takes place as a sub-text between fowk engaged in gossip. There was always a mutual incomprehension between him and Brian no matter how hard Jimmy tried to break it down; from those early days of his marriage to his death years later in his sixties.

Moira's and Jimmy's first house was an old stone cottage on the way up to the sprawling Field Head Council Estate on the edges of Birstall. (Uncle Jimmy spent some of his last years in a flat on that estate.) One Sunday morning after a Saturday night baby-sitting session, Brian was sitting with Moira downstairs in the cottage, with baby Tim tucked up in his pram nearby. Jimmy was upstairs, having a lie-in after the night before. Moira was full of plans for the cottage.

"It's gunner bi mi ideal contemporary-style house, kid. What d'yer think of ower new spiral staircase? It's grand, in't it? Jimmy got sum of is mates terelp im purrit in. An look, e's ripped out that manky owd black leaded fireplace. E's gooin teh build a Yorkshire stone one instead, all round chimney breast. E's startin tehday."

At this point Jimmy came down the new staircase from upstairs. He was hungover and in a sour mood, not bothering to thank Moira when she made tea and toast and handed it to him on a tray. He sat hunched in the easy chair beside the nearly-finished new fireplace, picking at the toast.

"I erd wah yeh wah sayin, Mrs. Est – abaht new fireplace. Ooo d'yer think's bahner bi doin all this work fer nowt then?"

"Oh come on Jimmy. Get yeh toast etten, an cheer up, will yeh?"

"Ah mean it, Mrs Est. Oo's gunner bi doin all tard graft?"

Moira's small chest started to heave with anger, on top of the heaving it normally did, just from the effort of breathing, trapped as she often was in her chronic bronchitic condition. She snapped at Jimmy.

"For your information, I'm not bluddy 'Missis Est.' I'm Mrs Colleran. What the bluddy ell's up wi you this mornin? Yer nasty, bad-tempered bugger!"

Jimmy hated swearing. It was a quirky something this hard-drinking brickie did not do and in particular he could not bear to hear women swear.

"Nah then, Miss Esti. Thes now need feh that language. If yeh gunner talk like that, ah'm off teh Nash."

He ran upstairs to change and Moira saw red. She chased after him, leaving Brian and baby Tim downstairs. There was an argument, with Moira shouting and Jimmy hissing, and some pushing and shoving, and bangings of cupboard doors, and thuds of bodies knocking into furniture – and maybe into each other. After a while Moira came down and stood, arms folded, at the bottom of the stairs, waiting for Jimmy to come down, her chest heaving monumentally with sheer angry temper. Jimmy appeared: dressed to go out. She tried to bar his way.

"An where the bluddy ell d'yer thing yoor off teh? Yeh long streak er piss."

He easily pushed her to one side, wincing at the swear words, and he hissed viciously at her before he escaped:

"You little – SEX POT."

And then he left, leaving Moira shaking and heaving, and Brian bemused.

Moira's ambitions for her contemporary home were never completed. When Michelle was born two years after Tim, the family moved out of the stone cottage to a three-bed council house on Field Head Estate. And by the time Paula was born four years later, Moira and Jimmy were settled in an uneasy truce in a council house on the other side of Staincliffe Estate from Chapel Fold. Moira must have been disappointed that the ambitions she had of moving-on in the world were never realised. But she showed no signs of that disappointment. Instead she concentrated on rearing her three children and keeping the household together.

As the marriage progressed, a pattern of relationship and behaviour developed. Jimmy had long spells when he worked hard and earned good money. For several years in the 1970s he worked on the massive building developments taking place in that "economic miracle" of the time, West Germany. During his working spells, Moira was settled and at ease. But Jimmy sometimes stopped working and went on boozing sessions for days at a time, drinking away most of his earnings and severing Moira's plans and ambitions yet again. She did the best she could to cope with an insecure marriage, including returning to work at

Rest Assured; an assurance that at least *her* money would be coming into the household during the times when Jimmy's earnings were soaked-up in alcohol. There was no question for Moira of ever resorting to state benefits to keep her household going: if Jimmy failed to bring in the money then she did instead.

Some memories of Moira in those later years of her life. It is 1970 and Brian has had a long and wearying journey from Dunstable to spend part of the half-term holiday in Batley. The journey has taken ten hours, by trains and buses. There is something different as he walks up the path and through the passage to the back door at Chapel Fold. What is it? Silence, mainly. No Mary; clattering about in the scullery, preparing tea. No younger siblings and nephews and nieces, playing in the passage and back garden. The back door is locked. Back doors in 1970 Batley are never locked until last thing at night – if then. He looks through the curtainless scullery and back room windows. The rooms are empty and bare. Next-door-Joan comes out to the bins.

"Ello, Brian. What yeh doin ere?"

"I've just got here. It's half-term. Where is everybody?"

"Eh, luv. Din yeh Mam tell yeh? Thiv moved. Sumweer Dahn Ba'ley."

"Do you know where?"

"Now luv, ah down't. Someweer on that new Central Estate. Why doo-ern't yeh bob ovver to yoo-er Moira's? Shi'll know weer thiv moved teh."

There is nothing else he can do. It is another ten minute traipse to Moira's. He is furious with Mary for not telling him about the move but he is feeling culpable too. There is no telephone at Chapel Fold in 1970 and Brian and Mary keep in touch through short letters. He knows it is some time since he told Mary in his last letter that he would be arriving home on this particular day, and he knows he should have sent a reminder. She has forgotten his half-term visit, among all the other things she has to remember every day.

At Moira's house he is upset to see how ill and exhausted she looks. Her hair is unkempt and lank and has lost its lustre. She is having huge difficulty breathing. Her chest is heaving with effort and every few seconds she is consumed by coughing. When the cough pounces it takes over her whole body and she is helpless in its grip. After a violent spasm of coughing, she makes a tortured rasping sound in her throat as she desperately tries to ease the agony by clearing some of the phlegm from her lungs. When her bronchitis is bad, the rasping sound sometimes transforms into a moan of pain, with frustration and anger mixed in, at not being able to rid herself of the burden of her congested lungs. It is also the sound of a defiant fighter: her bastard lungs are not going to get her down, not if *she* has anything to do with it. Brian knows all too well the sounds of her coughing and rasping; the sounds of her desperate efforts to breathe easily; sounds which echoed at Chapel Fold throughout his childhood and adolescence. His first feeling whenever he sees Moira like this is one of paralysis. He yearns for some power to come from somewhere and wrench this beast out of her and give her the full and active life she deserves. But he knows from long experience the worst thing he can do is offer sympathy. Even in the full throes of her condition, Moira insists on carrying on as if everything were normal. The cough is not going to get her down and you have to ignore her lungeing breaths, her coughing and rasping, unless you want your head bitten off by her angry response to any show of sympathy.

He tells her why he has turned up so suddenly. And she tells him – between coughs and horrible raspings in her throat – how Mary and Bob (mainly Bob) have suddenly decided to move from Chapel Fold. The new house at

Russell Close is smaller, brand new and cheaper to rent. The only children left at home now are the younger-end, and Stephen is going to college before too long. It is a miracle where she gets the strength from but Moira laughs with Brian when he tells her about turning up at the deserted house. They laugh at their Mam's forgetfulness and over how much next-door-Joan will have enjoyed the drama of "Poo-er Brian – an nubdi theer teh welcome im ome."

Brian made his way down to the new house at Russell Close. But the new house was not on his mind. Moira was. He knew she had not wanted him to see her in that state: ill, unkempt and exhausted. And he knew, though it was unspoken, that on no account was he to tell Mam how he had found her. He knew the sort of day she probably had, when what she really needed was a day in bed, restful and calm; but instead, she would have risen early that day to dress, wash and feed Tim and Michelle before school, while Jimmy was away in Germany. Or perhaps he was upstairs in bed, sleeping-off the booze from the night before? After the kids left for school she would have tidied the house before catching the bus to work. If Jimmy was on one of his boozing sessions, and money was short, she had no doubt worked overtime, to make up for the loss of Jimmy's earnings – and shopped for food after leaving work – and then picked up the kids from their after-school carer, Jimmy's sister Molly. A cooked meal would be partially prepared from earlier in the day, or the night before. A rabbit casserole, or dumplings and stewing meat in onion gravy, with potatoes and cabbage. (Fast food, except fish and chips – which was expensive – was virtually unknown in Batley in 1970.) Jimmy might have come down after Moira put the kids to bed, surly and satirical, and eaten some of the stew and then maybe there had been a blazing row before he left for another drinking session. What she did not need was Brian turning up on the doorstep; seeing her like that. All she wanted was to finish the washing up and the tidying and go to bed, to build up strength for the next long working day.

A happier day. It is October half-term again, one year later. This time Moira is expecting Brian's visit: maybe she bobbed-in to Russell Close the day before and he promised to call, to catch up on news. It is a bright blue crisp Autumn afternoon. The doors and windows at Moira's house are closed and a big coal fire is burning in the sitting room. The house is stuffy but they both know what can happen if she opens the door or windows – and the Autumn chill gets inside her. Her hair has regained its lustre and she looks happy and well. The cough is banished for now although her breathing is shallow and her face is drawn and thin under the artful make-up when you look carefully. She is full of plans and ideas. Jimmy is doing well in Germany and sending good money home. She has bought a new labour-saving washing machine which thrills and delights her with its ease of use. One of her famous casseroles is slow-cooking on the gas stove. It smells wonderful and they talk about where she found the recipe. Long before they became a fashion, Moira loved cookery books and she had her favourite chefs who gave her ideas – before chefs became TV celebrities. It was another manifestation of her wanting, her ambition for difference, this garnering of recipes by favourite chefs; like bringing home the Russian dolls in earlier times. She asks about Brian's job and his school and laughs when he imitates the Bedfordshire accent of his pupils.

"Mr. Hoist, Mr. Hoist! Danyel went let me share ewer bewk."

Brian is full of news of his very first small rented furnished flat on Icknield Street in Dunstable in a rambling Georgian house and Moira *has* to give him something for the flat. She finds a small pyrex mixing dish and a yellow tupperware container from a kitchen cupboard and tells him how to prepare perfect scrambled egg in the pyrex bowl and how fantastic tupperware is for keeping things fresh. Tupperware is a new and fashionable thing to have – and Moira has it. She tells him Michelle is bright and doing well with reading. Tim is no scholar but he loves helping her cook. Maybe he will go into catering, like one of his uncles on Jimmy's side? She has ordered a telephone. Everyone has one nowadays. She is going to learn to drive. She sparkles with happiness and contentment on this blue October day.

It is two years after that crisp sparkling Autumn get-together – 1973: the year Brian passed his driving test. It is tea time. He has just arrived at Russell Close having driven from Iver in Buckinghamshire, where he now works and lives, in his first car – a wonderful thirteen year-old 1960 grass green Triumph Herald. He is sitting at the Russell Close scullery table, enjoying a bacon, egg and tinned tomato tea. Mary is leaning by the sink – her favourite position for a long natter. Stephen, Lynne and Michael are in the living room next to the kitchen, lying on a chair, on the sofa, on the floor, laughing over a favourite TV show, ignoring Bob sitting in his corner chair by the fireplace, in a mood.

From where she stands at the sink, Mary can see any callers coming up the front path through the glass panel in the front door. Suddenly she stops whatever it is she is nattering about and straightens and peers. Moira comes in with Michelle. They are loaded down with shopping bags. They have called in for a natter before they take the shopping home. Moira drops the bags heavily on the floor and collapses on the chair at the other side of the kitchen table from Brian, just as Mam used to collapse on a chair at Chapel Fold a few years earlier after a hard day's graft at Percy Walkers. She has a bloodshot eye which looks blackened around the sides. She is exhausted and breathless after the short steep climb up the hill carrying the shopping bags. It is not long before she is coughing and rasping; trying to clear her chest of phlegm.

Mary's face is a picture of worry and anxiety …

Shi wants teh tell er off feh bein seh daft – carrying them 'evvy bags up that steep bluddy ill. Shi wants teh tell er shi shud tek sum days off on sick an gu teh see Dr. Hinchcliffe abaht that cough. Shi wants ter ask ovver that soor eye. Above all, shi wants ter ask if Jimmy's be'avin issen these days. But shi ses nowt. …

She knows from long experience that any interference will be met with a fierce wave of anger and resistance. Instead she puts the kettle on and makes more tea, quietly talking to Michelle, waiting for Moira's chest spasms to settle. It is astonishing, this prickly solicitude going on between mother and daughter: what they suffer: just to keep seeing each other. Eventually Moira's coughing and breathing calm.

"Ey up then, kid. Is that yoor green car outside? It's gorgeous, int it? Did yeh know ahm tekkin drivin lessons? In a Mini."

Brian is glad he can do something this time to help. He gives her and Michelle a lift home.

It is the second week of February 1979. A Saturday morning. Brian is in the house at Russell Close alone. Mary has gone out shopping and Bob is at the bookies. In January Brian moved from Iver to Derbyshire, to a Head of Department post in a small comprehensive school at Denby, near the pottery. Until he can find a more permanent place to live, he has been staying at a B+B in Matlock from Monday to Thursday, travelling the 75 miles every Friday after school to stay at Russell Close until early Monday morning, then travelling back down the M1 to the school at Denby. Bob and Mary have recently acquired their first telephone. It perches precariously on a tiny table in the small porch at the bottom of the staircase. It rings and Brian answers. It is Moira's Jimmy. For the first time ever, he drops the satirical "Esty" form of address. He sounds frantically worried.

"Is that yow, Brian owd lad? Is Mary an' Bob theer? Can ah talk ter em?"

"They're both out. I'm here on my own. What is it, Jimmy?"

"Brian, kid. I ad teh geh an amblance this mornin. Feh yoor Moira. Shi's in ospital. Et Steyncliffe. Brian, shi's reight bad. Can yeh tell Mary when shi gets back?"

Moira was still in Staincliffe Hospital the following weekend when Brian arrived at Russell Close. But she was feeling a little better. On the Sunday, he visited her, with Mam and Sheila. She was radiantly brave about her illness and, as always, thrilled to see him. She gave him the same big toothy greeting smile she always gave. She was lying upright in the high hospital bed, propped from behind by pillows and her body seemed full of plastic lines going into her veins. She joked.

"Look at all these tubes, kid. This one's feedin mi Sundi dinner. Ahm not sure wha tuthers are doin."

The following weekend she was still in hospital. Bob, Mary, Jimmy, Shirley, Sheila and Barry, and Jimmy's Mam and brothers and sisters, were with her, on and off, all that weekend. They were by her bedside, non-stop, willing her, urging her, to live and survive; not that she ever needed any willing or urging to do that. Stephen's wife Maggie rang Russell Close early on the Monday morning to see how Moira was doing, just as Brian was about to leave for the journey down a frozen M1 to Denby. He told Maggie he was in the house on his own. Bob, Mary and Jimmy had been with Moira at the hospital all night. He told her he had tried the hospital number repeatedly early that morning but had failed to get through. Maggie promised to phone him at the Matlock B+B each morning that week before he left for school, with updates on Moira.

A day or so later he arrived at school after a cold blizzardy thirteen mile drive from Matlock to Denby. One of the school's clerical staff, Josie, was waiting for him in the main entrance lobby as he came in from the icy cold car park.

"Brian. Your sister-in-law's been on the phone. Ah think y'should ring her straightaway."

Josie pointed him to the empty quiet medical room, where she had connected the telephone to an outside line. He dialled and Maggie answered immediately. Moira had died of a brain haemorrhage, brought on by her breathing difficulties, earlier that morning. It was February 28th 1979. She was forty two.

Brian taught his first lesson of the day just a few minutes after Maggie told him about Moira. He thanked God he had only been at the school a few weeks and had made no friends among the staff yet. He was frozen in shock and knowing no one well at the new school kept him in that numb, stunned state. Only Josie and the headmaster knew of his sister's death that day. He acted normally but was frozen inside. He worked all day, teaching classes and confronting the mountain of administrative tasks that needed to be done in his new post. He left the B+B in Matlock at 7.30am for the next two days and drove the thirteen miles down frozen snowy roads to the school at Denby, not returning to the B+B until 7pm. After a snack prepared by his landlady, he tramped the quiet, snowy, deserted streets of Matlock town centre and sat in empty pubs, drinking pints of strong Marston's Pedigree bitter, staring into emptiness. It was only when he returned to the B+B and lay in bed that the tears came. He wept himself to sleep every night that week and every night for months after.

Josie thought Brian should take the day off school to drive to Batley, two days before Moira's funeral, on snowy blizzardy roads but he decided to do a normal day's teaching before departing. The weather deteriorated during the afternoon and the news bulletin on the English department TV showed huge snow blizzard hold-ups on the M1. He looked at a map and decided to avoid the motorway, by driving the country way to Batley; via Matclock, the Snake Pass, Glossop, the Woodhead Pass and Holmefirth. They were just names on a map to him. He neither knew nor cared that the route he had chosen went over some of the highest and most treacherous roads in England in bad weather. It was fixed in his head to avoid the congested M1.

Everything was a blur, from leaving for Batley to returning to Derbyshire after the funeral. The dark evening drive to Batley was a dull blur in his head: swirling snow outside and the dim red lights of the vehicle in front. Occasionally the car skidded on ice and for a few seconds he came out of the blur to concentrate on driving safely. Somehow he made it to Batley. Later that year, in fine summer weather, he drove the same route and only then realised what bleakly beautiful country it traversed and what a miracle it was he made it at all in the blizzards.

The house at Russell Close was full of people throughout the two nights and one whole day he spent there. Brian barely caught sight of Mary, even though she was in the same house, until the morning of the funeral. She was in grief and shock and was constantly attended by Bob, Louie, Sheila and Shirley. Her keening, her sobs, and her occasional shrieking screams, filled the house. She sounded like an agonised wounded animal. Brian spent most of the time emotionally frozen in the small third bedroom, sometimes going downstairs for guilty tea and sandwiches. (What *right* had he to be eating and drinking?) He exchanged desultory mechanical words with whoever was in the kitchen. At night, alone in the small back bedroom, he started to drink, gulping down glasses of red wine from the supermarket litre-and-a-half plastic container he had brought with him, to carry him through, wanting only oblivion.

It was Ower John who penetrated his blur. He came up to the little bedroom and told him it was his duty to go to the pre-funeral wake being held at Moira's and Jimmy's house. He did not want to go but John insisted. He had no idea what to expect. When he arrived with John, the furniture had gone – to make more space for the dozens of mourners filling the house; most of them men; most of them Collerans. They were subdued and were steadily drinking beer, and whisky or rum chasers. Jimmy appeared and shook his hand and steered him to the front room, where Moira's body was lying in the open coffin. He had not anticipated this. He wanted to leave, having made an obligatory appearance. He looked for the briefest of seconds at the body lying in the coffin, in the men-filled house. It was not Moira. Moira was the toothy smiling woman he had last seen a few days before, lying on the hospital bed. He left the wake as soon as he could.

St. Mary's was packed on the day of the funeral. The whole world gathered to say goodbye to Moira. The Colleran women were mortified after the service: the priest had not conducted a full Requiem Mass: communion was omitted. Moira never converted to Catholicism but dutifully ensured her three children all became communicants at St. Mary's. The form of the service was not important to the non-Catholics in the Hirst family, especially not to Mary, who was too consumed by grief to care or notice.

After the service a large crowd gathered around Moira's burial plot at Batley Cemetery, behind St. Mary's. Apart from the family, Brian recognised some familiar faces from the past. Elsie Wainwright was there and Mavis Fryer, as well as a large contingent of Moira's co-workers from Rest Assured. Shirley pointed out a couple standing desolate on the edges of the mourners. It was Maureen and Jud. Jud had driven his black London taxi the 190 miles north, on that bitterly cold March morning: to be there. As the priest intoned the final words Mary was held and restrained by Bob, Barry and Young Bob. They were holding their hands over her mouth, preventing her from crying out, preventing her from going to pull Moira out of the burial plot. She was convinced her lass did not want a burial. Jimmy stood stiff, haggard and desolate to one side, surrounded by Colleran brothers. Auntie Louie was quietly crying, holding on to Michelle's heaving shoulders in front of her, stroking her with soothing motions. Tim was on his own, shivering and crying in the icy wind. Suddenly the burial was over and Young Bob was carrying Mary to the waiting funeral car and bundling her inside. It was the only way to get her home. She wanted Moira out of that plot.

Jimmy did his absolute best to rear his three children well after Moira died and the love between him and his children was strong. He drank steadily and unremittingly for the rest of his life until he died in his early sixties of cancer of the oesophagus. Tim is now forty one, nearly the age of his mother when she died. Michael and John, who know Tim best, say he never recovered from his mother's death: the image of him crying alone at the funeral still haunts. Tim had his difficult times after Moira died and was sometimes an aggressive and angry young man. He was never the chef Moira thought he might become. He works in the building trade, like some of his uncles on both sides of his family, and lives in Birstall with a long-term partner. Michelle is now in her late-thirties and a mother of three children, living in Batley. Her youngest child, Thomas, has cystic fibrosis and nurturing him has taken up much of her life over the last twelve years. The last time Brian spoke to Michelle was after Auntie Louie's funeral when she told him she had re-taken some GCSEs and gained a grade A in English. She was hoping to move on and do something with her new qualifications. Michelle has Moira's aspirations – and her face and toothy smile

– and when Brian sees her, he sees Moira. Paula is now a mother of two boys. She is a staff nurse and works full-time in a day care centre for the elderly in Batley.

Moira at Butlins: Late 1950s

MARGARET

Margaret was born twenty months after Moira in June 1938. We already know how she died, aged four. Mary has a small dog-eared photograph of Margaret with her older siblings, Moira, Shirley and Barry, taken when the four bairns were all under-sevens. They are carefully dressed, the three girls with ribbons in their hair. They are plump and well nourished. There is nothing in the image of Margaret to show how soon she would lose her young life.

Margaret's death was a wrenching searing tragedy for Bob, and for Mary, who ultimately took it more stoically. Whenever Mary loses a loved one her immediate response is unbridled grief. The first time her children experienced her grieving was after Grandad Wolstenholme died. The younger-end were kept away from her in the days following his death but they still heard her keening, like a wounded animal, in the bedroom upstairs. When she was younger there was none of the British stiff-lipped fortitude for Mary, when faced with a death. Her response to the death of a loved one was more akin to the women we see on our TV screens in Palestine, or Iraq: uninhibited visceral pain in the face of loss. Perhaps this emotional outpouring is her way of managing grief; her way of putting the matter to rest and normalising the loss into her life, which has to carry on.

Brian never knew Margaret but she always becomes a real person – another sister – when Mary speaks about those early years of her marriage and "Ower Margaret." Mary does not put Margaret on a Dickensian pedestal of maudlin infant death; she is still Ower Margaret: a part of her life; a part of her family; just like Ower Barry and Ower Moira, who were with her for much longer. Three of those four children in the dog-eared photograph have gone but they are still Ower Barry, Ower Moira and Ower Margaret – to Mary and her ten surviving children.

Shirley, Moira, Barry, Margaret. 1940.

YOUNG BOB

Robert ("Young Bob") was born in December 1939. Margaret died when Bob was still an infant, leading to a four-year gap between him and Moira. The first four children – "towder-end" – were born pre-war and had the benefit not only of Mary's but also Bob's nurture and care, in their crucial early years. Bob only became involved in his second son's life after he was invalided out of the army, when Young Bob was three. Young Bob is different from his three older siblings physically. He is taller and has dark hair and swarthy skin. In Barry's wedding photograph he is seventeen and already as tall as his older brother and several inches taller than Old Bob.

Barry, Shirley and Moira had a wide circle of friends. They socialised in pubs, clubs and dance halls. They were avid followers of popular music and jazz and they assiduously kept up with all the fashion trends of the day. Barry loved traditional and modern jazz; Shirley and Moira loved Sinatra, Ella Fitzgerald, Sarah Vaughan – and mainstream classical music. Bob, in contrast, was mad about football and fixing and mending things. He was (and still is) a participant rather than a spectator. He was passionate about football but it was playing it that he loved, not supporting a particular team, or endlessly pontificating over the game's niceties without actually playing it, as so many fowk do nowadays. Mary's relationship with her three oldest children was more like that of an older sister. Her relationship with Bob was different. As a boy and young man he was quieter, more shy, than the oldest three. He was practical, dependable and moderate in his ways and Mary came to rely on him a great deal. This reliance upon his steady practical nature has continued until today. It was Young Bob who took over the garden at Russell Close and kept it well maintained and attractive for some years. It was Young Bob who quietly and unobtrusively took control of Mary at Moira's funeral. And right up to today, Bob and his wife Dot, rarely have a week when they do not spend a morning with Mary at her Centenary Way flat, chatting about family, and this-and-that, helping with jobs and taking her shopping or to health appointments.

Bob is just *there* in the Hirst family: quiet, shy, practical. Aged eleven, he went to Healey Boys Secondary Modern School. He was good at sport, maths, science, and excelled at metalwork and woodwork. He brought home items he made at school: a wooden egg rack, a metal poker and stand. They were perfectly turned objects and he could explain precisely how they were constructed and held together. Healey Secondary was a rough boys school in the 1950s, where violence and bad behaviour sometimes erupted. The school had a fierce headmaster whose answer to misbehaving boys was simple: beat them into submission. Bob was among the more able boys at his secondary modern and he did not fall into the misbehaving category.

When Bob left Healey at fifteen he had no difficulty finding a full five-year fitter's apprenticeship at Walkers Engineers in Batley. The work itself, and the theory, which he did on day-release at technical school, fascinated and absorbed him and he became a fully qualified fitter at the age of twenty one. Not long after, he began work as a maintenance fitter at Fox's Biscuit factory which at that time was developing into Batley's biggest employer and which has expanded ever since. He stayed at Fox's until he retired at the end of 1999, rising eventually to machine maintenance manager, at what was by then a very large factory. Throughout his forty years of employment at Fox's, he worked on night shift: fitting, mending and maintaining the machinery, to ensure smooth and uninterrupted night-and-day factory production.

Brian never talked to Bob about his work until his last few years at Fox's and it was only then that he properly learned what "fitting" means. Bob, John and Brian were enjoying a Sunday dinnertime pint at the Nash and Bob was shaking his head in dismay over the lack of applied mathematical skills of some of the younger fitters he was in charge of by then. He talked about having to move a huge machine that week, from where it was housed to another part of the factory. The machine was crammed into a small space inside walls which had been built around it over the years. With no trace of boasting, just exasperation at the lack of applied skills in his juniors, and in his senior managers, he described his seniors fretting and shaking their heads over the problem of moving the machine, convinced it was a major operation involving demolishing walls, while his juniors futilely went to their computer consoles to construct models to solve the problem. Drawing complex sketches, and jotting mathematical measurements on the backs of beer mats, he explained his own practical, successful solution to the problem. He simply used the skills and formulas he had learned as an apprentice forty years earlier, where he was taught to measure fittings in thousandths of an inch, and where he was taught to get the measurement absolutely right, in order to fit something. It was only after that Sunday dinnertime conversation that Brian fully realised how complex and skilled Bob's work was and how able he was at it.

Not long after this conversation with Bob, Brian stayed with some German friends, Peter and Marianne Agert, at their house near Kempten in Bavaria. Peter was Head of Science at a prestigious grammar school in Kempten and one day, to Brian's surprise, he extolled the virtues of British engineering, describing how a British-made tool he used for jobs around the house was fine-tuned in its fitting to a degree he marvelled at. He described it as British engineering at its brilliant best. Brian told Peter about the VW and Audi advertisements back home, trumpeting the brilliance of German engineering and the general perception in Britain that German engineering is best. Peter thought it a shame he could not buy the old reliable tools from Britain any more and lamented the fact that these products are now produced by international conglomerates and have none of the refinement or beauty of earlier tools and machines, often made in Britain, such as the one he was still using.

During that same stay in the Allgäu, Brian went one day with Peter into Kempten. Peter's school, the Allgäu *Gymnasium*, is a highly selective grammar school and one of his main functions as head of science was teaching the Abitur (Alevel) in biology and chemistry, preparing students for science degrees, or medical, dentistry and veterinary school. Peter parked near the Kempten Technical School in the centre of town and Brian questioned him about the "Tech" as they walked past the site. Peter explained how it taught such professions as building, fitting, plumbing, catering and hairdressing. Sometimes pupils transferred from there to take more academic courses at his school and sometimes vice-versa, if it was found they had been placed in the wrong institution. Brian was fascinated by the egalitarianism and common sense pragmatism in German attitudes to education, inherent in Peter's remarks, unlike in England, where education from the 1970s, right through to the first decade of the 21st century, has been a chaotic rugby scrum of an argument between politicians, educational quango workers and bigots with bees in their bonnets over schooling, all of them constantly debating ideology, strategies, structures, instead of pragmatically getting on with the job of educating children to the best level of their abilities, as the Germans do. It intrigued Brian also how Peter knew exactly what is meant by the word "profession" in English and how he – a highly qualified academic science teacher – clearly thought the building and fitting professions worthy of as much respect as teaching, medicine or dentistry.

Bob was lucky enough to be educated in that brief period in English education just after the Second World War when there was a degree of consensus about schooling; when there was a genuine aim, and a flexible tripartite system that accommodated the aim, to give each child the best education suited to his or her talents. The sound practical education Bob received, which did not end until he completed his apprenticeship, set him up for life in a profession which had some of the highest standards in the world when he entered it. He did not have to pass numerous SATs, or jump through hoop after hoop of targets, dictated by people far removed from the reality of education, such as OFSTED inspectors, or education ministers, anxious to make a mark before moving up to more elevated cabinet positions. Bob only had to show aptitude in practical, maths and science subjects and his teachers, without the help of a vast network of advisers, inspectors and general busybodies, directed him to the right training: training suitable for Bob, the boy they taught and knew.

In his early twenties Bob married his girlfriend Dorothy and true to family tradition, less than nine months later the first of their three daughters, Jane, was born. Dorothy exploded into the Hirst family. She was the antithesis of Bob. She was loudness and assertiveness beside Bob's quietness and reserve. Bob kept his relationship with Dot quiet until they "had" to get married. But Bob always kept himself quiet, somewhat on the edge of the family. Dot made up for Bob with her noisy effort to be at the centre and soon after their marriage they became synonymous and were (and still are) usually referred to by the family in the singular – Bob'n'Dot.

One Saturday morning, when David and Brian were aged ten and eleven and Bob was eighteen, quite out of the blue, Mam told the two younger lads they would be going all the way to Battyford that afternoon to watch Bob play full back for Battyford Wanderers, a team he had played football with since leaving school. It was one of those Shirley-taking-them-off-to-New-Brighton situations. Mam had more than her hands full, with eight children still living at home and Bob must have offered to take his two younger brothers out for the day. Battyford in 1957 was a small Pennine village in the Calder Valley, between Dewsbury and Huddersfield. It was only a few miles from Chapel Fold but for Brian the journey was like discovering a whole new world. Bob was not as strict as Shirley or as bossy as Moira. He was more a distant stranger who had virtually nothing to say to his younger siblings and so they were subdued on the bus to Battyford. The three brothers sat upstairs on the front seats, admiring the views outside. As usual on these rare outings, David fidgeted with excitement and wanted to mess about but Brian was more interested in the scenery which to him seemed near, yet far, from Chapel Fold. He was fascinated by the gradual tranformation of the landscape outside, from the cluttered mills and cramped rows of terraced houses on Dewsbury's outskirts, to this vivid green valley, with its blue river, high fields and black drystone walls. Here and there, an isolated mill stood like a palace by the side of the Calder with its terrace of mill houses clinging to the valley slopes, the land and buildings in deep symbiosis. He loved the clarity of views and colours and as he gazed, he became acutely conscious of how clean, tidy and whole this landscape looked, compared with the rawness of red brick Staincliffe Estate, built upon land that must once have been as lovely as this Pennine scene he was seeing outside.

Brian was in the middle of a story inside his head, where he lived in one of those old stone houses surrounded by fields, with a posh Mam and Dad, and maybe just David for a brother, when Bob shook him, telling him they had arrived at their destination. David and Brian stared in wonder and amazement after they alighted from the bus. There was no town to be seen. Battyford Wanderers Football Club ground consisted of a rough field down in a green valley, with faded markings, leaning goalposts, a battered shed for changing and toilets and a serving hatch for half-time tea. The pitch lay by the side of the Calder and was surrounded by high green slopes, with only the noise of the flowing river, and sheep and crows calling, under a wide open blue sky. Before going to change, Bob left David and Brian by the side of the field, mildly warning them to stay there. Apart from the players themselves, there were just the two boys and a handful of earnest adult supporters.

A few years later David became a keen sportsman, like all the Hirst brothers except Brian, but that day at Battyford the last thing the two boys were interested in was watching a football match. They dutifully stood for the first ten minutes while the players lumbered around the field, chasing the heavy leather football, until the world seemed to wind down to an excruciating slow dullness. At first they were wary of the other spectators but they soon realised that for some inexplicable reason the grown-ups were interested in the match, not in them. As the minutes crawled on, they could not resist the open spaces around; the tumbling walls, fields, sheep, crows, river. They abandoned the game and ran, and climbed, and shouted at the sheep and crows, and splashed sticks and stones in the river.

"Ey up, yow tow. Cum away frum thah bluddy river, afoo-wer tha drahns thissens."

"Oo the bluddy ell ah them bairns ovver yonder? Theer gunner ave that bluddy wall dahn in a minit! Ow! Gerroff thah wall, yeh little sods."

"Them's Bob Est's bruthers. E wants teh geh them divils under controwl, e dus."

At half-time, Bob had words with David and Brian.

"Nah lissen teh me, yow tow. Thas bluddy shown me up, wi yeh bad be'avyer. Yeh can both stand reight theer durin second arf, an downt yow dare move. Ahm warnin both on thi. Understand?"

David and Brian solemnly nodded heads. Yes: understood. The last half of the match was interminable and cold and the lads yawned and shivered; utterly bored; indifferent to the game and who would win. They slept on the buses back home and Bob never took them to Battyford again. But the images of the pure Pennine landscape stayed with Brian ever after that day in 1957.

Another day: some time after the Battyford trip and Brian is twelve or thirteen – the age of discovering sex. A few bantams are kept in a pen behind the back garden outhouse at Chapel Fold. The bantams are John's but Bob helps look after them. Brian is fascinated by the sexual antics of cock and hens. He is inside the pen, holding one hen over another, trying to make them copulate. The birds are clucking in protest and trying to escape but he persists in trying to get them to "fuck." He has not thought through the fact that the hens are the same sex. It is seeing the sex act take place between the hens and the cock, and trying to understand its appeal to them, and by extension its appeal to humans, that intrigues him.

Brian looks up from his experiment and sees Bob outside the pen. He is holding a bag of feed grain and looking at Brian quizzically, hesitantly. He has watched Brian experimenting and understands what is happening but he is not sure what to say or do. The two brothers remain at the bantam pen for a few seconds in silence. Bob seems to be working up to saying something. Brian anticipates a scathing remark or a real telling-off or, even worse, a threat to tell Mam and Dad. Instead, Bob thrusts the feed bag at him, tells him to scatter the grain and then walks back to the house. Old Bob and Mary never uttered a word of sex education to any of their thirteen children. Young Bob had that one chance to educate Brian about sex. His hesitancy showed he thought about it for a few seconds but in the end he chickened-out.

Dot made up in more than good measure for Bob's reticence. From the very start of her incorporation into the family she made strenuous efforts to assert herself and become a pivotal part of it. On a one-to-one basis Dot could be as quiet and as discreet as Bob. But something seemed to happen to her when she found herself surrounded by a gang of male Hirsts and, in the early days of her marriage, the Hirst males were usually to be found in a gang. On the whole the male Hirsts are quiet and reserved; the two Bobs especially so. When Old Bob and his sons want to assert themselves in company it is usually done through a sardonic, sometimes cutting humour, rather than through a raised voice or visible assertiveness. The older females in the family are more outspoken and opinionated, and more than ready to assert themselves in a crowd, although they would draw-back from what they considered "showin-off" behaviour. Dot, on the other hand, has a strong streak of competitiveness and a deep need to have the last word. In the early days she found the quiet ironies of the Hirst males subtly challenging and her usual response was to become louder and louder, and more and more insistently assertive, faced with their rectitude and barbed humour.

Dot came into Brian's family just as he was moving into adolescence. She was still a late adolescent herself, being only seven years older than him. But she took it upon herself to be his mentor and guide in all worldly matters and she also gave him the status of being the intelligent sensitive one of her eight brothers-in-law; the one with taste.

"Aw, bugger off thee, John Est. Doo-ern't thee think thar can scare me wi thi shartin an bad temper. Ahm bahner talk teh yoo-er Brian; e's goh moor brains in is little finger than thars gor in thi ole body. Ey up, Bri. Did ah show yeh this luvli antique jug ah goh frum pot man on Dowsb'ry Markit on Wensdi? Look. Int it luvly? Ah berr it's werth a forchoon. I on'y peyed two bob ferit."

"Oo, yer, it's nice, int it? Ah berr it's and made, an all."

Brian was flattered and embarrassed by Dot's attentions, in equal measure. He deeply wanted to be what Dot was saying he already was: this deep, intelligent thinker with impeccable taste but he doubted her ability to assess his credentials and he often squirmed inside at their conversations, recognising them as nothing more than the bullshit they were, on both their parts. Dot was a capable person with her hands. She had a skilled job in a clothing mill in Dewsbury when Bob first knew her and many years later she performed an expert job of stripping and re-covering a set of 1940s dining chairs Brian acquired, taking great care to retain the original horse-hair stuffing under the new covers, which she measured, made and fitted herself. But unlike Bob, her practical skills and competencies never seemed to satisfy her fully. She aspired for something beyond.

Bob'n'Dot had three daughters with whom Dot had at times turbulent relations, especially Jane, the oldest, who was "a handful" and always in trouble at school. (She is a contented stable mother now with a steady, rock-like personality.) Dot reacted to the summonses to school to discuss Jane's bad behaviour with her usual belligerence and assertiveness, castigating Jane in private but publicly defending her blindly and blaming the school and the teachers. It was a difficult time for Dot, bringing up three girls who sometimes followed her loud and strong-willed example, while Bob remained distant both by temperament and circumstances; night shift does not fit in easily with a normal parenting day.

Dot threw herself enthusiastically into helping Brian learn to drive in his early twenties, giving him lessons in her first battered and temperamental Mini. She loved to lift up the bonnet to show him the engine.

"Nah then, Bri. Them's pistons theer. An them's brake linings. An petrol gus theer, an when yeh press starter, shi fi-yers up – an – WEER OFF!"

Bob, who really understood engines, was less enthusiastic about cars and driving and often he stayed silent, smiling sardonically while Dot, the greatest car mechanic to hit the universe, waxed lyrical over her Mini. Occasionally though, his exasperation with Dot's explanations rose to the surface.

"Aw, feh God's sake, Dot. Sometimes yeh don't arf talk sum chuffin shite."

Bob'n'Dot often came down for day visits during Brian's time in Derbyshire. They were in their forties by then and already grandparents but they were physically active and fit. They would arrive early at Brian's flat in Matlock Bath from their home in Mirfield, some eighty miles north. Brian was only just thinking about cooking a meal and so they cheerfully set off on a two hour pre-lunch walk, leaving him to prepare Sunday dinner. They described where they had been when they returned and Brian calculated they had walked a fast five miles altogether, over hilly and steep country. But they were not in the least tired. Dot is naturally thin, wiry and athletic in build. Bob is solid and sturdy and even now, in his late-sixties, there is little sign of flab: the result of a lifetime of regular physical activity.

When Bob'n'Dot are together without an audience of Hirsts around, Dot loses her assertiveness and they are very at ease together, like many couples who meet and marry young. They are good company and Dot gives Bob the space to express himself. The death of a loved one does sometimes bring those left behind closer. Bob'n'Dot's Derbyshire visits to Brian began not long after Moira died. The three of them rarely mentioned Moira by name but her death, and the way they all shared her life, was "there" and it brought them closer again. They enjoyed each other's company and talked comfortably; sometimes about work, though none of them fully understood what the others did. They also talked about homes, decorating, gardening, how to look for decent furniture: practical things. They joked about Mam and Dad and their siblings, and daft things they remembered from earlier times, some including Moira. They laughed over memories of her in a rage or a sulk with Mary. It was the best way to celebrate and remember her.

A few years after those Matlock Bath Sundays, Brian most often saw Bob in the Nash, on Sunday morning trips up to Batley from Derbyshire. The Nash's one-armed bandits stood by the wall just as you came into the lounge from the main entrance, and invariably Bob also stood there, obsessively pouring ten pence coins into the machines. He would catch sight of John and Brian coming in out of the corner of his eye and flash them a dry welcoming smile but Brian soon learned it was hopeless to try to engage his attention when he was playing a bandit. After a few minutes he would leave the bandit and sit for an hour with John and Brian, drinking four pints of beer in that hour with no apparent effects. He listened and laughed at the Sunday Nash natter, rarely joining in the conversation himself but enjoying the fraternity. And then he left, dragged off by Dot, who had driven over from Mirfield in her latest perfect car, to collect him.

When their three daughters grew up and left home and married, Bob'n'Dot took a B&B farm holiday in Somerset. They became close friends with the couple running the farm and they have repeated their visits over many years. Bob loves the hands-on holidays in Somerset, helping in every aspect of running a farm, from milking, to servicing the machinery. When he retired from Fox's Biscuits, he was glad to get away from the management culture and technology-worship which by then had invaded his expertise and the world he knew: the world of using your understanding of how the whole thing works and being able to utilise maths and logic to work out how things fit together, to make a machine work perfectly.

Bob is now a pensioner, although he does not look it. He was never against Information Technology as a practical tool, or as a research and development implement and he now finds all sorts of uses for his own PC. He also works hard on his garden and, with Dot's help, on the large garden of a doctor neighbour, a British Indian who has no time to give to his garden. Dot still aspires and, since Brian first knew her over forty five years ago, she has developed her own taste in interior design and she and Bob, with their combined skills, constantly work on perfecting their beautifully funished and fitted house. When he is not working on his own house, Bob spends time doing plumbing or carpentry jobs for his daughters and other members of his extended family, and Dot's family also. With difficulty Dot has persuaded him to travel abroad since his retirement, but Bob still prefers pottering and working things out on the farm in Somerset. The mass obsession, the fashion, of the British to travel south to blue skies and hot beaches has passed him by. He is still the quiet and distant older brother Brian has always known. He rarely speaks about things which are not in his immediate world and when he does he seems baffled, bemused by them, such as when Brian once tried to explain to him the difference between a master's degree and a doctorate. His unknowing about much of what goes on in the world is not the dumbed-down arrogance so often seen in social interactions in England nowdays. It is a kind of sureness, a certainty about knowing fully the things he knows, and doing well the things he knows he can do.

Bob at Centenary Way, 2000s.

OWER POOR JOHN

John was born in February 1943. He resumed the golden hair and freckly skin gene of the older Hirst children, which Bob broke. Barry and Bob were remote older brothers who Brian only came to know well as he grew older. John was there from the start. Shirley and Moira could both display the fiery nature which all redheads are supposed to have but John was even more fiery, volatile and quick to lose his temper. There was a simmering threat of latent violence in him, as a boy and young man; violence which sometimes became actual.

An early memory of John: being awkward and cantankerous toward Mary:

"Nah, cum on. John. Put yeh socks on. Yeh not gooin teh lake aht wi'aht yeh socks."

"Noo! Noo. Don't want no socks."

"Oo, am I bluddy fed up er *you,* sayin 'no' teh me. Ah's'll get this bluddy slipper off an leather yow, if you dooern't do wor ah seh."

Mary pulled off a slipper and made to hit John with it but as usual her blows lacked calculated precision and he easily dodged them and ran out of the room, ignoring her cries to come back so she could kill him. It probably ended with Mary half-laughing, half-crying, over the incident and John sidling back inside the house an hour or two later, embarrassed but unapologetic. Another picture of John aged around twelve; defying Bob over something or other. It led to direct action from Bob. Normally a look or a harsh word were quite enough to quell any rebelliousness from his sons, including John, but on this occasion Bob leapt up from the back room chair at Chapel Fold, small and wiry, his stiff dark hair seeming to stand up straight in anger and he furiously chased after golden-haired willowy John.

"Jesus, Joseph an Mary, lad. Wait till ah gerowd er thee. Ahs'll bluddy *kill* thi."

Bob chased John around the back garden and into the bantam pen behind the outhouse until John leapt onto the outhouse window ledge and scrambled onto the flat roof, at which point Bob abandoned the chase and went back into the house, threatening the direst punishment later. John stayed ages on the roof, the fire from his temper and the excitement of the chase dying down, with that familiar look of awkward wry embarrassment suffusing his face, until he finally climbed down to face the music from Bob.

Another day. John is aged around thirteen. David and Brian are playing in the back garden with a pet tortoise. Inside the house John is having one of his wild tempestuous rebellions against Mary. They can hear Mary yelling and John defiantly answering back. David and Brian are keeping out of it up at the top of the garden where they are lying on the grass, talking quietly to the tortoise. Suddenly John appears, his face full of rage and defiance: Mary has stood her ground against him.

"Gerroff Tommy. E's *my* tor-toyce. Not *thine*."

He grabs the tortoise from David's hand in sheer temper and stands, holding Tommy in one hand. David and Brian lie on the grass looking up. David giggles at John standing there with Tommy in his hand, more out of nerves than anything. Suddenly John throws Tommy straight at the outhouse brick wall with all the force he can muster. The shell cracks sickeningly as it hits the wall. After that: some shock; some horror; some whispering. At what has just happened. In Ower Back Garden.

John followed Bob to Healey Boys Secondary Modern and was not a model pupil. He struggled with literacy and numeracy and did not shine in any particular subject. He was no doubt as defiant and willful toward his teachers as he sometimes was with Bob and Mary. Some Secondary Modern schools (such as Healey) offered little to pupils like John in those days. There might have been basic provision of remedial education, where academically slower pupils were given extra help but a defiant, stubborn boy such as John would have been given no remedial attention to modify his negative behaviour. The reaction to poor pupil behaviour was brute force from the tougher teachers and nervous despair from the less confident. Contact between teachers and parents was kept to a minimum and disruptive pupil behaviour, and brutal teacher treatment of pupil insolence and defiance, were kept inside the walls of the school.

When Malcolm was a year or two below John at Healey, he swore Brian and David to secrecy one day before describing how John, in the notorious third year, had thrown a chair (possibly several chairs) at a teacher, in a classroom confrontation. Malcolm could well have exaggerated "several chairs" but one chair being thrown in anger by John did not at the time surprise Brian and David at all. Malcolm liked to invest John with the power of a hot-tempered Superman waging a heroic war against evil teachers. In reality, for three years and two terms at Healey Secondary, John was probably subdued into sullen dull quietude by the more fearsome teachers and he no doubt did occasionally defy the teachers with weaker disciplinary skills.

John left Healey at Easter just after he reached his fifteenth birthday in February 1958, half-way through year ten. The law at that time decreed children could finish schooling at the end of the term in which their fifteenth birthday fell and by April John had left school for his first job as a trainee miner at Shaw Cross Colliery near Dewsbury. Bob started hewing coal down the pit at fourteen in 1926. Thirty two years later we had progressed in this country: John began hewing at fifteen. He loved working as a collier. He liked the hard graft of the work and he loved the camaraderie of the community underground. He threw himself into becoming a fully fledged miner and soon acquired a reputation for toughness and hard work, as well as making deep friendships with lads his own age and with older miners. He would arrive home from a shift in those first weeks of working at Shaw Cross, his pale blue eyes shining in fulfilment and rimmed with black dust.

"Mam, honist. Yeh shuddah sin that see-erm wi worrin terdee. It wah that narrer, yeh cudn't even *fart* in it. An ah'm noo-en kiddin. An yer shuddah erd wot Mickie Tighe sed teh Johnny Backarse. E said -"

" – Orright, John. That's enuff. Bairns're lis-nin'."

For the first time in his young life John felt a real sense of worth and pride in himself when he ceremoniously put his brown wage envelope down on the kitchen table after the Friday shift and Mam took his "board and keep" from it, leaving the remainder – the spend – for him to keep. Some of John's spend went up in cigarette smoke and gambling on the horses and he soon developed a prodigious capacity for downing pints of Tetleys Bitter. What was not spent on cigarettes and beer went on clothes, and only the best would do. Brian was not aware of it at the time but John was a muscular and good looking young man, with older sisters who knew how to choose the right clothes for him. Brian was aware of the clothes, the cigs and the beer but it was only in comments John made much later that he realised girls also played a big part in his life then. But the girls were strictly outside the parameters of the family.

Brian was eleven when John started mining at Shaw Cross. Until Brian reached fifteen, the relationship between him and John was amicable and affectionate. John had a vile temper and could easily be provoked into violence but he was also funny and wry, specialising in self-deprecation. He was, and still is, generous and concerned for those less fortunate than himself. During John's first two or three years of wage-earning Brian was happy to run his errands:

"Ey, Bri'. Gu an' fetch mi a packit er cigs from shop. Thar can kee-erp change."

"Aw, shit. Ah'm gooin teh club terneet an mi soo-it's still et cleaners. Run dahn Perlwell an gerrit feh mi Bri, will yeh? Ah'll gi thi a tanner."

Keeping the change and a tanner was more than the penny or threppance that Mary rarely gave Brian for spend and he was more than happy to be John's errand boy. But trouble with John started when Brian reached adolescence. He began to resent John treating him as his errand boy and started to say "no" to his demands. It was not a major conflict between them but for a period there was simmering psychological warfare. It was partly adolescent sibling rivalry and partly mutual jealousy and incomprehension of the life and values of the other. Brian was jealous of John's smart clothes and how much money he had to throw around. He was jealous when Mary cooked John a full hot meal every day, buying the ingredients with the money he brought into the house, while Brian wore clothes from the rag-oyle, had little money and had to make do with free school dinners and treacle'n'bread or fat'n'bread for afternoon tea.

"Afore yer goo off teh ye shift, John luv, what d'yeh want feh yeh tea terneet?"

"Oo, ah dooern't nooer, Mam. Ahm late!"

"Steak? Gammon?"

"Aye, gu on then. Steak."

"I wouldn't mind sum steak feh mi tea an all, Mam."

"Sorry Brian, owd lad. Yeh'll have teh wait till yeh bringin a wage in teh get steak. Nivver eed, ah've got some luvli pork drippin feh yer tea, from yond stall on Dewsbury Markit."

One Saturday evening Mary fried a steak for John, which Brian longed to devour, when a sudden urgent hunger swept through him. But he made do with an egg fried in the steak fat that remained in the frying pan after Mam cooked the meat. It was one of the many times when he wavered about his decision to stay on at school. He knew if he left school and found a job and brought in a wage he also could eat steak. It was deeply tempting for a food-loving adolescent.

John loved his work but he often came home from a shift physically exhausted. When John got back home Brian might be reading, writing up homework, or sketching for O Level Art. At nineteen, John had already been grafting down the pit four years and here was his nearly sixteen-year old brother "doin nowt." There must have been times when Brian's "success" at school rubbed his nose in his "failure" and it must have stung, just as the privileges John had, as a worker, stung Brian. There was incomprehension too. Brian had no idea what it was like down the pit. He had no idea what the inside of the pubs and clubs that John frequented looked like. He had no experience of girl friends and he knew nothing about betting. Reading Shakespeare meant nothing to John, "O Level" did not exist when he was at Healey Secondary. And sketching was "messin abaht" as far as he was concerned. Mary kept the two brothers under control, acting in many and subtle ways. She was arbiter, referee and counsellor between them. But the tension simmered insidiously. Sometimes Brian would affect a total hauteur and superciliousness if John came into the back room when he was doing schoolwork.

John invariably retaliated with a sly thump and the threat of one of his violent temper outbursts, which Brian could not withstand.

Brian wreaked revenge on John in devious ways, in sheer frustration at not being able to stand up to him physically. Weekends were the best time for this when John rolled home hopelessly drunk late on a Friday and Saturday night. He would stumble up the stairs and undress in the bedroom he shared with Malcolm, throwing his smart clothes anywhere and then fall into a deep snoring sleep until late the following morning. This was when Brian acted, after Malcolm left for one of his mysterious assignations in the big wide world beyond Chapel Fold. Brian crept into the bedroom while John was still snoring, insensible to the world, and rifled through his pockets, taking cigarettes and loose change. He never stole above three cigs and never more than two shillings (ten pence) as John would certainly have noticed, no matter how drunk he might have been the night before. John would eventually leave his bed and come downstairs, a bemused look on his face.

"Ey up, Mam. Ah'm bluddy sure I ad mooer munny las neet i mi pockit than worrave goh this mornin. Aw bluddy ell – ave on'y goh two fags left in packit!"

"Humph! Don't you expect no sympathy from me, John Erst. Yeh kem back ome in a reight state last neet. Yeh gunner end up just like yeh bluddy Dad, if you aren't careful. Mark my bluddy words ..."

Brian smirked secretly to himself in the scullery where he was washing up, or from his chair where he might be reading, or nursing a younger one, enjoying John's bewilderment for all it was worth.

At this time Brian felt a visceral hatred toward John and John certainly disliked him. It was largely Mary's interventions and counsellings that stopped them from waging outright warfare. Things came to a head when

Brian was sixteen and nearing O Level exams. He was doing homework at the table in the back room at Chapel Fold one evening; it might have been history, or English: his best subjects. It involved a text book, exercise book, a bottle of Parker's Quink. All was quiet in the room: Brian at the table; Mam knitting by the fire; Moira curled up on a chair, listening to a classical music programme on the wireless. Suddenly John bursts into the room from upstairs, bad tempered and sour.

"Look worrave bluddy dun. Ah've cut missen, shavin. Thes bluddy blud ivryweer. An that bath watter were bluddy frozzen. Ah bet yeh dint put timmersion eater on, did yeh Mam? Ah'm pig sick er this. Ah'm bahner bi late meetin Micky an Jonny."

"Oh, ignore him, Mam. Cum ere, luv. Let me straighten yeh tie. There yeh go. Oo yeh do look lovely in that blue. It reelly suits yeh."

Moira is mollifying him, subtly controlling him. Brian tuts and pulls an ascerbic face. John explodes. He smashes his hand onto the table top and sweeps everything away. The ink spills everywhere, ruining Brian's homework and damaging the books.

"Watch it, thee. Tha sarky little sod."

Brian is devastated at what John has done. So is John, and Mam, and Moira. There is a still shocked silence broken by John escaping to meet his mates. It was one of those small incidents, lasting just a second or two, which hurts at the time but is a turning point. And after it happened, they left each other to get on with their lives – until John decided to go to Australia.

It was always "Ower Poor John" from Mary, right from the start. It still is.

After reading a school report: "Eee, Ower Poor John. E's nivver been ner good wi is sums, towd lad."

After an accident at work and his arm in a sling: "Ee, our poor John. E's reight accident prone yeh knaw."

After a temper outburst and his subsequent embarrassment: "Eee, our poor John. Is face went as red as a beetroot."

After John's sudden announcement of his decision to go to Australia: "Eee, our poor John. E'll not get neh further'n Leeds."

When John suddenly showed interest in a scheme involving migrating to Australia for a fee of £10 for the ship passage and a job guarantee at the end of the long journey Mary was, to put it mildly, doubtful Ower Poor John would make it. All families stereotype their members and John was stereotyped in the Hirst family as the wild but helpless one. It amazed Mary when he completed the application form to work in the gold mines at Kalgoorlie (with help from Moira, who doted over him) and it amazed her even more when he posted it. He continued to amaze her by proceeding, stage by stage, with the process of migration until he was finally offered the passage to Australia and a job in the Kalgoorlie gold mines at the end of it. When the time of his departure came, John turned down all offers to help him find his way from Batley to the ship at Southampton and Mary, still quite convinced he would turn back at Leeds, went along with the big farewell party organised by John's mates.

The party was held at the Batley Carr Working Mens' Club where John's namesake, Grandad John Wolstenholme, had been a lifelong member and sometime Social Secretary. It was a big day for everyone and there was a dispensation from the Club Committee for the whole family to attend, including the young ones. The leavetaking party began at lunch and continued well into the night. It was the first time Brian had been inside a Club and John was determined to wean him and David onto Tetleys Bitter, with the unspoken approval of Old Bob and, to a less extent, Mary. It was just expected then that all lads inevitably grew up into becoming big beer swillers. David and Brian drank too much beer. Brian left the party sometime in the middle of the afternoon and spewed endlessly, back home in the bathroom toilet bowl at Chapel Fold. But before he became intoxicated on Tetleys, he was both surprised and proud over how popular John was at the Club. Dozens of friends from all periods of his life, as well as the whole family, turned up to see him off. In the Club setting, Brian saw a different John: charming, confident and at ease, chatting and joking with everyone, in his best suit and tie, always with a pint in his hand. There was none of the temper and awkward gaucheness of the John he knew at home.

John did not turn back at Leeds. He made it to Kalgoorlie. All on his own. It was "Ower Poor Mam" when it finally hit her that her big bairn had really left, maybe for good, to live and work on the other side of the world. It was, of course, a common thing for English working class people (and other classes) to migrate or emigrate to Commonwealth countries, as it still is today, but it had never happened in Ower Family. John going to Australia grieved Mary for the first weeks of his going. It was before mobile telephones, texting and the internet and Mary behaved as if she had lost John for ever, fretting terribly until she finally received a letter.

Not long after John left for Australia, Brian began his teacher-training at Bingley College. John was enjoying his new life but he missed the family and Batley. Mary asked Brian to write to John. His first letter was short and shallow but to his surprise a return short letter arrived from John a few weeks later. It arrived at a time when Brian was beginning to realise how weak the written English skills were among some of the pupils in the schools he visited during his teacher-training course. Mam's letters were short but always clearly constructed and written in simple sentences with accurate punctuation and spelling. Ower Poor John's written English skills were the same as Mam's, quite contrary to the family myth that he could hardly write. But it was the content of his first letter, and letters that followed, that affected Brian, not their form. His letters were full of affection and a pride in what he was doing with his life and in what Brian was doing with his. They wrote regularly during John's time in Australia and John sometimes enclosed a present of Australian bank notes which, with difficulty, Brian managed to change into sterling at the bank in Bingley, neither of them knowing anything about international bank orders, or about banks for that matter. The money John sent was in generous amounts, from £10 to £20. This was between 1965 and 1968, when the Local Education Authority grant for the whole twelve week term at Bingley College was £50.

Brian rarely bought new clothes until he started to earn a regular wage after leaving college. Most of his clothes were hand-me-downs, a few were from the rag-oyle and there was a wonderful brand new Jaeger cardigan which Moira bought him for his twentieth birthday. Using John's money, Brian bought a heavy camel duffle coat, complete with wooden toggles and leather loops. It cost £12 and kept him warm in those bitter Pennine winter winds of the mid-1960s and lasted another ten years or so after he left college, for climes which always seemed warmer in the south of England. Brian is not a hoarder of possessions and things as Bob was. He a reckless discarder like Mary. But he kept the camel duffle coat for years after it fell into irreparable scruffiness. It meant a lot to him: the gift from Ower Poor John.

In one letter John told of flying by a private company plane several hundred miles across the Outback when he urgently needed the services of a dentist. Some fowk now casually hop on and off long-haul planes regularly, but how exotic and romantic the idea sounded in the sixties: taking a plane to the dentist! John earned well and played hard. He sent Brian two photographs with his letters. One photograph shows him standing by the side of a station wagon, just after he had learned to drive, with a blazing blue sky above and an endless empty Outback road rolling into the far distance behind. The other photograph shows him dressed only in shorts and boots, in a clearing in the Australian bush, perhaps taken when he worked on gathering sugar cane crops after he left the gold mines. He has golden hair and a lean muscular body with not a sign of his heavy beer drinking. There were times when he was in trouble with the local police and there might even have been a short spell when he was banged up in a local jail cell for drunken unruly behaviour. Bob was convinced the Australians had "barred" John from ever entering their country again, just as the Nash bars its members who do not abide by the Club rules. And John himself once hinted he left in something of a rush. But he grew-up in Australia and made lifelong friends and he loved the life and experience. Although he has never returned, a deep satisfied smile still comes to his face on the occasions when his time in Australia crops up in conversation.

After John returned to Batley, he began work in another ageing West Yorkshire mine, similar to his first mine at Shaw Cross, and not long after his return, he married his girl friend, Pat. They took out a mortgage on a back-to-back stone terraced house at the bottom of Clerk Green in Batley and less than nine months after their marriage their first daughter Kate was born. Their second daughter Moira came three years later. Not long after Moira was born John and Pat moved to a bigger terraced house, just across the road from their first house at Clerk Green, where they have stayed ever since.

It was only during Brian's adolescence that there was warfare between him and John. From September 1968, Brian worked just over ten years in four secondary schools in London and the Home Counties. John during that time was employed in the Yorkshire mines and was no longer the wild boy of the family but a young father of two daughters, and husband of a wife who expected him, "Teh be'ave hissen and tek is responsibilities seriously." During that period, Brian spent part of school holidays at Russell Close and whenever he was there a Saturday night spent on the town with John and Pat became a tradition. Like John, Pat left school at fifteen. Until Kate was born, she worked on the factory floor at The Briar in Birstall; where Shirley's Jimmy also worked. Pat is a small slim person, full of nervous energy and ideas and bursting at the seams with voluble words, which act as a release for her endless energy. She is from a close-knit, solid Batley Irish Catholic family and her world has always centred around three orbits: her family; St. Mary's; the Nash. Her family come first. At St. Mary's she communes with God. At the Nash she communes with the world. Sunday mornings for Pat might be spent at St Mary's but Sunday evenings are spent at the Nash with her friends and family, tearing the Father's homily that morning apart, if it did not accord with her own strong views on the state of the world – and everything!

Those Saturday nights out, in the early years of John's and Pat's marriage, followed a timeless pattern, beginning with a prior injunction to Brian, from John:

"Mek sure yeh cum ovver early, Bri. Mebbe that way wi'sll get teh t'pub afoor it shuts."

The ploy never worked. When Brian arrived early at the Clerk Green house, Pat simply sucked him up into her pre-rituals for going out on the town. To Brian, sitting on the sofa for an hour watching these rituals was like seeing a drama with many layers of theme, motive and emotion. It was a balancing-of-power drama between John and Pat. As far as Pat was concerned, Our Poor John was spoilt rotten by Mary and Moira and he was *not* going to be spoilt by her. No chance! She was seemingly oblivious to his tempers, tantrums and sarcasms: she was taming his wild side. By and large John wanted and needed to be tamed.

He capitulated to many of Pat's demands and whims but kept his ruefulness and irony, which invariably softened her, and he provided a quiet solidity in their marriage, countering Pat's volatile energy.

The first back-to-back house at Clerk Green consisted of just one big room downstairs. Stage left was the upstairs door, stage right the cellar door. When Brian entered the house on those Saturday nights Pat was usually standing at the mirror by the fireplace, putting on her makeup.

"Ey up, Brian. How are yeh luv? Just a minute. Let mi geh this lipstick on. Oo, ell fire! Is this seam on mi stockin straight, John? This is mi Uncle Mick – e's sittin fer us terneet, aren't yer Uncle Mick? This is Brian – one er John's bruthers."

"Nah then Brian. Nice teh meet yeh. Any road, Pat luv, like ah wah sayin, that new Fatther dahn at St. Mary's wants teh watch wha e says in them theer sermons on is. Doo-ern't yeh think?"

"Mmm, Uncle Mick. Let me just geh this mascara on."

"Ah doo-ern't knaw, Pat owd lass. Thes nowt weth watchin on telly, is the? Nor even on Satdis."

"Ooo, Uncle Mick. Ah forgot teh seh. Ower Kate's gorra a reight bad cowd. Can yeh mek sure yeh giv er sum coff mixcher if shi starts up agen? John! Ah think wi need sum moo-er coil on that fire. Goo an geh sum from cellar, fer Uncle Mick. Ave yeh gor enuff crisps Uncle Mick? D'yer want a cupple moo-er bottels er stout? Oo, d'ye knaw John, that beef joint's a bit small feh termorrer – an ah doo-ern't think wiv gor enuff taties norther. Oo God. In't it *awful*, what's gooin on i Biafra! Switch telly ovver, feh God's sake. Blummin news. Thes allus sumdi on strike these days ..."

John meanwhile hovered; half dancing in attention to her numerous frets: fetching more coal from the cellar, running upstairs to check on Kate, tutting at Pat.

"What time dus that clock seh? Twelve? That's it, then.

We've ad a reight grand Satdi neet aht, ant wi? Feh God's sake, Pat, gerra bluddy move on, will yeh?"

His agitated impatience appeared to largely wash over Pat but underneath she enjoyed dangling him on her strings:

"Ah, shurrup, thee," she would say to him over and over again, as she pursued her Saturday night pre-going-out ceremonies.

Once Pat was ready and final goodbyes were said to Uncle Mick, the pattern was always the same. They headed off to a pub in Dewsbury for the start of the night, usually standing at the passage bar with the wags and wits. Barry was often there alone, enjoying the bonhomie, standing in his solitary corner of the passage or more rarely he was with Sheila, whose natural gregariousness forced him into becoming one of the crowd. Brian soon learned he could not keep up with John's capacity for supping beer. After the second pint he drank a half pint to John's full pint and at the end of the evening he abandoned keeping up to John's pace altogether. Pat drank a half pint to John's every pint but she increased her intake at the end of the night, banking up the half pints before last orders were called. Often there might be up to two or three pints lined up for her to drink. But always in half pint glasses. In Pat's world, respectable lasses drank "halves."

After the first few pints with the wags at the Dewsbury pub, the three headed teh Nash afore its doors were closed to all comers at 10.00, members or not. A few more pints were supped here, inbetween John and Pat catching up on gossip with mates, friends in the St Mary's community and various family members, including Mary and Louie who were usually to be found sitting in the big Concert Room, tutting over the atrocious turn, or singing along happily if the turn was good. Mary made two half glasses of mild-with-a-dash-of-lime last all night; Louie's drinking capacity was greater.

It was on one of these Saturday nights at the Nash that Brian saw the violence and aggression John was capable of. One of the regulars liked to pick on someone to goad and outstare, just to provoke a fight. This Saturday night, he was playing his tricks on John at the bar in the Concert Room, giving him the evil eye and making snide comments. John seemed oblivious. Just before they left the Nash for last drinks at the Bull, John and Brian went to the Gents, the truculent club member following close behind. Having a weak bladder, Brian rushed to the urinal, desperate to expel the pints of beer he had consumed. From behind he heard the other man challenging John.

"Oo the fuckin ell der yer think yoor starin at Esti? Yeh ginger-nutted get!"

There was a loud smacking sound and a thud of something heavy falling to the ground. Brian turned round to see John, fists raised high, standing over the other man, now lying on the ground in a daze. After a few seconds the goader looked up:

"Nay, John, owd lad. The wah knaw need feh that. Ah wor on'y jokin."

"Fuck off, arse ole. Cum on. Let's get teh Bull Bri, afoo-er it shuts – and doo-ern't seh nowt abaht that pillerk teh Pat."

John said no more about what had just happened and Brian never saw him either provoke or be involved in fighting again, although he was sometimes an amused onlooker, such as on the night of the fight in the back room at the Bull, when Mary worked there. When they came out of the toilets after last orders had been called at 10.30, Brian, John and Pat found themselves in a tipsy swirl of a crowd making its way up to the Bull, a hundred yards away from the Nash, where last orders were officially called at 11.00 although unofficially the drinking often went on into the early hours. There was always an element of anxiety intermixed with drunken merriment, as they never knew whether David Foster might have closed the Bull if there had been "trouble" earlier in the evening. More often than not though the drinking was in full swing when they arrived and David was beaming or scowling behind the bar.

"Ey up then, young John Est. What time's thar call this? As Nash shut then? Expectin a drink frum us now are yer? Gu on then. Whatsta want, owd lad?"

At around midnight the threesome were swaying on the pavement outside with a few other stragglers, saying last goodnights. At this stage John was euphorically happy, his face suffused in a blissful – but always ironic – smile. Brian was desperately trying to stand straight and articulate clearly. Pat was in full discursive-argumentative flow, oblivious of the fact that both she and her interlocutors were all too far-gone on beer to utter anything remotely coherent. The night ended as it started, in a strange inverted way, with John now urging Pat home and Pat reluctant to go, wanting to prolong her monologue with the world outside the Bull.

The 1980s brought great changes for most people in Britain with the arrival of Margaret Thatcher and her co-idealogues into a position of complete political ascendancy, not least in "The Iron Lady's" decision to wage war against Britain's miners – "The Enemy Within" – in 1984, provoking the retaliatory one-year strike from the miners. John was just into his forties in 1984. He was active in the Miners Strike from the first day to the last and throughout that time he had the complete unstinting support of Pat. By 1984, Brian was five years into his Head of English post in Derbyshire, and four years into owning his first property, a two-bedroom cottage in Ripley, built to house a miner's family at the end of the 19th century, when coal mines still flourished in South East Derbyshire. When Brian moved to the Ripley cottage, he no longer stayed at Russell Close during school holidays, and so the Saturday nights spent with John and Pat stopped also. John, Pat, Kate and Moira went through deeply difficult times during the year of the Strike. Brian, during that year, was preoccupied with his own life, not least in the increasing interference from central government into his work as a teacher and he neglected to give John and Pat the time they both deserved and needed.

From leaving school in 1958 to The Strike in 1984, John led a carefree life. After they married, Pat tamed his wilder side and John himself fell happily into his domestic role as husband and father. But Pat appreciated the hard grafting work John did underground. She shared his love of pub and club life, and his love of beer. She understood his need for betting and for the camaraderie of his workmates and friends. She put the brakes on these activities when she thought he was neglecting his duties as husband and father but she never tried to stop these pleasures.

Everything changed for John and Pat in 1984. The Saturday nights came to a stop, as did the other benefits they had hitherto enjoyed, thanks to the good money John earned as a collier: quality clothes, good food on the table, holidays and high days for the children. Brian visited them at the second house in Clerk Green, several months into the strike. They were both resolute: they were fighting a good fight and no privation would turn them into "scabs." Brian was shocked when Pat showed him the food and gift parcels they had accepted from the miners of Europe and from supporters all over the world and Britain; all rooting for the miners. It was like being back in rag-oyle clothes again: a Hirst and his family, dependent for survival on the handouts of better-off fowk. But the change in John's and Pat's lives was not just material. The Strike changed their mindset, their ideology, their attitude to existence. In that over-used word of the time the strike "politicised" both John and Pat. A simple example of this was their abandonment of The Sun in favour of The Guardian as their daily newspaper. They were sceptical about the balance of the British media's coverage of the strike (as were all of us who supported the miners) and felt they might just get a little nearer to the truth by changing their daily newpaper.

Pat always had a strong left wing streak and the strike only strengthened and gave substance to her political beliefs. John was politically naive. He was shocked, hurt and baffled: there were people in his own country who considered the miners – and that meant him – as some kind of parasitical low-life; as people who could be discarded and thrown on the scrapheap. He had never had to articulate what it meant to him to be "A Yorkshire Miner" before. He just took it for granted he was doing a physically demanding and dangerous job but a job worth doing. As he saw it, it provided a basic need of humanity – fuel – and money to sustain him and his family.

In all walks of life – in mining, in teaching, in politics – there are people who love their work and take a deep personal pride in what they are doing. There are others who are doing a job just to earn a wage, and nothing more. There are others who try to do a job but are incompetent or not suited to the work. It is a cliche but it is true that the last two categories, the incompetents, the uncommitted, look for ways of escaping from the work they find so uncongenial. Very often their escape is via management structures, or becoming a union official, or re-training, or becoming an adviser: anything which keep them in the wage benefits, but enables them to escape from the actual work at the face.

The point about those who went back to work before the Strike ended (the so-called "scabs") is that they did not love their work, or take pride in it. The money, or the status that comes with earning money, mattered more to them than their work. John loved his work and took a deep pride in doing it. Pat respected and understood his love for his work and she shared his pride in what it meant to be a miner. By the end of the year of the Strike, John and Pat were considerably poorer financially than they had been at the beginning, and they were exhausted both physically and mentally by the privation and hardship they endured, and by the sheer will power it took to remain resolute during all that long year. But they came out of the strike richer than they went into it. Richer mentally and morally. They were able now to see clearly how power is distributed and used (but more often abused) by those who have it – in their own country and across the world. John's and Pat's perspectives were widened well beyond the family, St Mary's and the Nash, after that year. They came out of that strike richer as moral human beings, knowing what they believed in and in what they loved; knowing what is good and worthwhile in life, and fighting to the last against those who were determined to take what they loved and valued away from them.

Not long after the Strike, John returned to coal mining. But the old "uneconomic, unproductive" pits were being closed, relegated to history like fossils in a museum, in the shining new light of productivity and profitability at all human costs, in the post-strike world: a world that was just one big glitzy market, for those who could afford to shop there, and a closed shop for those who could not. John went to work at one of the new "productive" mines being developed in the Selby coalfield. He went with his head held high and his pride undiminished. He said little about what he felt at being forced to work in the new coalfield, under the new mining management regime imposed by Thatcher's goverment, except how hard it was to work with those he knew had been scabs. But he soon made new good friends and comrades at Selby and has kept in touch with them ever since. And it was not too long before his love of the work, his fascination with it, predominated again. Only a year after the Strike, he talked wide-eyed to Brian over a Sunday dinnertime pint, describing the huge

German-made drills and cutters that were brought to Selby to mine the new seams at a cost of millions of pounds. His fascination with it all was as fresh as it was when he first went down Shaw Cross, at fifteen.

John worked at Selby for several years but as he neared his fiftieth birthday the physical wear and tear of mining at the coal face for so many years began to seriously affect him. His knees were not what they were, his back and neck were weakened and worn and he began to experience a numbness in his fingers and toes, making it impossible at times to touch anything or stand firmly on his feet, without experiencing great pain. Meanwhile the "ethos" of the market and profitability (for a few) at all costs was relentlessly marching on and only a few years after the Selby coalfield opened, redundancy packages were offered to some of its workers. John took a redundancy package in his early-fifties and left mining for good. The deal was not good. Most of it was put into pension policies and investments which would mature and give him a small pension at the age of sixty: his "reward" for working hard physically, and with love and commitment, for nearly forty of his fifty-five years in this world. For several years after leaving the Selby coalface, he reluctantly found himself more and more dependent on state benefits, the experience of which for one such as him, always eager and proud to work, was deeply humiliating. Thanks largely to Pat's determination and the help of legal and medical people involved in the compensation claims of former miners for "white finger disease," after years of countless physical checkups, interviews and form-filling, he finally received a mining disability pension, and lump sum compensation for his illness and injuries, just before he reached sixty.

John is now sixty five and Pat is sixty. Kate and Moira live away from home but near enough to "call" (pronounced with a short 'a', as in the name Callum) on their parents every day. John still suffers from white finger and other bodily pains common to people who have spent a long life of physical labour. Pat too suffers from chronic arthritis and severe bowel problems. They still live in the second house they bought over thirty years ago, at the bottom of Clerk Green. John is devoted to his little terrier dog Gus and walks him every day. He is better off financially now than during that long year of struggle in the Miners Strike and the years after he took redundancy. John and Pat now spend an occasional week during the low season in their favourite resort abroad, Benidorm. It is a great sadness to both that their oldest daughter Kate and her partner Chris have been unable to have a child, and a substantial part of the money they now have to spare has gone on paying toward Kate's so far unsuccessful IVF treatment

John and Pat have lost the political fervour and idealism which so infused them during The Strike and for some years after. The world, and that includes Batley, has changed since the 1980s. John and Pat are now among a small minority of white British in the Clerk Green area. The majority of their neighbours now are Muslim British Asians, either first or second generation and the Clerk Green community is at the forefront of the tense 21st century debate over how well or how badly the British Muslim community is integrating into, or separating out of, mainstream British life. Ill health, worries about your children, coping with a rapidly changing world around, are difficult things to handle in late middle age but John at sixty five is not much different from the brother Brian grew up with. He still loves beer and gambling, and the Nash and St Mary's are pivots of his life. He is devoted to his wife, his daughters, to Mary and to all his brothers and sisters and their offspring. He "bobs-in" to Mary's flat daily on his way to place a bet at the bookies or on walks with Gus. And now Mary finds her scullery such hard work, it is John and Pat who cook wholesome meals for her two or three times each week, which John delivers for Mary to warm in the microwave later.

John keeps that wry sense of humour. His comment when asked about young British Asian girls living at Clerk Green who have recently taken to wearing the full burkha is typical of his humour:

"Ah wah cummin up Clerk Green tuther day an this yung lass, dressed in wun er them things, ses teh mi as shi's passin: 'Nah then, John. Ah's tah bahn?' Ah'd now bluddy idea oo shi wah! But she noo me."

Mary still sometimes shakes her head over Ower Poor John during her weekly telephone talk with Brian:

"Eee, Ower poor John. Yer shud ev erd im this mornin."

"What did he have to say for himself this morning then?"

"Well, yer know ow dry e can be, dooern't yer?"

"I do."

"Ah ast im ow Pat wah feelin this mornin. An d'yer know Brian, e nivver flinched a muscle. E just looked across at me frum settee an sed: 'Oo, yer knaw. Full er distemper this mornin.' Laff! Ah cudn't stop…"

John in Australia, 1960s

MALCOLM

Malcolm was born in June 1945. As a boy, he was obsessive about sports of all kinds and keeping physically fit. He still is. He is highly competitive and excels at any sport he takes up. He is at home in macho male situations, having spent most of his working life in the army.

An early memory of Malcolm. It is a humid summer's day. David is five, Brian six, Malcolm eight and John ten. They are about the same age as they were in the photograph taken of the four of them standing in a line, in the back garden at Woodsome. They are running down Wheatcroft, a narrow cobbled snicket in Batley. A red brick wall divides Wheatcroft from Fox's Biscuit Factory on one side and a high stone wall separates it from stone terraced houses on the other. Wheatcroft is three hundred yards in length – a long distance to a young child – and its walls seem to hem you in. Thick climbing plants hang down the enclosing walls in summer, adding to the sense of entrapment. One of the hanging plants stinks of urine and has huge white flowers shaped like trumpets. Wheatcroft is popular with the innumerable dogs which freely wander the streets and snickets of 1954 Batley and the cobbles down the snicket are covered in piles of various shades of brown dog excrement, upon which swarms of huge bluebottles settle. The older piles eventually lose their brown colour and turn into white piles of skeleton shit and, with the fascination children have for such things, the boys believe the turds turn this colour because the bluebottle flies have sucked the life out of them.

The top of Wheatcroft starts near Purlwell Hill, where Benjamin Hick's yard and stable are situated, so you smell the horse muck first before smelling the dog dirt and the piss- flowers. The bottom end of Wheatcroft comes out at a busy road. To the left is Nelson Hirst's butchery shop and to the right, after just a few yards, is a left turn into Batley Market Square which begins with Batley Public Baths on the right, and Batley Town Mission and the Technical School on the left. The Baths and Tech are imposing civic structures built of Yorkshire stone with intricate carved decoration in the masonry. The Mission, in comparison, is a low mean undecorated stone building.

The four boys are heading to the Mission. They attend Sunday School there most Sunday mornings, more to get them out of Mary's hair while she cooks a big Sunday dinner than for religious and moral improvement. It is a weekday during the six week school summer holiday: the day of the annual Mission Sunday School Trip to Filey. The boys are late and in danger of missing the coach. Malcolm and John are urging David and Brian to run, which they are both tearfully reluctant to do, having already run all the way from the house at Woodsome Estate. The oppressive heat and humidity makes Wheatcroft even more entrapping and stinking than usual. Halfway down the snicket, a violent hailstorm suddenly strikes. Huge bullets of hail pound heads, faces and arms, soaking thin summer clothes. It is the last straw for Brian and David. They stand stock still, wailing and crying to go home. Malcolm dismisses their cries and insists on pressing on. The usual street loafers and nosey parkers are hanging around outside the Baths across the road when the four soaked boys finally reach the Mission. The coach has left for Filey without them and one of the onlookers calls across:

"Ey up John owd lad. Tha's missed yon bluddy bus. It's just gone ovver market place nobbut two minits sin. Tha'd berrer tek them two young uns ome, so thi Mam can gi em a good rub dahn."

On the way back home John does his best to cheer Brian and David up. As the oldest he is afraid of catching all the blame from Mary if they arrive home wailing and crying. Malcolm harangues them for being softies and sissies but is careful to join John in trying to cheer the younger two brothers up as they approach home, fearing he too might catch some of the blame from Mary. John could be frighteningly violent and fiercely loving and protective but there was always transparency about him: you knew what to expect from him. Malcolm was more equivocal, more subtle; always keen to assert his superiority in quite complex ways over David and Brian – and even over John. Brian learned to look at him as a distant challenge from an early age although there was never at any time any overt hostility or rivalry between them.

Another hot summer day at Woodsome. Malcolm and John and some of the other older boys on the estate have been hunting wild mice in the wheat field. Glynne, David and Brian are playing in a makeshift den they have made in the corner of the back garden, using coats and old broom handles for its construction. Malcolm and John burst through the privet hedge from the wheat field. They are clutching a homemade wire and metal cage with a real live wild mouse inside. John is ecstatic about trapping the wild mouse and is thrilled to show it to the younger ones. Malcolm is equally thrilled. But just the fact of trapping the mouse is not enough for Malcolm as it is for John. Malcolm invests the occasion with a specialness which is peculiar to him and John, as the "old-uns." He is determined to make it clear to the "young-uns" how much more he knows than they do and he patronisingly explains how he personally trapped the mouse.

"Yer see, ah put this bit eh bait theer. An then when mouse cums an nibbles it, trap comes snappin dahn be'ind. An ah've gorrim!"

You would think it was entirely his idea, his cage, his superior skill and knowledge that caught the mouse, whereas in fact it was John's idea and it is John's trap and cage.

Some years later. Brian is aged ten. There is a chirpy blue budgie at Chapel Fold, Billy, who has become Brian's pet: his obsession. Brian loves Billy with an intensity he has never felt before for any living creature. He spends hours scheming and dreaming of ways he might magic some money to buy toys for Billy from one of the pet stalls on Dewsbury Market. To Brian, Billy's cage is his house and he wants to furnish it well and keep it clean. The cage hangs from a stand, a little higher than Brian, in the corner of the back room. He spends hours every day talking to Billy, lavishing him with love and attention which, to Brian's eyes, Billy reciprocates in full measure. Although he does not know it, his brothers have relinquished any claim on Billy; they accept and respect the fact that he is Brian's special pet.

Mary has given Brian money to buy sandpaper sheets to spread every Saturday morning at the bottom of Billy's cage, to keep it clean. He is alone in the back room and has closed the door and windows and opened the cage to let Billy out while he cleans the cage and changes the sheet. Billy is a poor flyer. He spends his first few minutes out of the cage perched on Brian's shoulder chirruping happily. He makes a few feeble failed efforts to fly and land on various objects and furniture in the room but then gives up and settles on wobbling around on the slithery lino floor, chirruping. The hook on which the cage hangs is above Brian's head and is tricky to release. He yanks at it. It releases suddenly and in surprise he drops the cage onto the floor, where it makes a loud metallic rattle on the lino. He realises he has dropped the cage onto Billy on the floor beneath. There is silence. He picks the cage up and puts it on a chair. Billy is lying on his side on the red lino: silent. A tiny trickle of blood seeps from his beak. He is dead. Brian has never seen death before but he knows it is irrevocable and final the instant he sees it. He has killed Billy. He is filled with remorse and grief. He runs from the room sobbing, to find Mam. When he finds her, she is shocked at what has happened. She tries to console him but he is inconsolable and after a while Mary takes him upstairs to lie on the bed. He lies there, limp after all his sobbing, for what seems hours.

Later he goes downstairs. Everyone is hushed; sad about Billy, telling him it was not his fault. But Brian knows he killed Billy and feels the horror of this fact will never go away. He is surprised when Malcolm beckons him outside.

"Cum on, Bri. Weer gooin in teh garden teh berry Billy. Ah've dug a grave fer im. Look. Ah've purr im in this big match box. It's is coffin. Ah've med a cross fer him an all, wi this lolly stick. Look. It says 'Billy. RIP' Cum on, les send im ter evvn."

He leads Brian to the end of the garden, with John and David in tow. When they reach the grave, Malcolm hands Billy's coffin to Brian.

"Gu on, Bri. Purr is coffin in is grave an then wi'll cuvver him up wi errth."

Brian places Billy's coffin into the hole in the garden and Malcolm and John fill the grave with earth, pressing it down tightly with their hands. The burial act fills Brian with a sense of consolation. It is Malcolm, with John's and David's silent support, who has released him from shock and found a way for him to accept Billy's demise. It is no mean feat for a boy of eleven.

It is a year or two after Billy. Malcolm's latest passion is cycling. His best mate Frank Wilson, who lives in one of the private stone houses further along Chapel Fold, has his own bike. Frank is the youngest of a line of boys and his ancient widower Dad owns his own car repair business and drives a battered Jaguar. Although the Wilson's have a modest house and lifestyle, they are better-off than the Hirsts. All the Wilson boys have their own bikes. There is no way Bob and Mary can buy their boys bikes but this does not stop Malcolm from achieving his ambition to have one. He has set about collecting all the bits you need to build a bike. The bits come from scrap yards and from the older Wilson boys, who slip him some of the parts he needs. Malcolm and Frank spend hours and hours, over days and days, solemnly and determinedly laying out all the bike bits and slowly assembling them into a whole, functioning bike. It is one of those exclusive-to-Malcolm situations again. Whenever David and Brian try to spectate or join in the building of the bike, they are dismissed by Malcolm and Frank, who put up a united front of superiority and knowingness against them. The bike is built eventually and for a year or so it works as well as any other bike, albeit with constant running repairs. The bike was one of the first signs of Malcolm's utter determination to succeed, once he set his mind on achieving something he wanted.

Malcolm followed Bob and John to Healey Boys Secondary Modern. He was bright and able at school and well behaved but his real passion was for sport, not study. In 1959 the two boys' secondary modern schools and the technical school in Batley were replaced with a brand new whole-town secondary: Batley Boys High School. From the start, the new school had a different ethos from the former secondary modern schools. It had an inspirational headmaster, George Locke. His new school took in a wider range of ability than the two old ones, and it enrolled technical and scientific-minded middle class boys from surrounding towns whose parents were attracted by the charismatic Mr. Locke, and the facilities offered at Batley High. Malcolm was fourteen when he moved to Batley High. He was already steeped in the tough boy image of a Healey lad and was by now even more passionate about sport above everything else. He had no interest in the opportunity to stay on at school after fifteen, which the new school offered boys of his ability. He excelled in the sports teams at the school but in July 1960, aged just over fifteen, he left Batley High, after four years of secondary education, to become an apprentice bricklayer with a small local building firm.

Malcolm was closest to John, in whom he confided – when it suited him. At junior school age, he was always out in the fields, hunting mice or enjoying other adventures. At secondary school age, he was riding his home-made bike, or chasing girls. After he left school, he seemed to grow even more distant, spending most of his spare time out of the house with his friend Frank Wilson and their circle, which by now included girlfriends. He even kept Mary and Moira at arm's length. Malcolm sought separation and independence, in contrast to John, who still depended on the women in the family for his emotional and material needs.

For the first year of Malcom's bricklaying apprenticeship, it was the best thing since sliced bread. He would arrive home after a day's work and talk enthusiastically and endlessly to Mary – who always loved to hear news of the outside world – about his day. Brian and the young-uns were completely excluded by Malcolm from these conversations. What Malcolm was doing was special and important – too grown up and complex for his younger siblings to understand. But the enthusiasm for bricklaying suddenly evaporated after two years and, aged seventeen, he walked out of the building trade and joined the army.

It is coming up to forty five years since Malcolm left Chapel Fold to become a soldier. The distance between him and many of the family has only grown over those years. He found his niche in army life and enthusiastically took up any sporting activities that came his way. In his early army years, he tried deep sea diving and loved it but it came to an end when one of his ear drums became perforated. He was in his early twenties when he took up skiing, never having been on skis before. Within just two years, he was competing for Britain in the Sapporo Winter Olympic Games in Japan, and four years later he competed in the Calgary Games in Canada. He took part in the Biathalon event, in which competitors ski long distances across country, interspersed with shooting heavy rifles at targets placed at strategic points on the course. He was up against Russians, Canadians and Norwegians who had spent much of their lives on skis. At Sapporo he achieved a respectable position; at Calgary he moved up a place or two. It was a remarkable testament to his total determination and dedication that he competed in the Olympics at all – in a sport he came across late in life, compared with his competitors.

When he reached his early-twenties, Malcolm married – in secret. Caroline lived at the other end of Staincliffe Estate from Chapel Fold. Ower John, Frank Wilson, Caroline's two sisters and the bride and groom were the only people present at the registry office wedding. The family never fully understood why the marriage was kept secret. It had something to do with Caroline's widower father, a hard man who might have raised objections to the youngest of his three daughters marrying. Or perhaps he had "gone bananas" when he learned Caroline was pregnant. Mary, when she found out, was devastated that Malcolm could have done such a thing: not telling her and Bob of his marriage and it was some weeks before she forgave him. The secret wedding did not surprise Brian;

he just thought it typical of Malcolm, knowingly separating himself off from the rest of the family (except John), just as he always did. Malcolm's and Caroline's first child Tracey was born less than nine months after the wedding and a second daughter Debbie followed soon after, followed soon after that by a son, Peter. Malcolm stayed in the army, rising to a sergeant, until he reached his middle- forties. Over all that time he was mostly posted abroad and he and his family lived in army accommodation in Osnabruck in Germany. And later, several winters were spent in the Norwegian Army house in Lillehammer, which Mary visited after her hospital operation.

The long visit to Lillehammer gave Mary the chance to get to know Caroline and the children. It also gave Caroline company, cooped up as she often was in the house in the depths of the Norwegian winter with her three young children. Mary and Caroline have stayed close ever since. Malcolm was away in the wilds of Norway during most of Mary's stay, ski training with the Norwegian army. On his rare appearances at the house at Lillehammer while Mary was there, she noticed with some dismay how he had become the stereotypical strict army father and husband. With difficulty she kept quiet, when she felt his discipline with the children went too far.

Some memory fragments from Malcolm's army years. After the Galgary Games, Moira telephones Brian down in Iver, thrilled, to tell him Malcolm had been awarded a BEM in the New Year Armed Forces Honours List. Malcolm accepted the honour but seemed far from thrilled, taking it with his usual distant cool. Moira on the telephone again, telling Brian of Malcolm's part in a film Mai Zetterling made of the Sapporo Winter Olympics. The film was shown on British TV a few months later. The brief shot of Malcolm crossing a vast white landscape on skis is artful and dramatic. You see his figure labouring across snow on skis from a distance, the heavy army rifle slung across his back. He pauses to unhitch the rifle and take aim at a target and the camera closes in, right up to his frozen face. Clouds of breath emerge from his mouth and nostrils and a stubborn small icicle hangs from his nose where sweat or mucus has dripped and frozen. He is totally focused and looks just right in this exotic setting: so far from Batley and those childhood Sunday School trips to Filey.

Moira telephones again. Malcolm has become involved in a government initiative to promote a more systematic approach to sports training in Britain. Captain Mark Phillips, a sports psychologist and Malcolm are featured in a short article about the initiative in a quality Sunday newspaper magazine. When Brian sees Malcolm next he asks him about the article. The old knowing, slightly dismissive grimace appears on his face. He praises Captain Phillips's prowess on the back of a horse in Olympic show jumping events but dismisses his mental acumen in understanding sports psychology. Some months later John tells Brian, over a pint at the Nash, how Malcolm spent hours in the summer months that year roller-skating with ski sticks up and down an autobahn near Osnabruck, which the local authority closed to traffic so that army skiiers from all over Northern Europe could simulate cross-country ski conditions. Listening to all this, Brian's feels his life "down south" as a teacher is flat, humdrum.

After he stopped competitive skiing, Malcolm spent his last years in the army involved in training younger skiiers, and after retiring from the army, he moved back to Yorkshire, to a house in a small village on the edge of Halifax, not far from Batley. His next step was a contrast to army life. He took out a franchise on a milk delivery round in an area near his new home. There was method in his apparent madness. He reasoned he could be done with the milk round by ten o' clock in the mornings, leaving the rest of the day for his new found passion: golf. But for reasons best known to Malcolm, the milk round did not last long.

Malcolm had the closest relationship with Bob of all his sons. It was the army that bound Bob to Malcolm. Perhaps Bob felt Malcolm was the only one of his sons who could begin to understand what happened to him in the war. Malcolm seemed to come close to Bob at times and Bob willingly stayed with him and his family in the army house in Osnabruck one summer. Mary once told Brian – with vengeful delight – how Malcolm would tell Bob off over his faults and eccentricities, during their stay in Osnabruck, criticisms which he accepted meekly from his special army son Malcolm. And it was Malcolm who came to an arrangement with Bob to buy the council house at Russell Close, which he sold for a considerable profit some twenty years later, after Mary made her decision to leave, for the ease and comfort of her one bedroom flat at Centenary Way. Malcolm has a generous side too, allowing his youngest brother Michael and partner Donna to live free of charge in the Russell Close house for several months after Mary moved out, before he put the house up for sale. Strangely though, at Barry's funeral wake in the Bull, when Brian drunkenly told Malcolm he had become reconciled to Bob's failures as a father, Malcolm seemed deeply bitter about Bob. It was the Malcolm of Brian's childhood all over again, hinting darkly and mysteriously that if Brian had known their Dad as well as *he* knew him, he would not feel so sanguine.

Malcolm and Caroline attended Auntie Louie's funeral. It was a bleak January day and both of them looked gaunt. Brian saw them briefly outside the crematorium after the service, sad and a little separate from the rest of the family. Later at the St Joseph's Parochial Hall in Dewsbury, where family and friends gathered for a goodbye drink to Auntie Louie's memory, Malcolm and Caroline left early. Brian met them leaving the Parochial Hall, as he was entering. Neither of them seemed to have put on an ounce of weight over the years. Caroline looked ill and even smaller and thinner than she was as a young woman and Malcolm was clearly in some pain, just standing in the cold. He was suffering at that time with arthritis in his feet; a result of all those years of intense physical activity.

The next time Brian saw Malcolm was on a beautiful October day in 2006, some twenty months after Aunt Louie died and only a month after the death of his lifelong bosom friend, Frank Wilson. He was sitting on the settee at Mary's flat with his ten year old grandaughter, Amber. He looked in much better shape physically than at Auntie Louie's funeral. There was barely a sign of grey in his hair and he had kept his lean taut shape, helped by his current passion for golf, which keeps him fit, as well as providing him with the competitive edge in his life which he so much needs. The love between him and Amber as they sat smiling and chatting to each other on Mary's sofa that beautiful day was transparent. When he stood up to leave, he looked mellow, contented, and just slightly stockier. Only a little stiffer in his movement than the Malcolm of old.

Malcolm in skiing gear, 1970s.

DAVID

David was born in January 1948, fourteen months after Brian. The two brothers were thrown together as children, whether they liked it or not. David enjoyed a long period of being the youngest of Bob's and Mary's then eight children. A whole four years and one month passed before Richard arrived. David was extrovert, excitable, outgoing and at times dangerously fearless. As children, David and Brian were lumped together because of the closeness of their ages. Brian tried to control and manipulate David during those early childhood years but on the whole his manoeuvrings had little effect. David's excitable outbursts usually dissipated Brian's devious efforts at control. An early example of Brian's manipulation of his younger brother occurred on the day the family moved from Woodsome to Chapel Fold. Brian deliberately played on David's excitability that day. He knew that splashing slushy snow inside the drawers and cupboards would land them in trouble with Mam but he carried on deviously encouraging his excitable, unthinking younger brother into greater and greater naughtiness, just to gratify his own delight in the reckless play. When the angry shouts, slaps and telling-off came from Mary, Brian half-expected them. Meanwhile, having been stirred by Brian into a frenzy of excitement, David was surprised and mystified by Mary's slaps and reprimands. To him, sloshing about in the furniture in the snowy garden was just fun; what was all the fuss about? Later he became wary of Brian's attempts to lure him him into the position of fall guy.

From the time they moved to Chapel Fold, to around the ages of eight and nine, David and Brian shared the same bed. They were a constant torment to Mary at this age. No matter how late or early they were sent to bed they talked, argued, played, or whispered conspiratorially for three or four hours before settling down to sleep. Brian was the main furtive instigator of this nocturnal insurrection. David was a willing and noisier follower. Brian needed little sleep and decided if he were not asleep then neither would David be. One of the more horrible games they played in bed was spitting-on-the-bedside-wall. The game involved spitting onto the thin wallpaper and the one whose spit ran furthest down the wall won. The horribleness did not end there. After spitting, they dug fingernails into the damp bits on the thin wallpaper and peeled off small strips and patches, revealing Barry's shiny blue RAF paint underneath, from years earlier. Sometimes Brian refused to play the spitting game or any of the other noisy grubby games they so much enjoyed. He wanted to "tell a story" instead and once David understood this he was invariably a willing audience, although he had a tendency to fall asleep long before the end. The story was whispered under the blankets and it was always the same:

"Wunce upon a time, the wor a very posh boy called Jirimy an a very posh girl called Jinnifah. They ad a very posh Mam an a very posh Dad. An thi lived in a big posh owse an the Dad ad a big posh car, an all …"

It went on and on in the same vein with some dialogue in which the posh boy and girl called their parents "Memmy" and "Deddy," just like people did in those virry posh 1950s middle class accents and voices on the radio, in programmes such as Mrs Dale's Diary which Mary (and Brian) listened to avidly.

In those pre-pubescent years, David and Brian were more often than not a threesome. Glynne, Auntie Louie's lad, was the third member of the trio. Glynne was three days younger than Brian and shy but his reserve fell away when he and David teamed up – and Brian became the outsider in the threesome. There were intensely idyllic summer days when the trio lay drowsily for hours on the grass in the back gardens at Woodsome and Chapel Fold, under homemade tents or inside ramshackle dens. Brian tried to tell stories, lying inside those tents and dens, but Glynne was highly resistant to his verbosity and David followed Glynne in stolidly resisting Brian's efforts to get wordy. When Glynne was not there, such as in bed at night, David's resistance was weaker.

On other days life was not so tranquil. The trio sometimes whipped themselves up into a state of manic excitement, especially when they were out of sight of adults. Glynne's excitement was modified by his natural shyness and Brian's was tempered by the fear of adults suddenly emerging from nowhere and catching them out in their wrongdoings. David's excitement, in contrast, was unbridled. He would do anything to keep it on the boil. David's face was invariably filled with a cheeky uninhibited grin at this time. There was often a large elastoplast stuck across his forehead, the result of his latest fall from a high wall or a tree, and his wobbly and many times mended national health spectacles looked in imminent danger of becoming detached from his face.

There is a story behind the spectacles. The trio went wandering one day well beyond the normal orbit of their usual playing grounds, across the busy Halifax Road and down a side lane leading to Staincliffe Hospital. The lane had a high mill gable end wall to the left and to the right was a low stone wall next to a mill dam. There was a Keep Out notice but it did not deter David.

"Les climb ovver this wall an gu teh dam."

"Nor Dave. We can't. It sez 'Keep Out.' Worriff a grown-up sees us? Wi'll get dun."

"Ah, cum on. Thes nubdy ere. Cum on, les climb ovver."

They jumped over the wall to the other side. It was magical there and it filled them with a great sense of awe and adventure. The whispery dry grass was waist high and as they ran it caught at their legs, slowing them down, and clouds of seedlings drifted up into the air, disturbed by their hectic plungings.

"Look at all fairies cummin off grass. Thi look like snow."

"Them's seedlins, not fairies."

"Orr, shurrup, you."

"Cum on, Glynne. Ah'm off teh look at dam."

"Nor, Dave. Don't! Yer'll drown. That watter's ded deep. An Ower Malc sez thes a *monster* innit."

They quickly forgot the dam, when a reed bed, spread whisperingly nearby, diverted their attention. The reeds were *miles* high, much higher than them, and they swished and swayed in the wind. The boys pounced, whooping and yelling like B-movie pirates capturing booty. All three had simultaneously envisaged the play potential in the reeds.

"Look, look! *Swords*! Wi can bi Muskatee-yers!"

Their favourite game at that time was sword fighting, inspired by a film they saw of *The Three Musketeers* on a Saturday morning Children's Matinee. The problem with the sword game until then was that they had nothing more than long pieces of grass, or one foot wooden rulers, to use as swords. Grass easily snaps or it wilts and flops lazily when swished soundlessly through the air at a mortal foe and the wooden rulers were unsatisfactorily short.

The high reed stems in contrast were firm, supple and shimmery, just like real swords.

"Look. Yeh can pull em aht, ded easy."

They uprooted the reeds and shook the mud from them, snapping off the soggy ends. And then they experimentally swished the reed-swords through the air.

"Listen! Listen teh mine. Woo, woo. Swish, swish, swish. Woo."

They soon discovered the reeds made wonderful sounds, when whirled around. David was ecstatic about the new-found swords and his ecstasy infected Glynne and Brian. They plunged into a wild contest, swishing the shimmering swords, chasing each other and feigning plunging, lancing blows. The sword fight continued all the way to the boundary wall and onto the hospital lane. The game grew faster, wilder, more reckless. Swish and plunge; swish and plunge: ever faster: until David suddenly screamed and dropped his sword and held his hands over his eye.

"Ah, oh! Mi eye. It *urts*. It's *bleedin*."

On this occasion there were no nosey parker adults around to tell the boys what to do. The hospital was nearby and common sense should have taken them there. But common sense deserted them. David was crying: really crying, and they ran home in a panic, seeking the comfort of Mam and Auntie Louie, David sobbing all the way. Dr. Hinchcliffe was called and David was rushed by ambulance to Batley Hospital, where he stayed for a whole week. Whenever something serious happened such as this, the adults closed doors on the children. Glynne and Brian were kept firmly out of the initial panic, distress and fear over the potential damage done to David's eye, until things settled down. Then someone, usually Moira, put them in the picture.

After the eye consultant decided David was going to pull through, Brian was allowed to visit him in hospital.

He giggled, wriggling nervously in the alien high-walled hospital corridor, before being taken into the children's ward by Mary. The corridor had shimmering green tiles, like being underwater at Batley Baths, and there were massive iron cream painted radiators, which emitted a stuffy coal-smelly heat.

"Nah then, Brian. Stop bein seh bluddy daft. You just be'ave thissen when we ger inside ward – ahm tellin yeh!"

They sat by David's high bed and after a while, a posh nurse came over, and Mary went to speak to the Ward Sister, leaving David and Brian with the nurse.

"Now then. You've been really naughty and silly, haven't you? David was nearly blinded, catching his eye like that. Doctor had to take his eye out and put it back in again. Straight. Did you know that?"

Brian solemnly savoured this gory detail. He was aware David had been in great danger but what he felt most was envy. As soon as the nurse left them alone, David grinned proudly, showing-off the huge white plaster covering his damaged eye. He was the centre of attention and was loving every moment. Brian was a mere visitor, a spectator in this strange world of the hospital. It was either Glynne or Brian who inflicted the wounding blow on David's eye, but stereotypes ruled and the incident was put down by Mary to David's excitability.

"Eee, ower David. He's as daft as a brush, tha knaws. Did I ivver tell yeh abaht that time e nearly lost is eye?…"

After the sword fighting incident David wore glasses for several years so that his eye could "correct" itself. The glasses were the bane of Mary's life. David lost them, trod on them, dropped them, smashed them, with constant and cheerful regularity, no matter how many dire warnings to take care were issued by Mary.

Around the same time as the sword fight Glynne and David had another adventure, one sunny Saturday morning. Every week the trio set off for Collins Picture House, which posh fowk called "a cinema," a real old fleapit at Batley Carr, for the Saturday morning children's matinee. The older-end would not be seen dead inside Collins. They preferred the sophistication of the newer picture house next to Batley Bus Station, or even better, the cinemas in Leeds and Bradford – the ultimate in style. The boys loved those Saturday morning films, hunkered down on damp smelly seats at Collins, watching the latest *Roy Rogers* or *Lassie* story, with that picture house smell all around: a mixture of pre-pubescent and early adolescent bodies crammed into the dingy hall and hot film cellulose whirring round the clattery projector wheel. It was during the time when "the slums" of Batley Carr were being demolished to make way for the sprawling estates of shining new post-war council houses. Brian's last memories of Collins, before it was demolished, are of it being surrounded by a huge building demolition site, where the Batley Carr stone terraced houses used to be. The demolition site grew bigger every Saturday morning during those late-1950s-early-1960s years, until the destruction spread right up to the top terraces, where Granma lived, and both Collins Picture House and Granma's terrace were reduced to rubble and never seen again.

At the same time as large sections of Victorian Batley were being wiped out of history, a new park was being created in an area called Hyrstlands, between Purlwell and Batley Carr. Hyrstlands had formerly been a grand house set in the middle of its own extensive grounds. Many of the mature trees and rhododendron shrubs in the old park were retained but large areas of the former private grounds were being landscaped to create the new public park. The trio were fascinated by the giant diggers and earthmovers on the site. Wire fencing barricades were put up, and big "Keep Out" notices were supposed to deter children and others from entering, while the park was being landscaped, but the boys ignored the signs. They wriggled through gaps in the fencing on their rambles from Chapel Fold down to Collins, all of them unable to resist the temptation of having a closer look at the gigantic diggers which stood dormant on Saturdays. And besides, what self-respecting eight and nine year old boys are going to walk the long way round to wherever they are heading when an enticing short-cut, in the form of a vast digging site, is on offer? That lovely sunny Saturday followed a week of heavy rain and the new park site, instead of being a place of dry mountains of earth and sand, up which they normally intrepidly climbed to the summit, only to hilariously slide back down to base, was now just an enormous mud bath. Being cautious and timid, Brian was unhappy with the mud. But David the reckless adventurer loved it and he charged straight into the area of the site where the muddy quagmire was at its worst. Glynne soon followed David. Brian stayed on the edges.

"Down't. Down't gu near mud. Mi Mam an Anti Louie'll kill yer when thi see mud all ovver yer."

The other two ignored Brian's whiny urgings. David was ecstatic, squelching around in the sticky bog and his excitement spread to Glynne, who joined him in the squelching game. Brian still hovered on the edges:

"Orr! Cummon. Dave, Glynne. Wi gunner miss *Lassie* if yeh down't cum nar."

But they continued playing in the mud. David was laughing wildly as the oozy mud gradually inched up his bare short-trousered legs, at first delighted to find himself sinking deeper into it. The mud crept higher and higher up his and Glynne's legs, until both of them realised they were well and truly stuck. No matter how hard they pulled, they could not extricate their legs and they were slowly sinking deeper. David's excited laughter and Glynne's quiet smiles changed to fearful scared cries and tears began to flow when they realised the danger they were in. Their tears and cries galvanised Brian into action. There was a small terrace of stone houses near the edge of the park where it bordered the top of Batley Carr. He ran round the edges of the muddy bog and headed for the houses, terrified David and Glynne were going to disappear and die, deep inside the mud. He banged on a house door crying, and in seconds a startled couple appeared:

"Missis. Mister. Mi bruther an mi cussin. Thi stuck. In mud. Up theer. In new park."

His terror-stricken cries persuaded the man and woman of the gravity of the situation. Like magic, men appeared from nowhere, eager to help in the rescue of Ower David and Ower Glynne. The men found planks, bricks and ropes and ran to where Glynne and David were now up to their thighs in mud. Calmly and miraculously, it seemed to Brian, the men extricated them from the mud. Afterwards it was the reed swords and the hospital all over again. David and Glynne were the centre of attention while Brian was on the sidelines, feeling left out and jealous. The three boys were taken back to the house of the couple and a small crowd of neighbours and onlookers gathered to witness the arrival of the two mud-soaked boys. Batley was such a tight knit town then, where everyone seemed to know everyone:

"Nah then, lads. Weer d'yow three live? Whah's yeh Mam and Dad called? Oo, bluddy ell fire, it's Mary Est's lads, an Louie Chadwick's bairn! Well, ah nivver. Ey up, Fred. Run up teh Chapel Fold luv, an tell Mary wha's appened. An thee Doreen, gerrup ter Eeli an tell Louie wha's gone off wi er Glynne. An tell em thed berra bring sum clean cloyes dahn wi em. Goo on. Run!"

Nowadays what happened next might make some fowk feel uncomfortable. But things were different then. A crowd of adults and bairns gradually gathered at the house to enjoy the rescue drama. The grown-ups decided David and Glynne were too filthy to be taken indoors to be cleaned, and so they ordered them to stay on the old stone flagstones in front of the bathroomless house until the family's tin bath was brought from its place in the back yard. The man of the house filled the tin bath with water from a hosepipe and David and Glynne were swiftly and unceremoniously stripped naked by the woman of the house and ordered to climb in the bath. They stood in the bath and the woman gave them a good clean with Fairy Household Soap and then rubbed them dry with an old towel. The two of them shrieked, squealed and giggled with delight – and a little embarrassment too – at showing their naked selves to the small crowd. Their largely uninhibited pleasure quickly infected the onlookers and soon everyone was laughing. What could have been a tragedy turned into an unexpected party, right there on the flagstones, outside the stone terraced house at the top end of Batley Carr, on a sunny Saturday morning.

Mary and Louie soon arrived with clean clothes. They were flustered, breathless and ready to give the bairns a good telling off. But they could never resist a party and before long big white cracked pots of tea appeared from nowhere and fat'n'bread sandwiches, the fat fresh from Dewsbury Saturday Market, and potted meat ones too, and a fairy cake or two. The men sloped off teh Batley Carr Club, "Teh tell tale theer," and the women stayed to gossip.

"Eee. Yoo-er Shirley works ont same bench as ower Mavis at Smiths, dun't shi?"

"By eck. Ah remember yoo-er Nellie at Burroughs. Yer could ear er laugh from wun end et shed teh tuther."

"Eee. E's as daft as a brush, is ower David. E nearly lost is eye, yer knaw …"

By the time they moved to secondary school, David and Brian were already growing apart. They still shared the same bedroom but now had their own single beds and the night time stories and insurrections ceased. Brian was making new tentative friends at secondary school, friends who suited his personality, and David was making a wide circle of friends who suited his, including Barry Summerfield. Barry lived next door at Chapel Fold. He was a badly behaved boy with no respect for adults. When Barry's parents told him off, he answered back, swore at them and pulled cheeky faces, before running away from their angry cries. He was one of those boys who was constantly stirring up trouble and mischief among other children, incapable of thinking through the consequences of what he was doing. Barry sometimes deliberately smashed a neighbour's window with a cricket ball, or trampled over a carefully tended garden, no matter how often David and Brian warned him not to. David for a time was attracted to Barry's wildness and followed him around, giggling nervously at his bad behaviour but not quite fully joining in himself. Mary swiftly weaned him away from Barry when David also began to be branded by neighbours as a bad and stupid boy.

Like all his older brothers except Brian, David became an able and enthusiastic sportsman as he grew older. After he was diverted by Mary away from Barry-next-door, he made friends with boys who were keen on sports and less "trouble" than Barry. David started Batley Boys High as a first year pupil in September 1959, the year the new school opened. He kept his sunny, gregarious nature throughout secondary school and was popular because of it, making many friends. Brian once saw David in a corridor during morning break when he was in year nine or ten. One of David's friends was holding him in what looked like a painful headlock, dragging him down the corridor. David maintained his cheerful grin and giggle even in what was clearly a painful situation. Brian wondered then whether David's relentless cheerfulness was just a mask; something behind which he could hide his deeper feelings and fears.

David was among the more able pupils at Batley High. The school was streamed by ability in each year and he was in the top stream throughout his time at the school. Unlike his older brothers, who tended to excel in one particular area – sport, or technical subjects, or English – he was a good all-rounder, although his favourite subject was maths. David was in a generation and a socio-economic class where children were still by and large expected to leave school at the earliest opportunity and go out to work, to bring some brass into the household for a few brief years, before marrying and continuing the same pattern with their own children. The official school leaving age by the time David reached year ten was still the end of the term in which the child's fifteenth birthday fell. In David's case, this meant he could have left school at Easter in year ten, after spending three years and two terms at Batley High. Although David was bright, his love of play and the big wide world outside school meant he lacked application. It was Mary at that time who made the big decisions about the Hirst children's schooling. Bob sat broodingly on the sidelines, only confiding his opinions about schooling to Mary in private. David wanted to stay-on at school an extra year to take O Levels. His reports said he could do well but lack of application was a problem. Mary was inclined toward him leaving school, as it did not look as if he was prepared to make the effort needed to pass O levels. It was a big decision: the money he could earn by going out to work would make a significant addition to the household budget. David, however, promised to work hard and he duly stayed on at school for the extra year.

When this decision was made, David and Brian still shared the same bedroom but they shared little else. Gone were the days of spitting games, stories in the night, sword fights and adventures with oozy mud. They led separate lives. It was obvious David was not applying himself to schoolwork during his extra year at school and it was only the urgings of his O level maths teacher that persuaded Mary to keep him on. With some effort he could easily have gained six or more good O Level passes. Instead, he gained just two basic passes in English and mathematics, subjects at which he was naturally able and which required minimum effort to pass on his part.

After his disappointing O Level results, David left school at sixteen and began his working life as a local bookie's assistant. Relations became even more distant between David and Brian. David never said so explicitly, but he was deeply disappointed with himself for not doing better at school. Meanwhile Brian was absorbed in himself and his own inner life during those mid-adolescent years, but he noticed how David changed – from a cheerful clownish younger brother, to a simmeringly moody person who wanted little to do with him. It was the only time the two brothers almost came to real blows. Brian was in the bedroom one evening, lying on his bed reading, escaping from the family downstairs. David came in to change his clothes, on his way to meet friends, or to a date with a girl. Brian was aware of David's resentment about him staying on at school to take A levels, but David seemed unaware how envious Brian was of his relaxed social skills, and the freedom he had to go out socialising whenever he wanted, which earning a wage gave him. They had a bickering exchange of words about something trivial as David was changing. Brian said something cutting about David's poor O Level results. It was the only time he saw his younger brother really angry. He shot Brian a look of visceral hatred and lunged at him. They scuffled for a few seconds, Brian fending David off. Neither of them were physically aggressive in the way their older brothers could be and David had asthma from a young age, like Mary and Moira, and it impeded him physically. It was David's fear of an asthma attack, and Brian's reluctance to enter a physical confrontation, that stopped the scuffle developing into a real fight. The scuffle ended and David stormed out of the bedroom, leaving Brian shocked and trembling at the hatred and near-violence which had erupted between them. It was like when John ruined his homework that time. Some tension was released and they left each other alone after. They never fought or argued again, but nor did they grow closer as they grew older, as John and Brian did.

David earned well at Frayn's Bookmakers and gradually he became an indispensable part of the small business. During Brian's first year at teacher training college, on a visit home, David invited him to a pub night out – to meet his first serious girlfriend. Her name was Elaine and she came from a large Irish Catholic Batley family who also lived at Staincliffe Estate. Her parents and older brothers were an integral part of the St. Mary's and Nash community and were known and liked by Bob and Mary and the older-end. The Staincliffe Estate community was varied and diverse by then, ranging from sober, hard-working, aspirational families, to drunken, slovenly ones, living on benefits. Elaine's family were at the hard-working aspirational end of the scale. She was taking A Levels at a Catholic Girls Grammar School in Bradford when Brian first met her at the pub with David and she had already gained a place at a Catholic teacher training college in Liverpool. She was a short, fresh, pink-faced girl with a wonderful mane of dark frizzy hair and Irish good looks. She was serious and earnest about life and about her studies and she was quite a religious person. She was already shifting from a Batley-Irish-Nash-working-class-lass, to a duffle-coated-heavy-knit-sweater-student, setting out on her way to becoming a professional middle class primary school teacher – even before she started training college. The three of them went out for drinks at pubs well out of the Nash and the Bull circuit, on several occasions.

A few years later, when John and Pat were settling into their adult selves and Brian into his, their jaunts to the clubs and pubs around Batley and Dewsury were a simple matter of bonding and enjoying the social scene. It was a little more complex between David, Elaine and Brian, just those few years earlier. They were all on the threshold of becoming adults. They were still developing and growing emotionally. David was showing off Elaine and Brian to each other: "Look at my bright clever girlfriend; my bright clever brother." And in the process he was proving to himself something of his own worth. When Brian pub-crawled with John and Pat, there was a sense of social and personal sureness. Nights out with David and Elaine were more tentative, more unsure. They were all three still formulating who they wanted to be, socially and personally, not to mention the fact that there was still some simmering residual sibling rivalry going on between the two brothers even at this stage, when they were starting to lead their own separate lives.

It was Mam who told Brian that David's relationship had ended, not long after Elaine started teacher training college and when he reached just nineteen, David married a girl called Mary, and less than nine months later they had the first of their three children, Donna. Mary was taller than Elaine, slim and pale skinned with a glorious head of blonde frizzy hair. Mary left school at fifteen and when David first met her she worked on the factory floor at Briar Carpets, where John's Pat and Shirley's Jimmy also worked.

From the start, David and Mary strove to make a success of their marriage. They found the deposit for a mortgage on a small back-to-back at Carlinghow, a still semi-rural part of Batley. Some years later they moved up the road to a brand new three bedroom semi, with its own gardens and driveway, where they have lived ever since. Soon after his marriage David left Frayn's and trained as a TV repairer. For some years he worked for a large TV retailer chain and for a shorter time he rented premises in Morley and he and Mary ran their own TV sales and repairs business there. After the television shop business ended, he made up for his two O Levels by passing an Open University degree in maths and IT, and later gained a job in computer maintenance. For some years now he has earned a good salary, with company cars thrown in, and he still works in computer maintenance as he nears his sixtieth birthday.

For the first ten years of their marriage, Brian kept in fairly regular contact with David and Mary and their three children, Donna, Tammy and Wayne, visiting them at their house in Carlinghow when he was staying in Batley. But Brian's contact with David and Mary has diminished more and more over the last thirty years. It resumed again when Brian was diagnosed with leukaemia, in his late-fifties. David telephoned him, soon after hearing about the diagnosis, from John. Over the years, David has developed a strong Broad Yorkshire accent, to present himself to the world. But on some occasions he has a quieter, more reflective, voice. It was David's quiet voice on the telephone that day and Brian knew it immediately, even though they had not spoken directly to each other for years. He said just a few words.

"Bri, it's me. Ow are yeh?"

It was the voice of David when he is distressed and bothered by something. The thin breathy asthmatic timbre was there; the sound of a voice Brian intimately grew up with. And the directness and uninhibitedness was there too. He was upset and concerned over Brian's health: testament to the deep ties that bind siblings so close in age together, no matter how much time makes them grow apart. They talked again briefly just a few weeks later – outside the Dewsbury Crematorium Chapel on a chill January day, just after they said goodbye to Auntie Louie for the last time. Brian was exhausted, pale with anaemia, breathless and drawn. David looked tired and weary too. He wanted to know how Brian was and was clearly relieved when told he was not as ill as he looked. At the funeral tea in the Parochial Hall afterwards, David sat at the same table as Brian, along with Sheila and her daughter Linda. The four of them shared anecdotes and reminiscences about Louie, and the memories brought smiles to all their faces. Brian could see David remembering, as things dug deep inside came back. And inside their talk, he felt a whisper of Glynne.

Glynne, Brian, Malcolm, John and David.
Club Trip, 1950s

David, Mary and Baby Donna with Lynne's friend Josie
looking on. Back garden, Chapel Fold, late 1960s.

RICHARD

Richard was born in March 1952. In Barry's wedding photograph, he is aged four and has flung his arms around his head to hide his face from the camera. Malcolm stands behind him smiling, holding onto his shoulders. You have the sense that if Malcolm let go, Richard would charge right out of the photograph frame, ruining the happy united family pose. From his earliest years, Richard easily turned to anger and defiance. He was a "brussen" boy, brussen being "Mary-speak" for belligerent and stubborn. Mary and Richard were often locked in conflict over something or other. It could be a battle over a pair of shoes he was refusing to wear as Mary tried to dress him. Or it might be a battle to keep him from running in and out of the scullery when the washing was being done. Richard in his early years seemed to be in a permanent state of seige and rebellion, forever shouting "no" to everything and everybody, just as he shouted "no" to having his photograph taken at Barry's wedding.

Mary started her part-time job as a rag-sorter at Percy Walker's Mill when Richard was eight. It was the time when Brian and David were put in charge of looking after the younger-end during Mary's shifts at the rag-oyle. Stephen and Lynne were placid, easily entertained and happy to eat the simple midday meals prepared by Brian and David.

Richard on the other hand was constantly saying "NO!" No to coming inside to eat his dinner; no to fried egg; no to "siding" his plate and pot from the table after he finished eating. David was more amenable than Brian. He was mystified and sometimes exasperated by Richard's brussen ways and made half-hearted attempts to get him to behave hissen, and conform, but when Richard was in full refusal mode, David just shrugged his shoulders and left him to his own devices. Brian on the other hand was determined to make him behave and if shouting at him did not have an effect, and it very rarely did, he resorted to slaps and pushes. When Brian inflicted brute force, Richard sullenly submitted, "an did as e was towd," but his assertively independent and contrary self soon rose again to the surface.

Richard began Batley High in year seven when Brian was starting year twelve. Aged seventeen, Brian was not prepared to acknowledge eleven year old Richard's relationship to him during school hours. It was not the done thing in those days to admit to your friends you actually had a *family* at all, and Brian was paranoid about other boys questioning him about his own exceptionally large family. To give him his due, Richard intuitively understood his older brother's embarrassment about him being around school and whenever the brothers did happen to be in the same corridor Brian studiously ignored him, and Richard likewise appeared to be unaware of Brian, apart from a glance and a quick flash of a cheeky grin. Whenever Brian saw him around school, he seemed happy and comfortable with his peers.

Richard grew into a stocky, good looking blond-haired boy in his middle teenage years. It was during these years when he developed asthma which sometimes laid him low, making him lethargic. He was passionate about cricket, a passion he has never lost, and he played for local and school cricket teams. He was able at High School but his main interests were social life and cricket and by the time he reached sixteen, beer, smoking and girls also came into his life in a big way. He was cheerful, gregarious and popular with his mates but the brussen, belligerent refusnik of the younger Richard was always there, and the struggles and conflicts between him and Mary continued throughout his teenage years. At fifteen he left school to train as a master butcher in a high-quality shop in Mirfield.

When they were both aged seventeen, Richard and his current girlfriend Lynne became parents. They rented a back-to-back house down Cross Bank and hurriedly married, before Nicola was born. A year or so later, their second daughter Joanne arrived. Mary fretted to Brian over Richard and Lynne, on one of his visits to Russell Close.

"Ah doo-ern't knaw, Brian. Thi both too young to be avin' bairns an tekkin on marridge. Norther on em's even alf grown up yet."

The small claustrophobic house at Russell Close often seemed filled with Richard and Lynne and the two small girls whenever Brian visited at that time. Downstairs, there was a small kitchen-dining room and a larger lounge. Upstairs, were three bedrooms and a bathroom. Sometimes the small house was bursting at the seams with people, when Stephen and his girlfriend Maggie were staying, and Brian, on top of the regular occupants, Lynne, Michael, Bob and Mary. When Richard and his family arrived, it brought the number in the house to eleven. If he was in one of his sour moods with the world, Bob was left alone in the main room, glaring at the telly or studying the horse racing form, while up to ten other family members squeezed themselves into the kitchen-dining-room in order to chat freely, uninhibited by Bob's surliness and glares. Even Mary, who loved seeing all her granbairns at all times, breathed a sigh of relief when Richard and family finally left for their own home in the early evening, after a long day with everyone cooped up in the kitchen.

"Oo, let me tek mi shoes off an sit dahn. Ah'm *that* tyeed."

It was obvious from the start that Richard and Lynne were finding the responsibilities of marriage and parenthood difficult. There was an occasion when the two girls needed new shoes and Richard and Lynne squabbled endlessly over when and where to buy them. Eventually Richard obtained a Saturday afternoon off work and a plan was carefully laid by Mary for him to meet Lynne at Russell Close at dinnertime, after his morning shift at the butchers, to take the children to Dewsbury in the afternoon, to buy the shoes.

"An you mek sure yeh ger ere at twelve. No slopin inter Nash on yer way back frum werk."

"Or reight, Mam. Ah'll be ere at twelve. Nor need ter bluddy gu on abaht it."

Richard duly arrived on time, tired out, surly and resentful toward Lynne. Mary made the usual Saturday dinner of tinned chopped pork sandwiches with salad, or bacon and egg, or home made fish cakes and chips. After dinner, it took Richard and Lynne what seemed years to prepare themselves and the children for their trip to the shoe shop. Lynne was expert at making mountains out of molehills. Putting on Nicola's coat, or wiping food from Joanne's face, became monumental, arduous tasks. Richard meanwhile was expert at totally ignoring her struggles, until her slowness exasperated him and he snapped at her, and a simmering mutual resentment between them boiled into loathing, until eventually they left with the children, thanks largely to Mary's cajoling and help in preparing the girls. Mary stood at the front door, watching the small family traipsing down the hill, crawling reluctantly inch by inch toward the bus stop. She sighed and murmured.

"Ee. Ah doo-ern't noo-er. Look at em. It'll nivver last."

Mary's own marriage was far from easy but largely due to her fortitude and hard effort it endured and she held the family together. The older siblings all had problems with their marriages at times, even steady Young Bob. But Mary had never quite seen a relationship in her own family as intractable and hopeless as that between Richard and Lynne. She was nearing sixty and it was a new thing she was seeing looming in the future as she watched Richard and his family from the front door: divorce. And it pained her.

It is a Sunday and Brian is staying at Russell Close. Richard and family arrive by eleven for dinner. A lovely joint of marbled beef, courtesy of Richard's job, is the centrepiece of the meal. At midday, Richard slopes off teh Nash, promising to be back by half two for his lunch, leaving a resentful Lynne and two fractious small girls with Mary, who copes with them, even with a Sunday lunch for eleven people to cook and Sam constantly under her feet, sniffing the joint of beef. Richard returns for dinner on time. As soon as he enters the house Lynne dumps the girls on him, making heavy weather of relieving herself of the burden. Richard is wheezing heavily and asthmatically after the steep climb up the hill from the Nash, and chain smoking, and downing six pints over the previous two hours. He is developing a big beer belly at the age of twenty and his breath reeks of alcohol. He plays with the girls, lifting them up high, pulling faces, making funny noises. The girls are delighted. Their adoration of him in this cheerful beery mood is transparent. He is a natural with children. He knows instinctively how to play with them and, when he has to, he is more than capable of washing, feeding, changing and dressing them. After all, like all his siblings, he has been surrounded by babies and toddlers (his nephews and nieces) from his earliest years and has been expected by Mary to entertain and care for the younger ones, almost since he could walk and talk himself. Perhaps Lynne resents his casual easy competence with children, set against the hard work she makes of parenting.

After dinner, everyone migrates from the kitchen-dining room to the sitting room, to pass the afternoon and evening watching Sunday telly. Bob has either not got up from bed at all or has sloped off to bed at some stage, escaping the noisy downstairs rooms. Richard lies on the sofa, struggling to light a cigarette, as Nicola and Joanne crawl all over him, touching his face, touching him all over, while Lynne tries to forget the children and being a mother, and gossips with Maggie and Ower Lynne. Richard calms the girls down and Nicola finds a quiet corner to play with a toy, while Joanne lies down on Richard on her back, sleepily watching the telly. It is not long before father and daughter fall into a deep sleep and Richard's asthmatic beery snores become louder and louder, easily topping the telly in volume. Looking at him lying on his back on the settee with Joanne, he could be her older brother. He is entirely comfortable with her and the profound depth of Joanne's sleep shows the total trust she has in her Daddy. There is a deep and natural companionship in their recumbent bodies which moves Brian and makes him envious. Mary is right. Richard is naturally competent and loving with his girls but he is not yet ready to be a father to them, and neither is he ready to be a husband to Lynne in the full sense, with all the decision making, negotiating, adjusting, and taking on of wider responsibilities beyond your own gratification that being a father and a husband involves.

Richard's first marriage did not last long. It was not Richard who stormed off in a refusnik temper, but Lynne. She left him, taking the girls with her, to live with her mother. Over the next few years, Mary despaired of Richard ever settling down. After his divorce, he became homeless and for some months lived at Russell Close. It was not a happy situation. He was drinking and smoking harder than ever and the belligerent side of his nature was erupting more and more. He argued with the butcher he had worked for since leaving school and walked out of a good job, in sheer temper. He argued with the steward and the committee men at the Nash and had his membership cancelled and was barred from entering the premises for several years. He seemed to be going from bad to worse but throughout this turbulent time he always found another job at which he worked hard, before arguing with the next boss and storming out yet again. Mary nattered herself silly over Richard but at heart she was still her old pragmatic self; she gave him a time limit to find somewhere to live on his own, which he eventually did.

Richard married his second wife Linda in March 1979, just weeks after Moira died, when he was twenty seven. Linda and Richard had two children, Gemma and Liam. The second marriage lasted only a few years. Richard's behaviour and work patterns continued much as they had done when he was married to Lynne: hard work, hard drinking and smoking, and storming out of jobs after arguments or perceived slights from his bosses. Linda differed from Lynne in that she drank as hard, and often harder, than Richard. The mutual heavy drinking and Richard's lethargy and impatience with the responsibilities of fatherhood and marriage led to a separation followed by divorce, when Gemma and Liam were still infants.

Richard now lives alone in rented accommodation in Heckmondwike. Throughout the years of Gemma and Liam growing up into teenagers, he maintained contact with them through regular Sunday dinnertimes spent at Mary's. By this time, he was re-instated as a Nash Member and he sometimes joined Brian, Bob, John and Michael for a Sunday pre-dinnertime pint or two. He mellowed as his two younger children grew into their teens and it was obvious Gemma and Liam treasured seeing him on Sundays at Granma's. Richard clearly valued seeing them and he had matured enough to show his appreciation of Mary's support. While he was still working in butchering, he supplied the meat for the Sunday dinner and he and the children cleared and washed up for Mary afterward, leaving her scullery spick and span. It was a time when he unburdened himself, discussing the issues in his life calmly with Mary in the scullery after the washing up, when everyone else migrated to the sitting room to watch Sunday afternoon telly. This Richard was a big contrast to the handsome, beery, snoring boy on the sofa some years earlier.

For years after divorcing Lynne, largely through his own peculiar mixture of indolence and pig-headed awkwardness, Richard lost all contact with Nicola and Joanne. It was Nicola who contacted Richard, not long after she graduated from Huddersfield University in Business Studies. By this time she had found herself a well paid management post in a prestigious national High Street company. Mary was thrilled when Richard first told her Nicola had contacted him to suggest they meet. She had rarely seen Nicola and Joanne for all those years since the divorce and it grieved her that she was missing out on the lives of two grand-daughters she had been close to during their first few years of life. It was Mary's suggestion that Nicola should join Richard, Gemma and Liam (and whoever else might be there) for Sunday dinner at Russell Close, and before very long Nicola became "a regular" among the Sunday dinner crowd, at Russell Close.

Nicola is a beautiful, intelligent, competent young woman, with every reason to be angry and resentful toward a father who neglected her for much of her early life. But she shows none of these feelings toward Richard. She loves him as much as she did before he went out of her life and it is clear he loves her, and there is mutual delight between Nicola, Joanne, Gemma and Liam, finding themselves with half-siblings, relatively late in their lives. It must be fifteen or more years since Nicola and Richard became reunited as father and daughter. The bond between them has tightened and strengthened, due to a combination of Richard always being willing and happy to give love and Nicola's ability to work on the relationship systematically and determinedly. It took Joanne many years longer than Nicola to forgive Richard for his long absence as a father from her life but she also now sees him. It was a special pleasure for Mary that both her long-missed grand-daughters turned up, with Richard and Liam and Gemma, for her ninetieth birthday gathering.

Richard left the butchery trade some years ago. Now in his middle-fifties, he is father to four grown-up children, and a grandfather. He has a loving bond with his children and grandchildren, in spite of the setbacks which sometimes he almost deliberately seems to create in his life. He currently works in a car accessories factory and redundancy looms on the horizon. But for someone so truculent when it comes to inter-personal relations, he works cheerfully and socially in the evenings as barman and sometimes substitute landlord, at a pub in Heckmondwike, owned by one of his friends.

"Younger-End" Richard, Lynne, Stephen. 1950s

Michael's wedding. Kneeling left to right: Brian, David, Richard, Lynne's Mick. Standing left to right: Shirley, Moira, Young Bob, Mary, Maggie, Sheila, David's Mary, Lynne, Auntie Louie, Sandra, Barry's Linda, Michael. Behind, Shirley's Jimmy, Barry. 1977.

STEPHEN

Stephen was born eighteen months after Richard in June 1953. Brian was eight before he really noticed his by then two year old brother. It was a summer's day. David and Brian were playing cricket in the passage between the Hirst house and the Dewhurst house next door. There was a permanently chalked wicket on the outhouse wall at the top of the passage and a crease line was scratched on the concrete path. They used an ancient hand-me-down cricket bat, originally belonging to Barry or Bob, and they bowled with a spongy floppy tennis ball, as proper cricket balls were banned from passage games, in case of smashed windows and black eyes. The bowler stood at the bottom of the passage and the batsman stood at the top; the enclosing passage walls negated the need for any other players. The boys made a noise in the narrow echoing passageway but no one minded, although there was a limit of rowdiness they knew they must not exceed, else the adults would ban them from playing before they could even blink. The house windows and back scullery door were wide open and Mary was busy inside. A gate had been put up in the open back doorway to stop the younger-end from venturing outside.

"Oo, Ower Stephen, e's a reight little buggerlugs feh wandrin off. If ah dooern't put that gate up, e'll be down that passage afore yeh can seh Jack Robinson. An norarf."

Stephen was determined to be let outside that day. He stood at the gate incessantly fretting and nattering Mary but she was happy with the situation as it was, with the three youngest inside, safe where she could see them and David and Brian peacefully playing passage cricket with no one winding them up. (They played quietly and amicably together for hours on their own but as soon as anyone else appeared on the scene – older brothers, or Glynne, or Barry Summerfield, or passing friends – they exploded into rowdy rivalries, arguments and scuffles.) Before too long, Stephen's constant whimperings got the better of Mary and she undid the gate and let him out.

"Nah then. Brian. David. Listen teh mi. Mek sure this little bugger dun't gu wandrin off dahn passage an onter road. Keep yer eyes on im."

It was around the time when Stephen, David and Brian were the ages they are in Barry's wedding photograph. Stephen was solidly built with vivid blonde hair and a perfect round face and he was already "steddy on is feet." Within seconds of Mary letting him out, he began to make moves to escape down the passage to the road. At first David and Brian halted their game and led Stephen away into the garden. Richard would have yelled in instant protest at being thwarted but Stephen was quiet and placid – on the surface. His outward calm though hid an underlying, unrelenting, determination to do what he wanted no matter what. No sooner had they led him into the garden, he headed straight back to the passage and made a charge for the road, sabotaging the cricket game again. After his tenth or more attempt Brian and David abandoned the cricket altogether and instead played the amusing new game of stopping Stephen from reaching the road, letting him go so far down the passage and then picking him up and taking him back to the back garden. He did not kick out, or cry, or yell, but as soon as they put him down, he charged toward the passage again, like some irreversible, programmed missile. It was not a game he was playing: it was a total determination to reach the road. They tried standing side-by-side, blocking him from going down the passage but their bigger bulk neither deterred nor intimidated him. He just persisted in trying to find a gap between them that would lead him to his destination – or should that be his destiny? Finally they grew tired of his unrelenting persistence and took him back inside to Mary. It was one of the first occasions when Brian objectively considered the personality of one of his younger siblings.

"Honest, Mam. Ower Stephen. E dunt alf know warree wants teh do, dunt e?"

Stephen was the fifth Hirst brother to attend Batley High. He had no idea then how big a part the school would play in his adult life. Brian was in the final year thirteen when Stephen started year seven. Unlike Richard, Stephen was determined (that word again) to recognise his big brother, on the handful of occasions they saw each other during the year they were both pupils at the same school. There was one embarrassing morning when Brian was in a main school corridor with a group of year thirteens, and a noisy gaggle of year sevens erupted from one of the classrooms. Stephen was among them. Stephen's hair was very blond. Brian's hair was dark. Stephen was cheerfully confident. Brian was moody and reserved. Stephen caught sight of Brian and a huge smile suffused his face. Brian's heart sank. Stephen waved and called out Brian's first name, quite unintimidated by the other year thirteens. It was a time when boys in school *never* called each other by first names. Surnames or nicknames were used instead, but Stephen was unaware of the convention. He was excited and pleased to see his older brother but Brian had not lost his paranoia over anyone at school knowing about, or worse still discussing, his huge family. Mercifully the boys he was with were merely mildly interested and amused to discover he had a younger brother. They commented briefly on the difference between their hair colour, and continued the conversation they had been having before Stephen's interruption.

Stephen was twelve when Brian left home to begin teacher-training. For the next six years they saw little of each other and Mary rarely mentioned Stephen in her short letters to Brian. Stephen followed Brian in taking O and A levels and gaining a place at Bingley College of Education. He also followed Malcolm's example. He was passionate about sports and pursued the sports he liked with single-minded determination. He was on the whole not as worrisome to Mary as Richard but this is not to say there were not conflicts. During his years eleven and twelve, he and some of his best friends veered well away from exam studies preferring sport, girls and socialising instead, enough to cause serious concern at school. The headmaster himself contacted Mary to tell her about Stephen's waywardness and stubborn determination not to listen when confronted with the error of his ways. Some fierce battles ensued between Mary and Stephen. Mary's battles with Richard were raucously noisy and involved lots of door slammings and stormings out. But with the quietly determined Stephen it was a case of bringing him back to the "garden" of his studies, away from the "road" of distraction, again and again, until finally he settled down.

At Bingley, Stephen trained to teach Outdoor Activities and Physical Education and it was there that his passion for activities such as climbing, canoeing and caving began. After he completed his teacher-training in 1974, he initially went into youth work in Halifax. An important part of his motive in taking his first job was the opportunity to pursue Outdoor Activities, in undertaking such work. He also told Brian at the time that he was reluctant to be sucked-up into the hierarchical and time-tabling rigidities of a school, and he hoped youth work would be less constricting than teaching. He did not stay long in youth work. He realised the job had financial limitations which he had not initially considered and after a year he left and took up a post as assistant PE teacher at his old school, Batley Boys High.

Within a year or two of starting work at Batley High, Stephen married his college girlfriend, Maggie. Maggie trained as an infant teacher and her first teaching post was reception class teacher at Warwick Road Junior and Infants in Batley Carr, the school where Mary and Louie were given an elementary education from the age of five up to the age of fourteen, fifty or so years before Maggie started teaching there. The Victorian school building was more or less the same as it had always been when Maggie was there but its catchment had changed enormously since Mary's and Louie's school days in the 1920s, when the children were entirely white and the vast majority were from working class mill and rag oyle families, living in the crowded terraced stone back-to-back houses in Batley Carr. The children in Maggie's first reception class in the 1970s were entirely British Asian, largely from Muslim families who had recently settled in the area.

Warwick Road retained its back-to-back terraces when the rest of Batley Carr was being demolished, and most of the children in Maggie's class lived in those remaining back-to-back houses. The majority of the children spoke no English and many were unfamiliar with aspects of living in a Western culture. Maggie once told Brian how one day she realised a five year-old non-English speaking boy in her first reception class desperately wanted to pee. He made his need clear to Maggie by signals. She took him to the outside urinals in a cold corner of the playground, the urinals probably being exactly as they had been in Mary's and Louie's time. The boy had only known fields or squat-down latrines in the village in Pakistan from which he came. A stand-up urinal was a completely new experience for him. Maggie, having all the unflappable attributes necessary for teaching reception class, helped him unzip and demonstrated as best she could where he should point and aim.

Stephen's and Maggie's first house was a three bedroom semi in the Wrenthorpe district of Wakefield. The house had its own driveway and small front and back gardens. Stephen was the first of Brian's nine married siblings at that time (apart from Malcolm, who had army married quarters) not to begin his marriage in a stone back-to-back terraced house in Batley. He broke another Hirst sibling tradition also: his first child, Richard, was not born until nearly two years after he married, rather than the usual less-than-nine-months. (Lynne and Michael followed in Stephen's footsteps in this respect.) Two years after Richard, came Elizabeth, and shortly after her birth, they moved to Maggie's childhood house nearby, when her parents retired to Heysham. Some thirty years later, they still live in the same house and Stephen sometimes works at Batley High, fifty years after it opened in 1959, when Brian and David were year seven and eight pupils there. Maggie spent two years at Warwick Road Infants School and then left teaching for several years to care for Richard and Elizabeth when they were infants. She returned to teaching once Elizabeth began Junior School and her second teaching post is at Wrenthorpe Infants and Juniors, a largely white middle class suburban school, where she has now worked for over twenty years.

Stephen became interested in gardening during his teenage years. Before he moved to Wrenthorpe, he maintained the gardens at Russell Close, often with Lynne's help. Stephen's and Maggie's Wrenthorpe house has a small front garden and a large rear garden which gradually climbs to thick shrubs and trees. The garden is Stephen's other main passion in adult life, alongside Outdoor Activities. He spends countless solitary hours in his garden, tending and perfecting it. Maggie tries to lure him away from the garden to come indoors for coffee and a catch-up chat when visitors call, but her efforts are often in vain. That old determination of the two year old, intent on getting down the passage to the road, is still there. No matter how much Maggie calls Stephen inside, he returns to his idyll outside: the garden.

Although Stephen's long career at Batley High was primarily in PE teaching, his work there ranged well beyond school-based teaching. For many years he was responsible for supervising the Duke of Edinburgh Award Scheme which had a big take-up of boys at the school. The headmaster gave his full support to the "D-of-E" scheme and money was raised to build a permanent Batley High Outdoor Activities Centre, at Stainforth, near Settle, in the Yorkshire Dales. At one stage Stephen seemed to spend most of his life – weekends and holidays included – at Stainforth, where he became a part of the Yorkshire Dales Outdoor Activities community. At a later stage in his career at Batley High, he worked mainly with years twelve and thirteen, until Kirklees Education Authority re-organised its education system and older pupils from Batley High were lured to tertiary colleges in surrounding towns, just before the school finally lost its sixth-form and became an 11 to 16 school.

Now in his mid-fifties, for the last few years Stephen has been on permanent secondment from schoolteaching, working as an advisor for the Kirklees Local Education Authority. Batley stopped being part of the West Riding some time in the 1970s or 1980s, when a government Commission re-drew boundaries and kicked several counties into oblivion. Well worn places, which had served their local communities since medieval times, disappeared. Parts of the East Riding and Lincolnshire suddenly became North and South Humberside. Bits of the old North Riding and County Durham became Cleveland. Westmoreland and Cumberland became Cumbria. Parts of the West Riding, including Batley, found themselves in this new, arbitrary, fictional area – Kirklees, which vaguely wanders from Huddersfield at its administrative centre and along the Calder Valley past Battyford and Mirfield to Batley and other fragmentary bits of the former West Riding Heavy Woollen District. Stephen's brief is to advise schools in "Kirklees" on ways of encouraging pupils to continue education beyond sixteen. His work focus is often centred on the large British Asian community in the area, although not exclusively so. When Maggie first worked with newly arrived immigrant children from Asia over thirty years ago, much of her work involved familiarising the children with the customs and cultural life in Batley. In some ways things have hardly changed at all in that much of Stephen's current work involves introducing British Asian and white teenagers to the opportunities available to them in further and higher education.

When Batley High opened in 1959, there were two British Asian pupils in a school of over one thousand white British boys. The two boys were the sons of professional parents – lawyers or doctors – based in Batley Carr. By 1962, George Miller, a black Jamiacan boy possessed of great cricketing skills and huge charm and friendliness, joined the school. George was the son of a single mother who emigrated from Jamaica to take over a midwifery round in Batley and, to Brian's delight, Mrs. Miller exotically drove around town in the first Volkswagon Beetle he ever saw. By the time Brian left Batley High in 1965, a British Asian teacher had joined the staff, as English as a second language teacher to twenty or so British Asian boys who were by then on the school roll, in the younger years. The school at that time had a thriving sixth form. Many of its pupils went on to apprenticeships, or to further and higher education. Just as Maggie did her best to introduce the infants at Warwick Road to British customs, similar efforts were made at Batley High, during those early days of Asian migrants arriving in the West Riding of Yorkshire Heavy Woollen District.

Brian's recollections from 1965 of the younger new British Asian boys consist mainly of the exotic spicy odours they left in classrooms. One of his weekly A Level English lessons was held in a room just vacated by an Asian special English class. Along with the rest of his A level group, he was both intrigued and a little repelled by the strange "foreign" odours that filled the room, as the newcomers left and his class entered. The all-white year thirteen group thought it was the smell of hair oil, as all the British Asian boys, to their eyes, had lustrous black oily hair. In the multi-cuisine world which is Britain today, those smells would be recognised immediately by almost everyone as a mixture of garlic, ginger, cumin, turmeric, cinnamon and the like – then exclusively the diet of the Asian immigrants, and now a universal "British" taste. There was ignorance on the part of most indigenous Batley people at the time of the lifestyle, culture, religions and cuisine of the immigrants, but there was minimal fear or hostility toward them. Although the woollen and shoddy industries were in terminal decline by the late-1960s, there was still an overall cultural confidence and cohesion among the indigenous population: there was still a real community. And confidence there certainly was at Batley High, led by its charismatic headmaster George Locke. There was a confidence at Batley High about what the future held for *all* its pupils, "home-grown" or "newly arrived" from the Indian sub-continent. School dinners were unvaryingly of the meat-and-veg-followed-by-pudding variety then but efforts were made to provide food which suited the newcomers, although it took some years before terms such as "halal" and "ghee" became fully understood and assimilated into the school canteen menus. Migrants in considerable numbers were not new to the Heavy Woollen District and the area had coped with assimilating large numbers of incomers in the past, including Winnie Hirst's large Irish family, arriving in Yorkshire from Ireland toward the end of the 19th century. In 1965, there was confidence, in spite of some mutual ignorance and incomprehension between indigents and incomers, that the community would cope again with its new wave of immigrants.

The confidence of the 1960s had gone by the 1980s. It was not until then that Stephen first spoke to Brian of his concerns about the school, when race became a burning isssue in the Heavy Woollen District, and the word "Islamaphobia" sprung into the language, often referring to attitudes among the white working classes, in towns such as Batley. There was a non-fatal stabbing one afternoon which took place on the Batley High School drive, just after school turned out, involving a white boy and a British Asian boy. The incident caused considerable shock in the school and in the Batley community. A stabbing just outside a school was still a very shocking event in the 1980s. (It would not be so shocking now outside *any* school.) Within just a few months after the stabbing, it became routine for police to patrol the main exits and steeets around Batley High, to try to prevent serious violence erupting between white and British Asian student gangs, when the boys turned out at the end of the school day. By the 1990s, many of the white parents in the school's catchment area were abandoning Batley High and placing their sons in largely white secondary schools in nearby towns. Stephen has never been a person to show or express outright his feelings, but it was when the sixth form fell apart, and Batley High became an eleven to sixteen school at the end of the 1990s, that he seemed to despair and lose hope of gaining satisfaction or fulfilment from his work there. He still spends one day a week during term at Batley High, where he is now largely involved in advising colleagues on strategies designed to include the pupils in further and higher education.

On the afternoon of Christmas Eve 2007, Brian visited Stephen and his family at Wrenthorpe. Stephen was in the garden, working steadily and doggedly on his winter vegetable patch. Brian talked to him for half an hour in the cold garden, knowing he was unlikely to abandon his current "destiny" to come inside to talk. He told Brian how Batley Business and Enterprise College (the new name for Batley High since the 1990s) had lost its sixth-form and the roll had dropped to around 700 pupils, from well over 1,000 pupils at its peak. In 2007, over 70% of students at the school were British Asian. Stephen went on to tell Brian he had taught one of the young men responsible for the London Bombings of July 2005. His recollection of the boy he taught was of a quiet, pleasant, conscientious pupil, who worked as a teaching assistant in a district of Leeds, some years after he left Batley High. Stephen was not especially surprised that the London Bombers, including the boy he once taught, had done what they did. He felt the problems of disaffection and alienation among a *minority* of the young British Asians in the former Heavy Woollen District had been simmering for years, and little was done to even recognise the problem, let alone alleviate it, or find solutions, by those responsible – in both the white, and British Asian communities. He did not say so directly, but he seemed to see it as just the next inevitable step among this militant minority: from a stabbing; to alienation; to "terrorism."

Stephen is one of the many ex-pupils of Batley High School for Boys who did well attending the school. He was born and brought up in a large lower working class family on a large council estate, where very few people he knew older than him stayed on at school after the age of fifteen. He took A levels followed by teacher-training and later gained a Leeds University education degree. He probably knows as much as anyone, and more than many who are put "in charge" of these things, about the problems and causes which beset many young people, including young British Asians, in run-down towns, such as Batley today.

In spite of now being permanently engaged in work which is a constant uphill struggle against fierce odds, he has a successful middle class life. Outside his career, he sticks doggedly and tenaciously to his passions of gardening, the outdoor life of the Yorkshire Dales and holidaying in France every August.

To a worker in the City of London – one of those people who does this amazing thing: "boosting the country's economy" and earning a bonus every now and then of £1m or more for doing so, Stephen's life achievements might seem tame and insignificant. But to Brian, his achievements are a reminder of that unstoppable two-year-old, determined to reach the road, no matter what.

Stephen and Maggie, 1970s.

LYNNE

Lynne is probably the second of his eleven brothers and sisters that Brian knows least, after Malcolm. He cannot recall any of her distinctive childhood character traits as he can remember Richard's bellicosity and Stephen's tenaciousness. Lynne was born a year after Stephen in June 1954, when Brian was seven and a half. He was mildly curious, in the amorphous way seven and a half year old boys do occasionally "think" of someone other than themselves, about having another sister at last, with three older brothers between himself and Moira and three younger brothers before Lynne. Bob and Mary were pleased to have another daughter after seven boys in a row. At first Mary put a barrier between the middle-lads and baby Lynne. They were kept at a distance from her when she was little "because she's a girl." But Brian created his own barriers between himself and Lynne. Sandwiched between three older and three younger brothers, a girl sibling was a strange and mysterious thing to come into his life at that point. Whatever its causes, "distance" seems to be the word that sums-up the relationship between Lynne and Brian for most of their lives.

Richard and Stephen were closer to Lynne in age and the three of them made up their own unit at the "younger-end" of the family. Auntie Louie's daughter Ann was born just a few months before Stephen and just as Glynne was "one of us" to Brian and David, so Ann was "one of us" to Richard, Stephen and Lynne. Looking at them as small children, a stranger might conclude it was Stephen and Ann who were brother and sister, with their blonde hair and Nordic good looks. Lynne has always had thick dark hair from her first few weeks of life. But although Ann and Stephen were strikingly alike in looks, the closest bond among the younger-end was between Lynne and Stephen. The reserve which exists between Lynne and most of her siblings does not exist with Stephen. Mary put it this way, when they were small and growing up:

"Look at them two. Thi worship each other, an norarf."

An early memory concerning Lynne. She is three and Brian is ten. She is suddenly ill and has spent some time in hospital, where doctors have conducted tests. The middle-uns, from John down to David, have been told virtually nothing about Lynne's illness by the in-the-know grown-ups. As usual, it is Moira who reveals to David and Brian a little about what Lynne's illness might be.

"Yer've not got teh say a word teh *nobody* about what ah'm gunner tell yeh: Ower Lynne might ave POLIO!"

They were not sure what polio was but they knew it was nasty – and Brian was duly impressed with the drama. Life was not always rowdy or scary at Chapel Fold in those days, with John throwing the tortoise at the outhouse wall, or Barry Summerfield being chased round the garden by his Dad, for telling him to "bugger off" when called to come inside from playing. During school holiday weekdays Bob and the older ones were at work and John and Malcolm roamed far and wide with their friends, doing the unknown things that older brothers did then. Mary was invariably indoors, busy with housework, cooking and looking after the younger-end. On days like this, the gardens and passageway at Chapel Fold were Brian's and David's almost-exclusive territory. When they wanted to talk privately, they wandered out of the back garden and down the passage to the bottom of the front path, where they spread themselves over the steps and garden wall. There was often a little gang of them: Brian, David, Glynne, and sometimes Barry Summerfield and Derek Brydon, who lived two doors down Chapel Fold. They talked disjointedly about things they only half understood. On the day David and Brian were told about Lynne, the gang gathered at the front steps. Tears stung Brian's eyes as he announced the portentous news:

"Ower Lynne's got POLIO. An shi's gunner DIE."

"Or, goo an get shifted, Bri. Thes nowt up wi er. What yer guin on abaht?"

"She is! She is! Ower Moira towd us. Din' shi Dave? Shi sed shi's got POLIO an" –

– "Yeh. But shi din seh shi were gunner DIE though!"

"But. But. Yer DO die when yer get POLIO, stupid."

"Oo sez? Ow du YOU know? Yeh just get poorly an then doctors mek yeh berrer."

"Yeh DO die. Yer DO. I KNOW yer do. So shut yer gob up, Barry Summer" -

– The discussion ended ignominiously for Brian. His voice rose to a hysterical high shriek as he tried to defend his case until the others grew tired of his histrionics and wandered off, leaving him alone on the steps. When he calmed down, he felt guilty and a bit of a fraud about making a drama, just for his own gratification, over what could well be a major blow to his young sister's future life. It might have been the first time in his life, musing on the front garden steps, that he became consciously aware of the layers we humans create in our existence; aware of our ability to say one thing and feel another; aware of being able to lie and deceive, while on the surface appearing sincere and honest. But even though he knew it was wrong, he enjoyed playing with that ability; he enjoyed the sense of power it gave him: to be able to control life and make it more interesting: by pretending; by embroidering; by adding to the bare facts Moira had given him about Lynne's illness.

In the end it did all turn out to be just a temporary drama. Lynne did not have polio and within a few days of the altercation on the front garden steps she was back to her usual good health. By the time Lynne went to Foxcroft Girls Secondary Modern, the school had moved from its old premises next to Purlwell Infants to the former Healey Boys School, after Batley High opened in 1959. It was a temporary measure until a large new girls comprehensive was opened at Howden Clough a few years later, replacing the three girls secondary schools in Batley. Brian was living away from Batley during Lynne's secondary school years. He hardly knew her at all during that time but she seemed quiet and reserved when he saw her during his visits to Chapel Fold and Russell Close. Mary is adamant Lynne could be strong willed and assertive – "from day one" – when it suited her. Mary was in her middle-fifties when Lynne went through adolescence but she was as feisty and indomitable as ever and she battled with Lynne as vigorously as she had done with all her children and, by Mary's account, Lynne gave back as good as she got.

Louie's Ann attended Batley Girls Grammar and she and Lynne grew apart but the close relationship with Stephen continued. Apart from Stephen, she seemed to have one other close friend, Josie, who was in her class at school and lived nearby. Josie was small, thin and dark. She seemed fascinated and terrified in equal measure by all the boys at Lynne's house. Lynne was an able pupil but there was not an aspirational ethos at Foxcroft. There was no sixth form and few girls went on to A level and higher education. Lynne took a course in office and secretarial skills, at which she did well, and then she left school at sixteen to work in the offices of a small factory down by Wheatcroft in Batley, where the four middle-uns were drenched on the day of the Sunday School trip to Filey years earlier. When Lynne was nineteen or twenty, on one of his stays at Russell Close, Brian was sitting enjoying the sun on the new patio in the back garden. He could hear Lynne's and Mam's voices, coming from the open kitchen doorway.

"Oo, nah then. An what did Wally ave teh seh abaht that then?"

"Well, yer know wor e's like, Mam. He won't like his fav'rite lad bein loo-werd away from im by another bloke, will he? He'll probably mek a fuss over it an' get Dave sacked, so's he can keep his mucky paws on Jeff."

"Ee. Onist! Ah doo-ern't noo-er. There's all soo-erts guss off wi fowk these days. An yeh'd nivver guess – teh look at im – he wor, yeh knaw, like *that* ..."

They were enjoying a bit of gossip over a gay boss at the factory where Lynne worked – although in those days he would have been called a queer, a puff, a fairy, or much worse. Brian had to smile. Mary was avid to hear everything Lynne could tell her. She had not changed at all from years earlier, when Moira used to recount all the scandal at Rest Assured, or all the goings-on of those prim old spinsters at the solicitors offices down Batley Carr.

Lynne was shy, reserved and distant as she was growing up but occasionally she came out of this mould and surprised everyone. Shirley and Jimmy once held a big family Boxing Day party at their house in Birstall, when Lynne was in her twenties. Almost the whole of the family turned up for the party, including Malcolm and Caroline, who were staying in Batley during one of their trips back to Yorkshire from their army house in Norway. Malcolm was at the peak of his skiing successes then and he could be highly assertive, if not arrogant, at times. Alcohol fuelled his innate aggression at the party and he decided to impress himself upon Lynne, who rarely and only lightly drinks alcohol. Lynne was standing somewhere quiet with her husband-to-be, Mick, when Malcolm cornered her.

"Nah then, owd lass. Are yer ignorin me an Caroline? Ave we dun summat ter offend yeh? Cos yeh norarf stickin yer snub little nose up at us."

Lynne passively soaked up Malcolm's attack for just a couple of minutes but then pushed him away.

"Piss off, you. Who d'yer think you are, an all? Talkin down teh me like that. Yeh nowt burra a bully, an a big gob."

Her attack shocked and silenced Malcolm – and everyone else – for several seconds, as the party-goers absorbed this visible confirmation that Lynne could be as explosive as her more volatile siblings, when under attack.

Lynne married Mick not long after Stephen's and Maggie's union. Just as Stephen and Maggie settled in Maggie's family house in Wrenthorpe, Lynne and Mick settled in a semi in Gomersal, a small town on the way from Batley to Bradford, just a stone's throw from Mick's parents' house. They have remained there ever since. Mick has progressed in his career over the years from technical assistant in a large engineering department at Bradford University, to IT resource manager in the same department. Lynne continued to work in the office at the factory in Batley for a year or more after she married, until her oldest child Hayley was born. Her second child Paul came soon after and Lynne never returned to office work after that.

A good few years after Lynne ceased regular work, Brian realised how able and competent she was at the work she trained to do at school, when he took a research degree at the University of East Anglia. The research involved writing a lengthy dissertation and Brian initially employed a person in Norwich to type the final copy, in the days before word-processors and PCs took over from typewriters. He spent endless hours proof-reading and correcting the numerous mistakes made by the university typist. On a visit to Russell Close, during the period when he was working on the final dissertation copy, Lynne and Mick and children arrived on their usual Saturday morning visit to Mary's house at Russell Close. In contrast to Lynne's reserve and distance, her husband Mick is a garrulous and sociable person. Mick and Brian were discussing their respective jobs at length that Saturday morning, while Lynne stayed mainly on the sidelines of the conversation, occasionally smiling or frowning at what Mick was saying but choosing largely to be occupied with the children, or helping Mary in the kitchen. Brian mentioned his difficulties to Mick over finding a decent typist.

"Problem solved, Bri. Your Lynne'll type it up foh yeh. Won't yeh Lynne?"

Lynne looked startled, then annoyed, then hesitant.

"An ah'll thank you, Mick Cribb, not teh go volunteerin my services wi'out askin me first. Gu on then. All right. Ah'll type it up for yeh, if yeh like. But don't forget – ah've not done any typing for years."

Brian never looked back. Lynne typed the thesis, inbetween housework and childcare: on time and with barely an error. Moreover, she spotted errors in Brian's draft and amended them. More surprising still, she followed the gist of the dull academic thesis and told Brian how she had enjoyed reading a section concerning child literacy case studies. As Mick was not slow to point out, Lynne could have been a real asset in a university department clerical-administrative team. But for her own reasons, she did not pursue a career while her two children were growing up, or after.

There may well be an element of lack of confidence, or just shyness, in Lynne's makeup but as Malcolm found out at the Boxing Day party, there is also an underlying strong personality, more than capable of asserting herself when necessary. All of those closest to Lynne have persistently over the years nagged her to stop smoking – a habit she started around the age of fifteen. To date she has resisted and ignored the attempts from others to make her end the habit. Except when she is really pushed and roused to anger, her style is not to loudly argue her corner, but to stick to what she wants to do: quietly but immovably.

On the whole it is domineering, extrovert, aspiring personalities who seem to lead things in human affairs. Quiet introverts such as Lynne are often pushed into a corner and ignored. But if you take time to observe them, the quiet introverts are sometimes more interesting than loud extroverts. As Lynne grew older and became a mother and a grandmother, when he could, Brian observed her in family gatherings in Mary's crowded kitchens and living rooms at Russell Close and Centenary Way. He noticed how, when she is enjoying the family banter, Lynne is very like Barry, sitting or standing in her own space, inside the company she is among. She does not throw herself into the centre of things but stays on the edge. Sometimes she is entirely herself: a person with no need to be like anyone else. When she is not interested, or is unhappy with the people she is with, she has a capacity to withdraw into herself. There is a kind of immovable unspoken barrier there when she is in this mood. She can block people out, completely ignore them, and they know not to intrude. It could be seen as great rudeness but you can also see it as a great strength: to be able to quietly withdraw into yourself, in a human world where there is so often too much pointless noise and babble.

When her two children grew into their teens, Lynne took a job as a classroom assistant at a difficult, socially deprived primary school in the middle of a run-down drugs-ridden housing estate, a mile or so from her middle-class home in Gomersal. Her role was to support teachers in their dealings with the many difficult children in the school. She worked at this taxing and badly paid job for several years with real commitment. She clearly derived satisfaction and reward from her work and, like most of the people (overwhelmingly women) who do this sort of job, she willingly undertook extra work above and beyond the terms of her contract. Lynne had been doing the classroom-assistant job for some time before a new headteacher was appointed at the school. The old headmaster was sensitive in his relations with non-teaching assistants and flexible in the demands made of them. Lynne liked his approach and it was partly because she liked his working methods that she willingly did extra unpaid hours. The new headteacher was determined to be a new broom but in her zeal for success she seriously misjudged Lynne's character. She took the quietly spoken Lynne to be someone too timid to say "no" to her unreasonable demands for extra hours of work, demands well outside Lynne's job description. The new head expected Lynne to begin her working day an hour earlier than usual, as her first Open Day approached. She wanted everything ready and up to the stringent standards she had set herself. Lynne was already quietly irritated by the new head's lack of management and inter-personal skills in dealing with her staff.

"I'm sorry, Mrs X. I can't come in for that extra unpaid hour on Monday. I'm looking after my gran'son Callum that morning."

"I said I want you here by eight on Monday, Lynne. And that's EXACTLY when I expect you to arrive."

"Well, in that case. You know what you can do with your job, Mrs X. I'm off. And I won't be coming back."

Richard has a tendency to storm out of job situations he does not like. Probably a red mist of anger and emotion comes down on him and he is swallowed by it. He might regret his impulsiveness later. Lynne did not storm out of her job; she walked out of it on a point of principle, the principle being that she would not be bullied by her boss. It was the Boxing Day Party situation all over again, when she stood up for herself and refused to be bullied. There is something of John and Pat in what Lynne did, when they stood up to a government and Prime Minister who deliberately picked out a group of workers to prove and assert her will and power, which she disingenuously called her "mandate." There was something of Bob in Lynne as well: remember the fourteen-year-old boy who started work in the year the British Establishment bullied its workers into submission in the General Strike: remember the man who put the funeral of his dead baby daughter before army discipline in 1942.

Lynne is now in her fifties with two grown up children, and grandchildren, to whom she devotes much of her time, including weekends. She is still that quiet reserved person with a strong underlying personality and will; a person who resists being bullied or demeaned. She is still a smoker who seems to ignore the dismay of her spouse and children over her habit and who now does part-time cleaning jobs, possibly to pay for cigarettes. A smile comes to her face when she talks to Mary of her summer holiday plans. For nearly thirty years, Stephen and Maggie, Lynne and Mick, and children, took holidays in France together every August. In the early days, they travelled by coach from Yorkshire down to camp sites in Provence, Aquitaine, or Brittany. Over recent years, now the children have grown up and lead their own lives, the four parents have moved upmarket and purchased a static caravan home, situated on a site very near the Pyrenees and the Spanish border. It is a great escape for all of them every summer.

Picture the scene. Stephen, Lynne, Maggie and Mick are enjoying a warm summer evening, stretching into night, over a barbeque meal and bottles of wine, on the patio garden of their holiday home in France. Mick and Maggie make most noise but in the background Stephen quietly but determinedly eggs them on, keeping the pleasure in the company going. Lynne for the most part listens, just happy to be there with the other three. She is laughing mostly or reacting, quietly indignant, to Mick's and Stephen's teasing and Maggie's feisty redhead's responses. But occasionally this quiet smiling woman bursts into words and noise; this slow fuse fizzes into explosion and the others stop what they are doing and saying and listen and stare, amazed, before they pick up the pieces and resume their usual roles. And later, when the four of them gather at New Year at Stephen's and Maggie's house, and reminisce over last summer, and look forward to next, it is Lynne's rare explosions they remember best. Lynne came as a surprise after a long line of seven boys. She keeps her capacity to surprise.

Lynne at Russell Close, 1980s

MICHAEL

Funny manifestations occurred in the house at Chapel Fold, when David was ten and Brian eleven. A second-hand royal blue Silver Cross pram appeared in a space especially cleared under the front hall stairs. A baby's cot arrived in Mam's and Dad's bedroom one day. A pile of white nappies on a chair. Baby's clothes in a drawer. A conference was convened on the front path steps.

"Oo d'yer think new pram's feh, then? An thah cot? An them nappies? Is Sheila avin another baby?"

"Down't be seh daft. Coo-erse not. Shi's on'y just ad Ower Christerpha, an yeh can't ave anuther baby till after anuther year's gone."

"Oo sez? Ow d'you know?"

"Ower Moira sez. See, stupid."

"Well, sumdy's gooin ter ave a baby. Oo is it?"

"Yeh don't think – yeh don't think – it could be: MI MAM?"

"MI MAM? Not mi mam. Shi's too owd!"

They became spies in their own house, hiding behind doors to rooms where the older-end were talking, hoping to pick up clues.

"David! Listen! Ah'm gunner tell yeh summat. Bur it's a secret, an yeh've got teh swear yeh wee-ern't tell nubdy."

"Ah promise. Ah promise. Tell me."

"Well. Yeh know babies?"

"Mmm. Ye–er?"

"Well, thi grow in wimmins bellys, afoor thi geh born."

"Urgh. NO! No, Bri! Thi dooo-ern't, thi DOO-ERN'T!"

"Onist. Ah'm not kiddin. Ower Moira towd mi. Listen. If mi Mam's avin another baby, all wi'v gorra do is: see if er belly gehs bigger."

"Oo, NOO! NOO! Well. Oreet then."

Every day they surreptitiously monitored Mary's belly, trying to assess if it was swelling or staying the same. They did this for several days, a lifetime then, but thought they saw no change. A few days into their top secret survey, they were standing in the hall scrutinising Mary's belly through a crack in the partly-open front room door, watching her folding some nappies and stacking them on a chair. They were whispering: assessing Mary's shape. Moira put them in the picture when she sneaked up behind and heard their whispered speculations.

"Shhh! Come on David. Brian. Come in teh back room, wi me. Listen teh me. Yes. Yer right. Mi Mam's avin another baby. Orrite? So just stop messin about, an accept it."

Michael was born in July 1958, already an uncle to Barry's two children. Mary was forty three and Bob forty six. Nowadays the media regularly present features aimed at middle class professional women expecting a first child in their forties. It was not so among most working class women in the North of England in 1958. Most of Mary's and Bob's contemporaries married young, had children in their twenties and became "old grandparents" in their forties. Mary thought Lynne was the last of her childen and you could have knocked her down with a feather when her body first signalled Michael's arrival inside. But pragmatic as ever, she accepted she was "expecting" for the thirteenth time and rolled up her sleeves. Mary was fifty three when Michael was ten, and sixty three when he reached twenty, but she got on with the job of being his mother as vigorously as she did with her first twelve children. And true to form – at least with the children who were born after the war – Bob left Mary to it.

Mary was already child-minding Linda and Christopher when Michael was born, so that Sheila could pursue her career in the Batley law firm. Shirley's two oldest children, Julie and Linda, came not long after Michael, and Mary also took care of them when called upon. In effect, Michael was as much a part of the next generation of the family as well as being the last of Bob's and Mary's children. In his early years Michael was just one of the five little ones Mary regularly looked after, the only difference between them being: he lived at Chapel Fold permanently, while the others came and went.

Richard, Stephen and Lynne were still close enough in age to Michael and the oldest nephew and nieces to feel left out, but jealousy and resentment were not major problems among the younger-end – although Lynne was distinctly cool toward Barry's Linda throughout their growing years. Linda inherited Sheila's outgoingness and vivacity, in contrast to Lynne's quiet reserve. By the time Michael was born, the older-end were already adults with lives of their own and the middle-uns were nearing adulthood. After everyone recovered from the surprise of Mary's final pregnancy, Michael was accepted as yet another addition to the ever-extending family.

Brian and David were used to younger siblings being around and they took pleasure in playing with Michael and caring for him when called to do so. A typical day at this time might go like this. Brian is in the back room at Chapel Fold, pleased to have bagged one of the two easy chairs. He is reading a Just William book or playing with a Dinky car on the arm of the chair. In his head he is a character in the book, or he is driving the car on a fast mountain road, somewhere a long way from Batley. Mary is baking, washing, cleaning, preparing baby bottles in the scullery. Michael whimpers in his pram in the corner and Mary picks him up and plonks him on Brian's knee, ignoring his book or Dinky car.

"Here y'are Brian, luv. Look after Michael fer a minute while ah see teh these buns in tuven ..."

Or:

"Brian, luv. Gi Michael is bottle whilst ah finish this washin..."

Or:

"Brian, owd cock. Play wi Michael till ah've done these chips ..."

Brian regarded Michael with wonder, affection and interest. There was none of the interfering rivalry and jealousy which constantly exists between siblings close in age. He loved playing with Michael: pulling funny faces; counting "one, two, three;" bouncing him on his lap before saying "plop"; playing peek-a-boo. And he delighted in Michael's delight in these simple games. He loved having him plonked on his knee and giving him feed and watching his face and gestures as he held the bottle to his mouth, observing his varied suckling noises. He was absorbed in, and fascinated by, this small human being. Those times of looking-after-or-playing-with-Michael were moments of great pleasure for Brian; moments of peace and security. They were time-out, from the stresses and strains of being in the middle of a large family; time-out from anxiety about Bob being in a funny mood, or John deciding to torment him, or Malcolm looking down his nose, or Richard being a pain in the neck, or himself nagging Mary for some spend to buy some sherbets, and feeling guilty about nagging. Michael was born with golden gingery hair, resuming the colouring that was last seen in John, with six bairns inbetween who were either dark or blond. In contrast to the blue eyes of his four older red-haired siblings, Michael's eyes are dark brown, almost black. It is the golden hair, vivid dark eyes and huge life-loving grin that Brian recalls most of Michael as a small child.

Throughout his childhood and adolescence, Brian was fascinated, obsessed, with cars. Cars were not so numerous then as they are now in Britain. In the Hirst family, only Ower Barry had a car and at Chapel Fold, in the late-1950s, only a handful of neighbours owned cars. At Batley High, half a dozen teachers out of forty or so, were car owners. Mr. Parkin, the Deputy Head, who lived in the posh private housing estate near Chapel Fold, had a huge sage green Vauxhall, with acres of chrome. The Vauxhall used to glide down Chapel Fold sometimes, making a wonderful swishing sound as Brian sat watching from the front steps. The only cars Brian ever rode in were Barry's first ancient Austin Seven – and once, kindly Mr. Margetts, a teacher at Healey Boys, rescued him from a hailstorm and gave him a lift home in his neat Hillman van. Those rare car rides were moments of exquisite pleasure. Brian loved the sound of cars and could recognise most makes and models from their engine noises, well before they came in sight. He loved the bump and roll of the rides in Barry's and Mr Margetts' cars, and he savoured every detail of the interiors.

Even in the 1960s, a car ride was still a rare thrill. Sometime during 1965, he marvelled over how quickly and quietly the Austin Cambridge of a new drama teacher at Batley High swept up Clerk Green Hill when the teacher gave him a lift back to Staincliffe after a year thirteen evening theatre trip to the Bradford Alhambra. *The Winter's Tale* production that night disappeared from his memory quite soon, but the luxury of the car's interior and the purring whir of its engine made a lasting impression. When Brian was not lucky enough to be riding in a car, which was most of the time, he was imagining owning one, playing with Dinky cars on the floor or on chair arms. And when he grew too old for toy cars, he spent hours sitting on the front garden wall, or standing at bus stops, imagining he was the owner and driver of the car passing by.

In Brian's mind Michael's Silver Cross pram was a Rolls Royce or a Jaguar (no Mercedes or BMWs then, in Yorkshire) and when it gently bobbed and swayed on its springs, in his imagination, he was not pushing a pram but driving a beautiful limousine over perfect roads in a glorious Pennine landscape. Enjoyable as it was, driving the Silver Cross was difficult in that first year of Michael's life. Brian could barely see over the top of the hood, so his driving was akin to those little old men and women you sometimes see inside powerful cars – with their heads, from their noses up, just visible above the steering wheel. He struggled with the steering at times; the heavy pram had a tendency to veer to one side; the brake was stiff and did not always respond to the pressure of his hand. There were other difficulties too, the main one being the strict limits Mary set on his driving.

"Or reight then, Brian. Yeh can tek Michael fer a pram ride. But yow just think on! Bi back in ten minutes. Down't gu further'n bunglows crescent – and DOOERN'T RUN! WALK!"

Driving became much more exciting and thrilling when Michael graduated from the Silver Cross to a racy little maroon Tansad, a Tansad being the 1960s equivalent of today's baby-buggy. It helped that Brian could easily see over the top. And he was older, stronger, and able to drive it with ease. The Tansad had a good effective brake when it was new and Mary was more trusting of his good sense and driving ability by then and she imposed fewer restrictions. During the Tansad years, being sent on an errand was not a chore.

"Brian, owd cock. Slip onter teh Co-op, an geh mi two ounces er best boiled am, foh yeh Dad's tea. An doo-ern't ferget teh tell em it's foh Miss-is Erst – An gi em divi number – 10-11-2. An tek Ower Michael wi yer. It'll do im gud teh geh sum fresh air."

At the mention of taking Michael out, Brian happily stopped whatever he was doing and Michael himself, no matter how many times it happened, treated every trip as if it were Christmas. His mouth stretched in a huge grin and he wriggled in anticipation of the thrill that was to come, as Mary wrapped him in his outdoor coat and strapped him in the Tansad. The drive began at a decorous slow pace down the front path and steps and along the first twenty yards of Chapel Fold, where you could be seen from the front windows of number 77. Brian made ear-splitting screeching noises as the brakes were applied for the tricky manoeuvre of driving down the front path steps. He purred along, the engine revs steady and gentle, for those first few yards. Michael hunched up his shoulders and clasped his hands, enjoying his grandstand view of the road ahead, his ear-splitting grin becoming ever wider. As soon as they crossed the spot where they could no longer be seen from the house, the engine roared into an explosion of energy and speed and Brian raced nail-bitingly through the gears, the Tansad squealing on two wheels as it roared round the bungalow crescent, rocking from side to side, gliding over cracks and causa edges. There were no speed cameras then but just after Frank Wilson's house, an avenue veered off to the right and opposite were two "coppers'" houses, so Brian prudently reduced the speed to a sedate purr till they reached the Co-op, on Halifax Road.

After a couple of years of heavy use, the Tansad was in a sorry state. The maroon paint was scratched to buggery; the tyres were worn to nothing; the wheels were inclined to come off when not wobbling dangerously; the hood was broken, its wire frame poking out through the worn material; the brake no longer worked. Michael was an agile walker by this time and growing out of needing wheels. But one day during the summer holiday when Michael turned three, before the Tansad was finally discarded, Brian, David and Michael enjoyed a last glorious drive. It was one of those days when Mary was overwhelmed with work, and children, filling the house and garden. Grateful to be temporarily rid of three of the bairns, she gave in to Brian's and David's pleas to be allowed to take Michael for a long afternoon Tansad drive, down to the new Hyrstlands Park, where David had nearly disappeared under the mud just a year or two earlier.

Michael was thrilled to be out on a drive. He was starting to speak a few words by then but he was usually silent. Brian was in a valedictory mood. He knew on a conscious level it was going to be one of the last of the Tansad drives. On a deeper level he knew things were changing. Michael was walking and talking; David and he were growing; soon the carefree Tansad drives would end. He decided to go further than Hyrstlands and easily talked David into going up Howley Moor instead. Howley Moor was a good deal further away from Chapel Fold than Hyrstlands Park. They had been before when they were younger, when Moira had taken them on walks there, giving dark warning of dangers in strange places. And they went there once with Bob and Mary, and all the younger-end, for a summer picnic. It was a lovely, arduous walk. From Chapel Fold you headed down Clerk Green Hill, with the field on the right where shaggy ponies grazed, then past Cemetery Road, the Parish Church and the Fleece Inn – which everybody called the "Church Steps." Then there was the long climb up Field Hill past the drive to Batley High and down again briefly, past the posh houses behind the school, before another climb through Upper Batley until eventually, on the hill that climbed further up the Pennines to Morley, a path led off to the left, through Briar Wood, to Howley Moor.

The views from the high moor were fabulous. You could see all the outskirts of Batley and the settlements around. The buildings seemed carelessly scattered across the hills but when you looked closely, you could discern patterns of streets and junctions. The centre of Batley was hidden in its deep valley and on the far high western horizon were the higher Pennines and somewhere, just out of sight beyond, lay Oldham and the eastern outskirts of Manchester. You felt insignificant and tiny there. It made you aware of the small space you occupied on this huge rolling earth and how infinitesimal Batley was in the world. Being there on the high moor filled Brian with excitement. He was normally a cautious, timid lad, but up there on Howley Moor his customary caution and timidity disappeared on the wind.

In reality the moor was a small remnant of what it had been before the industrialisation and urbanisation of West Yorkshire, but the moorland that remained that day was empty, high and blowy. It seemed vast to Brian. Sandy footpaths and animal tracks criss-crossed the moor, each path like: a racing track! He could not resist. He pressed the accelerator down hard, revving and rocking the Tansad into juddering vibrations, before launching into the race. David added to the revving sounds and Michael grinned, clutching the Tansad sides, anticipating a thrilling ride. They roared off from the startline, accelerating and accelerating, faster and faster, racing over sandy paths and bumpy hillocks. Michael adored it but he made no sound; his grin just grew bigger and bigger, threatening to split his face apart.

It ended in a crash. It was Brian's error. He thought they could soar over another hillock and give all of them, especially Michael, that sickeningly wonderful stomach-lurching sensation you get in a car when you crest a hill fast and then descend over the other side. But they crashed instead. The Tansad rolled over, with Michael underneath, while David and Brian fell in a heap nearby. They picked themselves up and turned Michael and Tansad upright. Michael's knee was grazed and he was shaky, but with a little clowning from David and cajoling from Brian, he cheered up and was soon ready for the next surprise. The Tansad looked a sorrier mess than when they started. The crash calmed them down and they started the long drive home, excuses at the ready in the face of Mary's inevitable wrath when she saw the damage done to Tansad and youngest child.

It is a hot summer's day at Chapel Fold in 1963, when Michael is five. He is playing on his own in the garden, making a pile of toy bricks, concentrating on them not falling down. The back door and all the windows are open, bringing some breeze into the stuffy rooms. Malcolm is tinkering with his bike near the outhouse with David watching. Brian is reading in the back room. Mary is there knitting, her lips counting out the stitches, just as her lips mouth out the words when she is avid in one of her love books. Michael talks to himself as he plays with the toy bricks. Suddenly his construction falls down in a heap:

"Aw, FUCKIN ell! Look whah yeh've gon an dun!"

It is Ower Michael saying these words. In Ower Back Garden. Brian puts down his book, not believing what he has heard. Mary drops her knitting, her mouth wide open in shock, speechless for some seconds. David, Malcolm and Brian exchange secret grins, waiting for an explosion from Mam. She goes outside to Michael and speaks to him: quietly: dangerously:

"*What* did I ere you jus say, yung man? An down't yow look't me like that, wi yeh big black innocent eyes! You listen teh me! Doo-ern't you EVER, EVER seh that nasty word agen."

Then it is all over. A landmark in Hirst family history. In history really. The F-word being said out loud by one of the children – outside, in the garden, where the neighbours might hear. How language use among everyone, and not just council estate fowk, has changed since then.

A couple of years later. The summer term of 1966. It is near the end of Brian's first year as a student at Bingley

College of Education. Michael is nearly eight and Mary has brought him and Christopher to college for the day. It is as big an adventure for Mary as it is for the two boys, catching all those buses to travel the twenty or so miles from Batley to Bingley and then the long walk up the steep hill to the campus from the High Street in the valley below. Brian is young and callow, cruel and cold, socially confused. He wants Mary and the boys to enjoy the treat but does not want to introduce them to any but a few trusted friends, for complex reasons which he has not fully faced. It is a Sunday and the halls of residence are virtually deserted, which suits him: it keeps his visitors to himself and it also means there is plenty of food available from the basement kitchen, as the college caterers have not grasped the fact that halls are deserted by most students on Sundays. The basement kitchen table is groaning with buffet-style Sunday tea for a full hall of students but the hall is almost empty.

Mary and Brian spend the first two hours of her visit chatting in his room, while Michael and Christopher run riot along the long basement corridor which interconnects the five halls of residence. Michael has hardly changed since Tansad days. His big brown eyes are full of fun and adventure. He loves being with Christopher. They are best friends. His grin is as constant and huge as ever. Mary enjoys the chance to put her feet up from her usual Sunday chores and marvels at the food when they go down to collect it from the basement kitchen, nervous about whether she and the boys should really be eating it. Michael and Christopher behave just as young lads are supposed to. They want to eat everything, especially the synthetic cream buns and they want to continue charging up and down the empty, echoing corridor as they eat.

Mary tells Brian how Michael is doing at school. She says he is, "As daft as a brush and no scholar," but the love and affection between her and her late child is transparent.

She is more relaxed, more tolerant, more demonstrably affectionate with him than she was with the middle-uns when they were his age. Brian shares Mary's affection for Michael. He is not an introspective indoors child. He has huge energy and loves "lakin aht." He loves running, jumping, climbing. When he is dragged indoors to join his elders, he gives back in full measure the affection he receives from them. He still likes being hugged; sitting on your knee; being fussed over. He chats away happily when an adult demands his attention before he runs off to his next game.

Not long after Mary's day out at Bingley, three of Brian's college friends became fascinated in church brass rubbings. Brian was interested in them too – mainly as decoration for his college room walls. The three friends scoured churches around West Yorkshire and the Dales, seeking decent brasses. They did serious research and discovered that St. Peter's Batley Parish Church, where Mary and Bob were wed, had especially good brasses. Brian wanted to separate his family from college but his friends persuaded him to join them at the Parish Church and because they were so close to Chapel Fold, he felt compelled to invite them for tea there, after making the brass rubbings. When Brian and his college friends arrived, it was the usual scene at Chapel Fold: children everywhere: Bob on his own in the front room: Mary doing ten thousand jobs at once. Richard, Stephen and Lynne were in their early teens and kept their distance, not sure how to respond to the three strangers (four, if you count Brian) with their weird accents and talk, ranging from broad and garrulous Black Country, to middle class, reserved, Kent. Michael, on the other hand, boldly came forth, turning on his huge smile, expecting attention. Within seconds he charmed the three friends and took turns in sitting on each of their knees, enjoying the fuss. Years later at a college re-unioin, the friends remembered Michael – and Mary's "tea" that day: fried egg, ham, tomato, mountainous slices of white bread to soak up the juices, and milky sweet tea, in cracked white pots.

Michael was the last of six brothers to attend Batley High. His nephew Christopher was in the same year as him. Christopher went on to take O and A Levels and progressed to a teacher training college in Northumberland. Michael struggled with academic lessons but was quick and able in practical subjects and PE. He remained in what were then called "remedial" classes until he left school after five years, with CSEs in Woodwork and Metalwork. The other one of Mary's twelve children who struggled with learning was John. But schools had changed since John's days at Healey Secondary Modern. Batley High held Parent Evenings where children's progress was discussed in an open way. Mary scrupulously attended these events for all six of her Batley High boys. She must have been a familiar figure to the many staff who taught at the school throughout the sixteen year period during which her six youngest lads passed through the school. In his early years at the school, the teachers were bothered by Michael's low ability and poor concentration, especially those who knew his five able, and varyingly conscientious, older brothers. The teachers' worry made Mary worry too. A few years earlier she was not so bothered by John's poor performance at school because in his day life was pre-destined for working class boys who did not take to school: "Thi went dahn pit, inter mill, or onter dole." Or, if they turned-out bad, they went "inside." But by the 1970s, Mary was seeing how a school like Batley High could provide something more than pre-destination for her children. She nagged, cajoled and nattered Michael to do better. In return, she received little more than his charming sheepish grin. By the time he reached his last two years at the school, the teachers and Mary had given up on the idea of Michael being a "scholar" and instead they talked about how charming, friendly and likeable he was, hoping his appealing personality would get him on in the world.

Michael left school aged just sixteen in July 1975. The minimum school leaving age had only recently been raised. It was not until then that *all* children, in one of the world's first great "democracies," became entitled to a minimum five years of secondary education. Michael's first job was as a trainee painter and decorater, in a business based in Cleckheaton. He loved the work and after a year with the Cleckheaton firm, he moved jobs and began working in George Harwood's painting and decorating firm in Batley, Goerge being Barry's best mate, since their days at Batley Grammar. Everything went well until he reached the age of seventeen, when something awful happened: he was sentenced to serve time in a Young Offenders Centre for the alleged crime of assaulting a police officer. Everyone in the family was shocked to the core. How had naïve, happy-go-lucky, charming Michael ended up in this situation? It upset the family even more than what had happened to Barry, a few years earlier.

It is a fairly ordinary story really. A thoughtless callow youth goes to Sheffield, on a football match outing with his mates. He drinks too much and starts showing off, and after the match, he allegedly takes a swing at a policeman, caught-up in a street melee, trying to impose order. The essentially harmless youth is arrested, put before magistrates and banged up inside for being a menace to society and civilisation. It is the sort of story you might read every day in your local newspaper. If you are of a liberal frame of mind, you might shake your head in disapproval at the punishment meted out and at the narrow retributive midset of those who imposed the sentence. You might spend a minute or two thinking how a community service order, or making the youth face the victim of his mindless violence, would be both cheaper for the tax payer and possibly lead to reform. Then you might forget it and read about something else. If you are of a less liberal temperament, you might wish for the return of the birch, to really sort the problem of savage youth out. But you feel better that at least this particular vile monster ("Ower Michael") has been incarcerated and kept apart from decent fowk, like you.

It is different, of course, when the youth happens to be a much-loved younger brother; a middle-aged mother's adored youngest bairn. Brian spent the weeks of Michael's incarceration worrying and fretting over what the experience would do to him and raging inside at the people who had done this mindless brutal thing to him, remembering other slights from "betters" that the Hirst family suffered, such as Barry's Open Prison sentence – and those awful people in the New Brighton boarding house, all those years earlier. It did not help that he had recently read Ray Minton's stark novel *Scum,* set in a Young Offenders Institute, at the same time as Michael was banged up in one. When his day's teaching and evening marking and preparation were over, the thought of Michael banged-up haunted Brian, long into the night and the early hours. He was enraged to think how casually cruel, thoughtless and random life is, more for some than others, including his younger brother. It was devastating for Mary but she responded in her usual way when one of her young was in trouble. She succumbed to initial visceral distress at the awfulness of what had happened to Michael, but the distress was quickly supplanted by a stoicism found from deep within, a determination to see it through, and after, to mend and nurture her child.

And Michael? Did imprisonment do him harm? Good? He once spoke briefly to Brian about that time, when he was in his early fifties. He seemed to remember the affair philosophically, with none of the anger, bitterness or anguish that Brian felt about it, at the time.

"Well, actually, the wah two on us goh dun. Me an mi mate. An it wah mi mate oo it copper, not me. Wi bowth goh five weeks. An, the tell yeh truth, ah think it did mi a load a good. Med mi think. An ah've never forgottn them lessons norther."

Michael had just begun his first serious relationship before the being sent away, and to Mary's delight and approval, his girl friend Sandra supported him unstintingly, accompanying Mary, or travelling to the prison alone, on every visiting day of his incarceration. When he came out, Michael resumed work at George Harwood's firm, in the painting and decorating trade and a year or so later, not long after his nineteenth birthday, he married Sandra, only months after Stephen's and Lynne's marriages. Sandra was the youngest of six children. She had four surviving brothers. Her older sister and parents all died during her teenage years. Three years after Michael and Sandra married they had a daughter, Michele. But by the time Michele was an infant, the marriage came to an end. Mary had warmed to Sandra and was deeply sorry when she knew the marriage was ending. Sandra was at the time a vivacious, fun-loving person who often behaved as if there were no tomorrow. Perhaps it was to do with losing her parents and sister at an early age: live while you can, you may be gone tomorrow, might have been her motto.

Not long after Michael had completed his first five years of training in painting and decorating, some time in his early-twenties, he set up his own one-man business. He was adept at his work and was soon in great demand around Batley. Not long after he started his own business, Michael met an interior designer from Harrogate who introduced him to a number of wealthy clients, and after that he was in demand with posh fowk as well as Batley fowk, and never short of work. One of Michael's pals at Batley High, nicknamed "Arty," after his surname, Hart, eventually became "posh fowk." Arty worked on technical support at rock concerts, for some of the world's leading stars, and made a great deal of money. Michael has worked, on and off, over many years, on the various substantial properties Arty has owned: in Suffolk, London and the Yorkshire Dales. Norman Tebbit would no doubt extol Michael's and Arty's virtues. They both had humble origins and troubles in their teens, but they "got on their bikes" and became self-made entrepreneurs, earning good money. Michael found himself in a scrape as a young man, a scrape which might have had disastrous consequences on his future life. But he learned some lessons about life and picked himself up. And by dint of sheer hard physical work, considerable talent, skill and charm, he became a successful self-employed decorator, often working for the very rich, including once working on a chateau near Bergerac for a City asset-stripper whose own assets came to £300m.

Several years after his divorce from Sandra, Michael re-married. His second wife Sue was a steady, career-minded person. Like Michael, she made a mistake early in life which she subsequently worked hard to overcome. At seventeen, she became pregnant and had a daughter, roughly the same age as Michele. Sue was a more academic person than Michael. She went to the Catholic girls grammar school at Tong, where Shirley's two daughters, Julie and Linda, were her contemporaries. Sue raised her daughter as a single mother and at the same time established herself in a successful career as an administrator with a national charity for the aged: another self-made successful person of whom Tebbit would be proud. During the years they were married, Michael supported Sue in gaining a Leeds University diploma, which led to her move to a senior administrative post in work for the aged.

Michele lived with Sandra after the divorce, but throughout all the years of working far away from Batley, Michael maintained close contact with his daughter. His relationship with Michele is intense, close, sometimes explosive. At sixteen, Michele took a joy-ride with friends, which ended in a crash. One of the friends was killed and Michele had multiple injuries. Several weeks after the crash, Brian met Michael one Sunday for a lunchtime drink at the Nash. His marriage to Sue was breaking down and coming to an end, and Michele was a patient in Leeds General Infirmary, miraculously being re-constructed by a brilliant surgical team. He was working at the time on the house of a wealthy Harrogate client which was being used as a film set depicting the house of a family of lottery winners, in a popular ITV series. Earlier in the week, he had fallen from a ladder onto an iron garden fence at the big house in Harrogate and seriously damaged his ankle. The huge grin of the younger Michael was just a trace behind his rueful smile as he told Brian how the client was insisting he should be on site to supervise the last-minute touches to the decorating project on his film-set house. The client was sending a driver in his own personal Mercedes on the following day to transport him to the house at Harrogate, where he was to supervise the completion of the job from the back seat of the Merc. It was ridiculous. It could easily have been incorporated as a scene in the TV series.

Michael bounced back again just a few years ago after two divorces and the trauma of Michele's injuries, and all those anxious hours spent in hospital, while she was being re-built by the superb surgical team at St James's Hospital in Leeds. It was Mary, of course, who told Brian the news, during a phone call. In her eighties, Mary was still as close, intimate and affectionate with Michael (when he let her), as she was in her fifties, when she came to Bingley that day.

"Did yeh knaw Ower Michael's gor issen anuther wuman? Oo, aye. Donna. Shi seems a luvli lass. Shi's sixteen years yunger'n im. But shi's frum Ba'ley. Shi lives up Sut'ill."

"Oh, well that's all right then, if she's from Soothill! Well, I'd better go."

" Ave yeh ad yeh tea yet?"

"No, not yet."

"What're y'avin'?"

"Oh, just some sausage, potato and steamed celery."

"Mmm. Steamed celery. That sounds nice. Thi ad a weekend in Filey, yeh knaw, lookin at ouses. Thiv seen wun in Brid thi like …"

Now nearing his fiftieth birthday, Michael lives in Bridlington with his partner Donna and their two children, Scarlett and Otis. He still has his one-man painting and decorating business. Occasionally he sub-contracts workers, to help with bigger jobs, but essentially he has scaled down his working patterns. He is happy being a father again and chooses customers from his local area when possible, to avoid travelling and being away from his new family. He is determined to enjoy family life and experience fatherhood fully, which he feels he missed during his two marriages. Michele is now in her twenties and adores her younger half-brother and sister and she has learned to drive – a psychologically huge move on her part – which enables her to travel to Bridlington from her home in Birstall, to spend a weekend spoiling her younger half-sister and half-brother.

Michael must have endured a difficult time during his spell in a Young Offenders Prison, where he met and mixed with young men and boys who were already hardened criminals, some of them perhaps destined to criminality for life. Brian once encountered one of the young men Michael knew during his time "inside." It was at the Nash. A Sunday dinnertime and John, Brian and Michael were enjoying a quiet drink or two, laughing over Mary's lifelong habit of running through several of her lads' names, before reaching the right one:

"Barry, er Bob, em John, er Malcolm. Oo, bluddy ell, ah mean BRIAN! Will yeh just ave a look fer Ower Richard's, Stephen's – oo, ell – Ower MICHAEL'S dummy? Ah think e's thrown it down sumweer, an ah down't want im yellin is ed off fer it..."

The conversation was interrupted by the young man, approaching from the bar. He was seriously drunk and wildly unsteady on his feet but somehow he manged to blunder his way to the table where the Hirst brothers were sitting.

"Ey up, yung Esti. Yeh li-el fucker. Ah thowt it wha thee wen ah wor ovver theer et fuckin bar. Ah've not fuckin seen thee sin – yer naw – wen wi wha bowth -. Whah's tha be-ern dooin wi thi fuckin sen sin then, eh?..."

The young man continued talking for several minutes more, in the same vein, the expletives gradually outnumbering everything else. John supped his lager steadily, and puffed on his Golden Virginia roll-up, and stared silently, inscrutably, at a point somewhere up on the ceiling. Brian surreptitiously examined Michael's former co-inmate; he had wild dangerous eyes and a pent-up inner violence hovered around him. Listening to his colourful history, it seemed he had spent much of his life in prison since Michael knew him, thirty years in his past. He reeled off the names of the places he had been banged-up in, like a champion listing his trophies. Brian could see Michael was discomfited by the young man's presence at the Nash. He smiled stiffly at him, and responded to him monosyllabically, when necessary: "Aye, owd lad," "Mmm, aye." "Yeh – ah do remember." His eyes looked trapped; as if he was locked in a place from which he wanted to escape.

Watching Michael's eyes, Brian thought of that famous opening sentence in *The Go-Between*: "The past is a foreign country: they do things differently there." He thought:

"That time in Michael's life has passed: he lives a different life now." He thought: "We all have a past that we tend to forget, if we can." He thought of his own past, and how things were done differently then, from now. But the people are the same. They continue to live and survive, the lucky ones, that is. He thought how he might write it all down, one day, before it passed forever: the story of his rag-oyle town family.

Michael with monkey, 1966?

Mary aged 90 with daughter Shirley, Grandaughter Linda, Great grandaughter Vicky and great great granson, Conor.

DIALOGUE

English spelling is not a phonetic system, when it comes to many words. You only have to think of "ough" words, such as "through," to get my meaning. Phonetically written, "through" is "throo." When it comes to the spelling of dialogue, especially the dialogue of characters speaking in a strong local accent, finding the right spelling can be tricky. The West Yorkshire accent is a good example of this. The definite article is almost always "silent" in West Yorkshire speech, when it comes before a word starting with a consonant. For example, "He walked up the road," in W.Yorks is, "He walked up road." Many writers of dialogue seem to worry that this won't make sense to the non-Yorkshire reader and so they insert a "t" followed by an omission apostrophe: "He walked up t'road." To my mind this is nonsense and moreover it distorts the speech – as many comedians have discovered when they want to portray the Yorkshire voice. So I have kept "the" silent, where it *is* silent, in actual Yorkshire speech.

When "the" comes before a vowel in W. Yorks, the "t" is said, but it slides into the following word; it isn't separate from it. For example, "She's gone with the others," is not said as, "She's gone with t'others," but instead it's said like this: "She's gone with tothers." So I've followed the sliding rule when it comes to "the," before vowel-starting words.

"She's gone with the others" is a good example of another problem that frequently comes up when writing W. Yorks speech on the page: when do you use the omission apostrophe? If you are over-anxious, the tendency is to include it rigidly and strictly: "She's gone wi' t'others." To my mind that is just fussy pedantry and so I have not used the possessive apostrophe in my written dialogue, except where the meaning is seriously lost without it. So my version goes: "She's gone wi tothers."

But actually, even written that way, it still sounds nothing like the West Yorkshire voice I've been hearing in my head while writing this book, especially the West Yorkshire of my childhood, in the 1950s-60s. In the inside-my-head W. Yorks, "She's gone with the others," actually sounds like this: "Shis goo-ern wi tuthers." In my head at least, this is as close as I can get to capturing the sound of the voice into written language. Have a go at reading it aloud to yourself. But remember: the "i" in "shis" and the "u" in "tuthers" are short and hard, not long and soft.

Another tricky problem involves words ending in sharp consonants when spoken in standard English accents. Words such as "was," "what," "for" "that." These could be written as "wa'" "wha'" "fo'" "tha'," to show the silent end-consonants in spoken W. Yorks. But again, they are rather "fussy" on the page. For example, "What was that for?" Becomes, "Whah' wa' tha' fo'." Ugh! Horrible! I much prefer: "Whah wah thah foh?" It's about the nearest I can get to the *actual* sound.

Another "rule" I've followed concerns words such as "your" and "to." They are said differently when they occur before consonants and vowels. For example: "Your dad is here," sounds like "Yeh dad's ere." But "Your uncle is here," sounds like, "Yer uncle's ere." In other words, "your" is "yeh" before a consonant, and "yer" before a vowel. It's the same with "to." It genereally sounds like "teh" before a consonant word, but "ter" before a vowel.

This is becoming another book. So, to cut a long story short: I've followed these basic rules:

1. All dialogue is written as phonetically as possible;

2. I've used omission apostrophes only where absolutely necessary;

3. I've followed the rules where a word sounds different, depending on the follow-on consonant or vowel word.

4. But the best rule of all is: say it out loud, or say it aloud in your head, as you read the dialogue. You'll soon "gerrit."

Dialect, and words which are now almost completely lost, are explained in the glossary.

GLOSSARY

aster – have you/has to
afoo-er – before
allus – always
aipney – half pence
as'll – I shall
ah's ta bahn – how are you?
atter – have to
bairn – child
bee-ern – been
brass – money
bahn – going
bahner – going to
claat – cloth
cowd – cold
cloo-ers/cloyes – clothes
coyle – coal
coyle-oyle – coal store
causa – pavement
coit – coat
dusta – do you
fowk – people
gorm – notice/heed
gerrart – get out
goo-ern – gone
gunner – going to

loo-erd – lured/load
lakin aht – playing outdoors
noo-en – not
neet – night
nubdi – nobody
oyle – hole
owme – home
owd – old
rag-oyle – shoddy mill
sen – self
slopin-off – sneaking away
summat – something
scullery – kitchen
snicket – alley
spanish – liquorice
soo-it – suit
sumweer – somewhere
sin – since
shartin – shouting
see-erm – seam/seem
sithee – listen/look
seh – say
sumdi – somebody
thee – you
thine – yours

thisssen – yourself

towd – told/the old

tha'll – you will

tha's – you are

thar – you

thy – your

tan – hit/beat

Woodie – Woodbine cigarette

wee-ern't – won't

weers – where is

AFTERWORD

First, a few words to my family. This book is entirely based on *my* memories and "memory" is a subjective thing. It's something that happens inside our minds, and the human mind is an individual thing. People remember things differently. People see things differently. And with the passing of time, we forget details, or we add details on – things that didn't happen at all. I had a choice when I finally got down to writing this family memoir. I could *either* tell you, my family, that I was writing this book, and check the details of my memories with you: Did it happen like this? Did it happen at all? *Or,* I could just rely on my own memories and admit there might be bits – maybe very large bits – which are "mis-remembered." They didn't happen as I've remembered them, or they didn't happen at all.

I chose in the end to rely on my own memory. One reason for this decision was the sheer logistics of consulting everyone included in this story – Mary, Sheila, Moira's three children, my seven brothers, two sisters – and others. I doubt if it would ever have been written if I'd gone down the "consulting" route. The second reason I chose to rely on my own memories was that I soon realised it was going to be "a story," rather just a straightforward factual memoir. In other words, I wanted to conjure up atmosphere, feelings, a *sense* of the places and people, not just give strict facts about them. So I'm not going to argue with anything you say did not happen at all, or did not happen as I have "remembered" it. And I am definitely not going to argue if you say I've got the speech wrong. After all, (very stupidly) I expended great energy in my younger life, trying to get rid of my "Batley-speak" and it's so long now since I spoke it myself, and heard it being spoken around me every day, that I probably *have* got it badly wrong. And besides, accents nowadays seem to be gradually merging. Even The Queen "talks common" now and "poor Batley fowk" talk a lot posher now than they used to – including you lot. But putting the weaknesses in my story to one side, I just hope you enjoy the story, and are touched by it as you read it, as I was when I wrote it. And that you realise, as I gradually did, that it's actually a tribute to *you,* my family – warts an' all!

A few words to my Mam. I have spent a lot of time over these last few years, while writing this story, asking you about things you remember from the past, without telling you I might be using what you told me, in this book. I'm a cynical "young" devil. I was frightened if I told you about the book, then you might "mis-remember" bits yourself – I had a feeling you wouldn't talk as naturally as you did, if I'd sat there writing it all down. So quite a lot of the pieces in the book, where it is your voice, remembering things, are virtually what you actually said. I wrote them down, as near as I could "remember" your very own words, as soon as I got back to Scarborough from Centenary Way. Sorry, owd lass!

To my friends and anyone else who might read this book: just a little about its progeny.

It all started on August 16th 2004 when I was "only" 57. My GP phoned me out of the blue to tell me a blood test I'd had for a bowel problem showed traces of something called "Chronic Lymphocytic Leukaemia." Of course, the only word that registered with me was that last one: "leukaemia." In other words, cancer – of the blood. At first, the doctors hoped it would be a "mild" leukaemia. Alas, that was not to be. It quickly developed into quite a nasty condition and a lot of the last six years of my life has been spent in chemotherapy treatment rooms, or in hospital beds, keeping my survival going. (The writing has kept me going too.)

When you get to the age of 57, and you're told your chances of survival are so-so, you realise you have a lot of "history" behind you. Some of it very personal and private. History you've never really spoken about or revealed before. Some of it quite special, quite different – like the story of my family. Some of it quite public, quite political, ideological – issues you care about, things you really believe in. Till gradually, you start thinking: "I've got all this history inside me that only me knows. And yes, all this private, personal stuff that's haunted me for years. I *must* write it down, before I die." So that's how my memoirs started.

At first, I was a bit lost about how to get going. Then I read Lorna Sage's memoir, "Bad Blood," which I mistakenly thought might tell of a childhood similar to mine. It didn't. The nearest she got to my background was the bit about "The Duckets" – the large, poor family living next to her Grandad's vicarage. Brilliant as the rest of "Bad Blood" is, the bit about the Duckets is full of the usual patronising, insulting tosh in "literary" English, when it comes to depicting large poor families. Professor Sage covers herself by presenting the depiction ironically, the Ducket family as seen by her small-minded grandmother, but that doesn't absolve her from my accusation. She says the Duckets made her "feel lonely," but other than that there is just a page of mean description, which isn't developed, but is just left hanging in the air: "(The Duckets) bred like rabbits and spilled out of their house wearing ragged hand-me-downs for all to see ... You could see Mrs Ducket with her hair in curlers running about barelegged in slippers ... Their kitchen drain disgorged a slow stream of soapy slime and tea leaves ..." And so on.

It was just the sort of stuff them fowk in the New Brighton B&B would have said. It infuriated me. But the fury inside me turned out to be a good thing: it launched me into writing what has eventually, over the last six years, become "Rag-Oyle Town Family." At first, I started a semi-angry, semi-nostalgic book, written in first person, but found I couldn't cope with this voice, when it came to remembering the bereavements – Glynne, Moira, Barry, Shirley's Jimmy and Bob – and so I switched to what is really this semi-first semi-third person voice – "Brian" – which helped me continue and finish the project. The private, personal stuff is in the next book – nearly finished – which covers the first eighteen years of my life. I want the last book, only just started and maybe never to be finished, to focus on politics, ideas, issues which have engaged me throughout my adult life. But that's a long way off yet ...

I think I actually finished the unedited bulk of Rag-Oyle Town Family three years ago. A lot can happen in three years. The worst thing that's happened in the family was the death of fifteen-year-old Thomas, my niece Michelle's son, (the grandson Moira never knew). Cystic fibrosis took him away, far too soon. His funeral at St. Mary's was incredibly moving, with so many of his friends, and teachers, from St. John Fisher's School in Dewsbury there, many of them taking an active part in the Mass. And all the family there, to lend whatever support they could give to Michelle, Chris, Georgia and Sophie.

John and Pat have moved, after over thirty years of living down the bottom of Clerk Green. Not very far – to Cross Bank. The new house looks over Batley Cemetery, where quite a few of the family's graves are, and John often walks there on his various errands, and pays his respects,